A CONTRIBUTION TO
DEMAND ANALYSIS

A CONTRIBUTION TO DEMAND ANALYSIS

BY

I. F. PEARCE

PROFESSOR OF ECONOMIC THEORY
UNIVERSITY OF SOUTHAMPTON

OXFORD
AT THE CLARENDON PRESS
1964

Oxford University Press, Amen House, London E.C.4

GLASGOW NEW YORK TORONTO MELBOURNE WELLINGTON
BOMBAY CALCUTTA MADRAS KARACHI LAHORE DACCA
CAPE TOWN SALISBURY NAIROBI IBADAN ACCRA
KUALA LUMPUR HONG KONG

© *Oxford University Press 1964*

PRINTED IN GREAT BRITAIN

PREFACE

A PREFACE might seem an unnecessary and unwelcome addition to a book which already includes a lengthy Chapter 0 designed to explain the aims and objects of the work. There remains however a duty to acknowledge as far as possible my debt to colleagues and others who have knowingly or unknowingly contributed.

Among the unknowing contributors it is my privilege to be able to mention my teachers at the University of Bristol, in particular Mr. J. Miles Fleming and Professor H. D. Dickinson. I am also much indebted to Mr. S. F. James and my colleagues at the University of Nottingham who patiently corrected a prodigious number of my early mistakes.

The general approach to demand theory adopted in Chapter I is based upon the recent work of what might be called the 'Stanford School'. In particular I made conscious use of Professor Hirofumi Uzawa's masterly synthesis *Preference and Rational Choice in the Theory of Consumption*. Other specific plagiarisms are mentioned in the text, although, of course, no list could be complete without reference to a long line of demand theorists beginning not later than Thomas Aquinas.

I am grateful to Professor J. R. Hicks, Professor W. M. Gorman, and Professor T. W. Swan and others too numerous to mention who read the manuscript in whole or in part or who discussed specific points with me.

I have to thank the editors of *Economica* and *Australian Economic Papers*, for permission to adapt material previously published therein and the editor of *Applied Statistics* for permission to reprint Tables 1.7.1 and 1.7.2 taken from an article by Gabor and Granger.

It is doubtful also if the book would ever have appeared without the technical assistance of Miss Diana Marshallsay, who, among other things, prepared the index.

Finally I record the enormous debt I owe to the Australian

National University where most of the work was carried out;
and to my colleagues there, who encouraged me in my belief
that what I was attempting was worth while.

I. F. P.

University of Southampton
February 1964

CONTENTS

0

A READER'S GUIDE

0.1. Prologue

FOLLOWING the precedent set by a distinguished mathematician† this book begins with a chapter 0, so designated because it is not, properly speaking, part of the book. Indeed it was written *ex post facto* on the advice of a number of friends who very kindly read the original manuscript and who, with impressive unanimity, felt that the essential argument is too often held up by over-rigorous discussion of minor points, the most important ideas of the whole work being introduced much too late.

One way to meet this criticism might have been to undertake a major reconstruction transferring to appendixes all of the more tedious sections. There are, however, compelling reasons for not following this course.

First and foremost it is my earnest hope that there is nothing in what follows which might be widely considered to be not worth writing. And the relegation of material to an appendix is too powerful an invitation to the reader to ignore it to be entirely consistent with such a hope.

It is also a fact that 'one man's gnat is another man's camel'. This is particularly true of economic theory, where there are a great many levels of understanding of the same problem and a great many routes by which each level might be reached. A point which seems very ordinary and obvious to one person may look new and important to another. Nor is everyone prepared to condone the erection of a vast edifice of economic theory upon foundations which we no more than hope can be strengthened later, however exciting the final structure may appear to be.

Again it is sometimes the case that the casual pursuit of an apparently trivial analogy yields to the imaginative reader the

† J. L. Kelley, *General Topology*.

most fascinating new insight. By way of illustration consider the following myth. Suppose that an expedition to the planet Mars discovered there a society with an almost parallel technical industrial development to that on earth but where, in every country, economic activity had always been centrally organized. Money and prices might be used simply to bring consumer demand into line with arbitrarily determined supply. In such a society economic theory could well have developed along analogous but startlingly different lines from that on earth.

Interest would be centred, not upon the response of consumption to price changes, but upon the response of prices to quantities offered for sale. No government would ask 'What changes must we make in the rate of exchange to correct our balance of payments deficit?' It would frame the question in the form 'What will be the effect on prices at home and abroad of a planned change in exports and imports?'

More important still, the attempts at answers developed by Martian economists would almost certainly consist of formulae involving, not elasticities of demand, as we know them, but percentage price responses to percentage quantity changes. These parameters are not simply the reciprocals of the familiar demand elasticities. They are related in a much more complicated way. Martian economic theory would look very different from our own even though the same fundamental truths would be expressed.

In due course also some Martian Slutsky would have recognized that almost every planned increase in sales *ipso facto* increased total money expenditure by the amount of the increased sales. He would notice too that, when an expression for the price response is written as a function of all sales, using the hypothesis that equilibrium implies maximum utility, a term appears which is precisely the change in price which would occur if total expenditure were reduced by the amount of the increased sales. In other words he would see a connexion between a purely algebraic element in a formula for the price response and a real phenomenon. He may be tempted as a result to divide his price response into 'income' and 'substitution' parts which bear no relation whatever, except that of analogy, to the 'income' and 'substitution' parts of the demand elasticities familiar to us. Using second-order conditions for a maximum the Martian mathematician might then have derived meaningful theorems capable of empirical refutation which, in certain circumstances, set signs on his (very different) concept of income and substitution parts. He would notice also properties of symmetry which may or may not be satisfied in fact.

In section 1.5 of this book some of the basic Martian theorems have been worked out for no other reason than that they can be, and it may well be thought that, interesting and amusing though such an exercise is, it has only marginal importance when compared with some of the econometric work of later chapters. Here is material perhaps for an appendix.

But who can be sure that it may not one day turn out to be more useful to teach qualitative economic theory to Martians (or to planners in general) than to prepare doubtful numerical estimates of elasticity of demand? The reader who remains unconvinced might still be persuaded by the fact that, as it turned out, one of the planning theorems of section 1.5 seemed in the end to lead to the neatest solution of a very relevant problem in oligopoly theory discussed in section 5.5. It is hoped that no more need be said to justify at least a certain reluctance on the part of the author to pronounce finally on the subject of which of the following pages should be read and which need not.

The search for a compromise suggested Chapter 0. This is intended to be a reader's guide. It will, if it is successful, both fortify the patient by describing what they might expect to come to at last, and indicate to those with less time or interest where, if anywhere, to browse.

0.2. Ends and means

Paradoxically the theory of demand, as it is commonly presented, is both too general and not general enough. It is too general because all goods are treated symmetrically; it is not general enough because it applies strictly only to a single individual who does not save and only to commodities which are totally consumed in one time period. It is an evident feature of the real world that consumers' wants fall into more or less distantly related classes, that is, that there exist 'marked gaps' in the chain of substitutes. But, beyond noting the fact, little has been done to trace its implications either from a theoretical or from an econometric point of view. Again difficulties connected with the proper integration of the theory of saving into the theory of demand are too often solved by omission. In textbooks the problem of consumer durables is rarely treated explicitly. Where progress has been made in this field it often appears as an uncomfortable exception to, rather than an integral part of, accepted theory.

The present work owes its existence primarily to the fact that, at various times, the author has found himself perplexed or dissatisfied with his own arguments on one or other of the points referred to above. It became necessary to invent some more or less satisfactory way of meeting the objections, or of exploiting the possibilities mentioned. It then seemed worth while to set down in as concise a manner as possible the results of these inquiries if only to let it be known what paths have been explored. The occasional encounter with colleagues apparently struggling with similar difficulties served also to suggest a possible demand for a monograph carrying the subject to a rather more advanced level than the ordinary textbook.

It is now hoped that the whole is reasonably complete in the sense that there is very little known about the theory of demand which is not at least referred to in the pages which follow. The book might therefore be used as the basis for a series of advanced lectures. On the other hand, it has not been thought desirable to give long and tedious accounts of propositions which are today of only historical interest. For example, certain theorems connected with the 'revealed preference' approach to utility theory are not proved although they are stated. Nor is any attempt made to make peace with mathematicians by establishing with full rigour the precise conditions under which we might accept the obvious, particularly when the required conditions are almost certain to be met by economic data. But in all such cases suitable references are given.

For two very good reasons symbols rather than words are extensively used throughout. The first is simply that it is a great deal easier to write and to print 'x_i' than 'the quantity consumed of one of the goods'. The second is that when statements about economic relationships are set out symbolically it is often possible to recognize immediately, and without further effort, a number of important consequences already discovered by mathematicians. In such cases we need only refer to the relevant theorem in the textbooks with considerable saving in time and space.

The irresistible appeal of this procedure to the lazy writer can hardly be a matter for dispute. What is more debatable is how far it is likely to be acceptable to the reader. If the greater number of the theorems referred to are known to him he will appreciate brevity. If they are not he may still appreciate brevity provided he is willing to accept on trust all the propositions alleged to be well known. The reader untrained in mathematics who is at the same time very properly sceptical is, however, more difficult to cater for. It is hardly possible to imagine in what terms the more important points of the pages which follow could be made if at the same time it were necessary to develop from first principles all that has been taken for granted.

Fortunately there can be very few economists at the present time who do not have at least some acquaintance with the terminology of mathematics. It is also a fact that the amount of mathematics contained in this book is quite small and easily learned. Indeed it could hardly be otherwise for the writer is himself entirely without formal training in the subject. This book is directed therefore to readers of classes I and II above rather than class III. It is hoped that these will represent the majority.

With readers class II in mind rather more clumsy techniques and notations have been chosen than are currently fashionable among mathematicians, partly because they are better known to economists and partly because they often give deeper insight into the economics involved. Care has been taken also to explain the meaning of some of the more obscure terms when they first appear. Some general comments on notation are given at once.

0.3 Notation

The symbol x is consistently employed to represent quantities of consumer goods used up in each time period. With subscripts, e.g. x_i, it usually means a quantity of a single commodity, namely the ith. Without a subscript or with a superscript, e.g. x^0, it means a quantity vector or consumption pattern; that is, a set of n quantities of commodities used up.

The symbol p is used in an analogous way for commodity prices.

Where it has been necessary to distinguish between the quantity consumed, or used up in a time period, and an actual quantity in use, we put q for the latter, retaining x for quantity used up.

y is either income or expenditure according to context. C is used for total expenditure and y for income where a distinction is made.

When we write $$x = f(p, y)$$
a vector value function is usually implied. We mean, in fact, a set of n equations relating n quantities x_i and n prices p_j and expenditure y.

The notation $$x^0 P x^1 \quad \text{or} \quad x^0 R x^1$$
expresses a relation between the commodity bundle x^0 and the commodity bundle x^1. For example, x^0 is preferred to x^1, or x^0 is chosen rather than x^1.

Following the usual conventions a bar over a symbol, e.g. $\bar{x}$, means the arithmetic mean of all values taken by the variable x, *except* that a bar signifies also the negation of a relationship. For example, $\overline{x^0 P x^1}$ is to be read x^0 is *not* preferred to x^1.

When we write $u(x)$ we mean that the number u depends upon the value of the vector x.
$$x^0 \geq x^1$$
implies that every element in the vector x^0 is greater than or equal to the corresponding element in x^1, at least one element being greater. $$x^0 \geqq x^1,$$
on the other hand, includes the case where both vectors are identical.

$$[x \in S: u(x) \geqq u(x^0)]$$

defines the subset of the set S which includes all x such that the corresponding u is greater than or equal to a particular u defined by the particular vector x^0.

Two familiar notations are ordinarily used for the partial derivatives of functions. Thus u_i is the marginal utility of the ith good, i.e. the rate of increase in the value of u due to an increase in the quantity of the ith good consumed. And $\partial x_i/\partial p_j$ is the rate of response in consumption of the ith good to changes in the jth price. The second notation is employed wherever a partial derivative might otherwise be confused with a particular element of a vector. In general the expression 'rate of response' is used to distinguish between partial derivatives and elasticities which are logarithmic derivatives. u_{ij} is, of course, the partial derivative of u_i with respect to the jth commodity and so on.

The symbol σ_{ij} represents the substitution part of a demand response, i.e. the difference between the response in consumption of the ith good due to unit change in the jth price and the response due to compensation for that price change by a sum of money x_j. The writer was unable to resist the temptation to write v_{ij} for the 'substitution' part of the price response to quantity changes in the mirror-image theory of section 1.5. In this connexion I am grateful to Professor J. R. Hicks for pointing out that every hieroglyphic should have a name and for suggesting the term 'anti-sigma' which it would be hard to improve upon.

C_i commonly replaces $p_i\,\partial x_i/\partial y$ and may be read, 'marginal propensity to consume the ith good'. In Chapter 3 in particular it becomes necessary to distinguish between demand functions for the individual and demand functions for the community as a whole. In this case capitals are used for aggregates, e.g. X_i is community demand and x_{ir} is consumption of the rth individual in the community. Γ_{ij} is the aggregate of σ_{ij}.

λ is used in Chapter 1 to signify the marginal utility of money. This should not be confused with the λ_{ij} central to neutral want association theory. The connexion between the two is remote as explained in the text.

dx_i is *any* small change in the quantity x_i.

Determinants† are not written in full except where necessary to make an important point. Normally

$$|u_{ij}|$$

signifies a determinant with the general element u_{ij}.

$$\begin{vmatrix} 0 & u_j \\ u_i & u_{ij} \end{vmatrix}$$

is the same determinant bordered with a row and column of u_i's.

Finally attention is drawn to the system of numbering sections and equations. Each chapter is divided into sections identified by Arabic numerals. Equations are numbered consecutively within each section, Roman numerals being used. Thus any equation referred to in the text can be rapidly located, e.g. 5.2 (iv) is the fourth equation occurring in section 2 of Chapter 5.

We now proceed to survey and locate the topics discussed below, not in the order in which they appear, but in an order which, in view of critical comment already referred to, seems best.

0.4. Neutral want association

One of the central objects of this book is to introduce the idea of 'neutrally want associated' groups of commodities. It will be suggested that the boundaries of such groups correspond to the intuitively appealing idea of gaps in the chain of substitutes which might, in some instances, mark out the domain of an industry operating under conditions of oligopolistic competition. If such groups can be shown to exist in the sense defined the consequences both in the field of economic theory and econometrics will be far reaching.

It has been suggested that the reader will expect and wish to learn something about the concept of neutral want association and its possibilities before, and not after, a tedious justification of the foundations upon which it is based, i.e. before we reach

---

† See A. C. Aitken, *Determinants and Matrices*.

Chapter 5. With the intention of remedying this defect of presentation a brief account will be given here of the circumstances which first led to the development of later ideas.

In the theory of international trade it is sometimes important to know whether the ratio of the increases in consumption of goods i and j, due to an income compensated rise in the price of good w, is greater or less than the ratio of increases in consumption which would occur if income rose with no changes in price. Symbolically it is of interest to know if

$$C_i/C_j \gtrless \sigma_{iw}/\sigma_{jw},$$

where C_i and C_j are marginal propensities to consume goods i and j and σ_{iw} is the substitution part of the demand response, $\partial x_i/\partial p_w$, of the ith good to the wth price [these terms are fully explained in section 1.4].

It seemed clear that the required condition must have something to do with the relationship in consumption between good w and good i on the one hand, and good w and good j on the other. For example, if i is a better substitute for w than j, then the effect of a price rise in w (and a consequent fall in consumption of w) will be to increase demand for i rather more than j. If income rises without any price change so that consumption of w increases as well as consumption of i and j the bias towards i is no longer present. In other words,

$$C_i/C_j < \sigma_{iw}/\sigma_{jw}.$$

The opposite is the case if j is the better substitute for w.

This observation led naturally to consideration of the marginal case where
$$C_i/C_j = \sigma_{iw}/\sigma_{jw}. \qquad 0.4\text{ (i)}$$

Such a case might arise for two reasons. First, $i, j,$ and w could all be very closely related, that is, they may all be close substitutes, as, for example, three kinds of household detergent. Or they may all be highly complementary, e.g. knives, forks, and spoons. Second, w may be very unlike i and j. It may satisfy a completely different kind of want. For example, w might be entertainment whilst i and j are two different kinds of food. Entertainment is a substitute for food, but only in so far as one

kind of utility can always be substituted for another to keep
total utility constant. It is not a substitute in the sense that it
satisfies the same kind of want. In this case also there is no
reason to suppose that w will be a better substitute for i than
for j or vice versa. The equality 0.4 (i) will hold.

We might now introduce a notion of groups. In case (i) i, j,
and w might be classed in the same group, in which event we
should expect 0.4 (i) to hold however we interchange the subscripts. In case (ii) we might say w is located in a different
group from i and j. Condition 0.4 (i) holds with subscripts in
the order shown but

$$C_w/C_j = \sigma_{wi}/\sigma_{ji}$$

does not *necessarily* hold. In case (ii) we have a 'marked gap'
in the chain of substitutes between w and the rest.

Thus we have immediately

(a) A rational principle for the classification of commodities
which suggests a practical solution to the time-hallowed
question 'are bedsocks "textiles" or "boots and shoes"?'

(b) A series of new equations, 0.4 (i) which, if we can identify
groups in practice, must enormously simplify econometric
work in the field of consumer demand.

(c) An attractive definition of an oligopolistic industry.

(d) Additional information which must lead to new qualitative conclusions in almost every field of economic theory,
particularly the theory of international trade from which
the inquiry began.

(e) A challenge to work out the full consequences of the
existence of groups.

Further work showed that groups imply nested utility functions of the type illustrated by equation 5.3 (vi) below; and that,
where there are more than two arguments to any sub function,
additivity is implied within the sub function. Thus a connexion
is established with earlier investigations into additive utility
and a powerful generalization achieved.

The systematic treatment of the theory of commodity groups
begins in Chapter 5. The reader who wishes to study this subject

alone, rather than demand theory in general, need only look first at the remarks on notation in section 0.3. Sections 5.1 and 5.2 describe the formation of groups and the obvious computational advantages. In section 5.3 utility implications are considered. Section 5.4 proves theorems stated in section 5.2 where computational procedures are suggested.

In section 5.5 attention is drawn to the wider implications of the theory of groups. In particular we consider the possibility of identifying and computing the 'share of the market' which would be enjoyed by firms operating under oligopolistic conditions, according to relative product prices.

Chapters 6 and 7 set out the results of some simple computations based on national income data.

0.5. Aggregation

It will not escape the notice of the reader of Chapters 5, 6, and 7 that the theory there developed is applied to the demand for goods of the community as a whole, as opposed to individuals. On the other hand, appeal is made throughout to results deduced from utility analysis which has a meaning only in the case of the individual. In particular it is taken for granted that the substitution parts of demand responses are symmetric (see equation 1.4 (xv)). This is only another way of saying that there exist what have elsewhere been called 'community indifference curves', a matter which has been the subject of a great deal of inconclusive debate.

The purpose of Chapter 3 is to suggest a solution to this problem. The intention is primarily to justify later work. It is a fact, however, that there are as many definitions of the substitution part of an aggregate demand response as there are definitions of community welfare. The definition of a substitution part implies, of course, that the residual is the income effect. Inevitably we are drawn into some discussion of community welfare. In particular this is the subject of section 3.4.

The main approach of sections 3.2 and 3.3, on the other hand, is strictly operational. We proceed by defining income effect, rather than substitution effect, in such a way that it can be identified with the aggregate effect of a proportional rise in individual incomes with prices constant. Substitution effect is now the residual. It is shown that in general such substitution effects are not symmetric, but that only a negligible error is involved in assuming that they are. On the same basis all of the ordinary theorems of demand analysis are established for aggregate data.

It is further shown in section 3.4 that, despite the operational approach, the resulting behaviour curves do still have the limited welfare significance required to justify the usual normative conclusions of established welfare economics.

0.6. Saving

Most of the data available to econometricians working in the field of consumer demand consist of observations of total spending and the patterns of spending and prices in the *current* period. Total incomes, and hence saving in the period, can also be measured, but not the effect of current price changes on future planned expenditure. Unfortunately future planned expenditure and the current pattern of spending are not necessarily independent, and future planned expenditure cannot be observed. Explicit recognition of this fact casts some doubt upon the validity of accepted theory and particularly upon results central to the work of Chapter 5.

It is the purpose of Chapter 2 to determine the conditions under which the current demand for each good can be expressed as a function of current prices and total expenditure *alone* with all the usual theorems still intact. The work of the econometrician is once again enormously simplified if such a condition holds. Only current consumption patterns, prices, and total expenditure need be observed in this case. With the relevant parameters calculated consumption patterns can be predicted from price and total expenditure estimates or vice versa.

Not unexpectedly it turns out that the required condition is, that there should exist a marked gap in the chain of substitutes between goods in current consumption and planned future consumption precisely in the neutral want association sense of condition 0.4 (i). This assumption forms the basis of later theorems.

In the course of the work a number of subsidiary problems are explored. It is worth pointing out that once again the investigations of Chapter 2 were originally provoked, not by any direct wish to carry out econometric studies but by a question in international trade. What in fact is likely to be the effect on saving of a movement in the real terms of trade? So far economists have been unable to provide a conclusive answer to this sometimes crucial query, even in terms of signs alone. The whole problem is reviewed in section 2.5 in the light of the results of Chapter 2.

Since completing Chapter 2 the writer has noted also, in the learned journals, a new round of argument related to the so-called 'Pigou effect' which is, in its most general form, the secondary effect upon the consumption of a particular good due to a revaluation of stocks of wealth following price changes.

On the assumption of a 'marked gap' between current and future satisfactions the Pigou effect appears simply as an influence upon saving in general. The conditions under which it is likely to be zero are discussed at various points in Chapter 2. The whole chapter, in fact, constitutes a model, within the framework of which a number of currently controversial questions can conveniently be put. The prediction (see section 2.5, para. 1) that the work of the chapter would again become a centre of debate was in fact fulfilled rather sooner than expected.

0.7. Short-run saving

The concept of short-run saving (positive or negative) is introduced to distinguish savings proper from that which is designed simply to meet irregularities in the flow of payments for the continuous use of durable consumer items. The one is an operation designed specifically to shift consumption intertemporally, the other simply smooths the payment for current consumption.

Attention is drawn to the fact in section 1.3, that it is impossible to buy a consumer durable item without at the same time buying a loan service provided either by self or by a finance company. This opens the question of what is really meant by the quantity, x_i, of the ith good. A notion of quantity is suggested which is a function of physical quantity q_i, the rate of interest, the technical life of the item, and the time in use per period of time. It is in this sense that the quantity x_i used up in each time period is employed throughout the book.

0.8. Durable consumer goods

In view of the definition of quantity used up, introduced in section 1.1 and developed in section 1.3, the theory of demand for consumer durables fits naturally into the whole. All concepts are operational involving only entities which are observable at least in principle. Definitions of quantity are used also to sustain the hypothesis of continuity upon which all theorems are founded (see section 1.1).

0.9. Foundations of demand theory

The foundations of demand theory are examined in sections 1.1 and 1.2. The assumption that the consumer is able to order in his mind all relevant bundles of goods is introduced and the evidence for it critically examined. The basis of the theory as presented is an arbitrary order-preserving function rather than a utility function although this term is freely used.

The assumption of transitivity of the ordering is made directly rather than via the so-called axioms of revealed preference which have been shown to be equivalent. This method is simpler and more directly invites examination of the plausibility of the assumption.

Revealed preference is briefly discussed in section 1.6 from an historical point of view.

The principal results of demand theory are set out in section 1.4 in a straightforward way.

0.10. The planning view

Section 1.5 outlines the Martian demand theory already referred to under 0.1. No further comment is necessary except to express again the view that but for an accident of environment this might have been the principal content of our textbooks. And it may still be yet.

0.11. On Chapter 4

Chapter 4 is probably the most difficult and at the same time least satisfying part of the book. A reader's guide to this section is most needed yet the hardest to prepare. The author, if no one else, is left with the impression that there remain facets of the problems discussed which are not yet fully understood. Perhaps for this reason Chapter 4 may, in the end, be the most worth while.

The central point of section 4.1 is a simple one. Almost the whole of qualitative economic theory which, despite the right and proper aspirations of econometricians, remains the basis of most policy decisions, rests upon statements about the sign and rough order of magnitude of single price elasticities of demand. On the other hand, relationships like complementarity, substitutability, and neutral want association are relationships between pairs or groups of commodities. It ought to be, and it is, possible to use such ideas to make qualitative statements about the sign and possible magnitude of more complicated functions of demand elasticities involving several commodities, for example, determinants of elasticities. This may be important when such functions appear in formulae expressing the answer to particular policy questions. Examples of such functions as they occur in international trade theory are in fact given in section 4.3.

With this in mind section 4.2 re-examines definitions of complementarity and substitutability between pairs of goods, developing a measure which turns out to be a function of elasticities and cross elasticities of the two commodities involved. It is now clear that this procedure ought to be extended to groups of three or more goods but no obvious next step has occurred to the writer.

Section 4.4 carries over the idea to the notion of independence between goods, a discussion which leads, by a circuitous route, once again to neutral want association, which forms the subject of the remaining chapters.

1

DEMAND THEORY—THE SINGLE CONSUMER

1.1. The foundations

INTROSPECTION and common observation suggest the initial hypothesis upon which generally accepted demand theory is based. It is usually taken to be self-evident that the satisfaction derived from the consumption of goods and services, which command a price, can, in principle, be defined for each individual by a utility function, and that market behaviour is the outcome of attempts by individuals to maximize that function subject to the constraints imposed by prices and available incomes. Unfortunately, for various reasons, it is not at all an easy matter to devise experiments which would test directly this basic assumption. Nor can it be said to have been fully confirmed by indirect evidence; for, although the utility hypothesis is rich in consequences, controlled experiments on a macro economic scale are impossible. In practice, other things not being equal, it is usually easier to give *ex post facto* 'explanations' of the failure of predictions than it is successfully to predict. On the other hand, some testing is possible, and it is part of the purpose of this book to suggest new ways in which this might be done.

We remark especially on the difficulty of finding objective confirmation of notions which are at least partially subjective, because this has been the source of a great deal of criticism which must be faced. At least two lines of argument can be distinguished. First, it is sometimes claimed directly that the whole idea of a utility function is a myth and that the massive edifice of economic theory which rests upon it amounts in consequence to little more than elegant speculation. Secondly, more constructive critics have proposed alternative approaches thought to be more objective.

In order to be in a position to assess the significance of the various objections it is considered desirable to examine more closely what is meant by, and what is implied by, the existence of a utility function. To this end we reduce our original hypothesis to a set of more primitive axioms which can then be considered in turn. These sub axioms are best thought of as conditions on a 'preference' relation, which is assumed to exist in the mind of the consumer, so that he is in a position to order, or choose between, *any two* commodity bundles which might be offered to him. It is convenient to express this symbolically as follows.

First we define a commodity vector x, as a set of quantities $(x_1, x_2,..., x_n)$ of n goods constituting a 'bundle' to be consumed in a given time period. For the moment we need not say precisely what is meant by a commodity or a time period; an everyday notion will do. This crucial question will be dealt with later when we come to discuss the utility function.

Next we use the notation $x^0 P x^1$ to indicate a relation between the bundles x^0 and x^1, meaning that x^0 is placed before x^1 in the consumer's ordering; that is, it would be chosen if x^0 and x^1 were offered as alternatives. P may be read as 'preferred to' if desired but attention is drawn to the fact that this might be a question-begging term which, in its ordinary meaning, implies all of the axioms we are trying to enumerate. It is not easy to rid the mind of the notion that 'chosen' does not necessarily mean 'preferred' in the sense of giving higher satisfaction. It may help, therefore, to recall that the community as a whole chooses a definite pattern of consumption but only in a restricted sense can it be said to prefer it.†

In the notation defined our first axiom is:

(i) That for every conceivable pair of commodity bundles x^0 and x^1 contained in the whole set, S, of bundles which could be offered, the consumer is able to say *either* $x^0 P x^1$, *or* $\overline{x^0 P x^1}$, where $\overline{x^0 P x^1}$ is the negation of P meaning x^0 *not* ordered before x^1.

Notice that $\overline{x^0 P x^1}$ does not imply $x^1 P x^0$ since we might have also $\overline{x^1 P x^0}$. In the language of preference $\overline{x^0 P x^1}$ and $\overline{x^1 P x^0}$ would

† Cf. Chapter 3.

mean indifference between x^1 and x^0. In terms of ordering it would indicate simply $x^1 = x^0$ in the ordering. For the moment, however, we treat it only as a way of saying that any choice between x^1 and x^0 is made at random.† It is worth noting in passing that indifference does not imply, as some writers have supposed, that the consumer being, like Buridan's ass, unable to make up his mind, must remain dithering between two possibilities for ever. Dithering is, of course, an observable phenomenon but it is one which arises because of *uncertainty* and not because of indifference. One might pick at random without hesitation one of two identical pots of jam offered, being sure of indifference. On the other hand, a great deal of time might be spent over a choice between two motor-cars whose relative merits are uncertain.

Consider just how innocuous axiom (i) really is. We are supposing no more than that the consumer, if offered the choice of either x^0 or x^1, will be able to select one or other with certainty *or* will recognize that he is choosing at random. This is a simple testable hypothesis which is in fact so much a part of our ordinary experience that we scarcely need to test it. If x^0 is chosen with certainty rather than x^1 then we write x^0Px^1. If the choice is made at random then we write $\overline{x^0Px^1}$ and $\overline{x^1Px^0}$. We hold that the individual will know whether his choice was made at random or with a consciousness of ordering and is capable of indicating which is the case.

It is important to notice that we have not assumed that if we write x^0Px^1 then x^0 yields more satisfaction, except in the very widest sense of this term. We do not have to argue about subtle distinctions between Professor D. H. Robertson's 'ecfare' (satisfaction derived from goods) and 'welfare' in a wider sense. x^0 might be ranked higher than x^1 because it is fourth in line, or because it gives less satisfaction than x^1 but the chooser prefers not to appear greedy. Nor do we have to debate with

---

† On the other hand, it is clear that x^0Px^1 does imply $\overline{x^1Px^0}$, which is the essential requirement for the existence of a binary relation. If the consumer is able to choose x^0 rather than x^1 with certainty, it would be a contradiction to say that at the same time he is able to choose x^1 rather than x^0 also with certainty.

philosophers whether or not it is possible to be indifferent. Either some individuals have feelings which would force them to make choices at random or they have not. Whichever is the case makes no difference to the logic of what follows; for it is not necessary to the axiom that we should be able to write $\overline{x^0 P x^1}$ and $\overline{x^1 P x^0}$ for any pair x^0, x^1. It is quite sufficient that we should be able to write something even if it is always $x^0 P x^1$ or $x^1 P x^0$. The fact that the existence of indifference classes can be inferred from later assumptions regarding the nature of an order-preserving function is not a valid ground for criticism of axiom (i).†

Finally we remark that, so far, we need not even be concerned with the possibility of uncertainty or ignorance of the technical want satisfying properties of various goods; for the individual actually faced with a choice must of necessity order any pair of commodity bundles, or decide that he cannot order them, whatever the state of his knowledge. Nor is it essential to assume that the consumer is capable of comparing pairs of commodity bundles of which he has had no experience since we shall not attempt to establish the existence of a utility function beyond a relatively small area containing the existing pattern of consumption; that is, beyond the area where there is the greatest awareness of the possibilities. This means, of course, that any results obtained cannot be used to explain large changes, but we are in any case unlikely to be able to treat large changes for other reasons. Indeed in practical economics we are very seldom required to.

It follows that we scarcely need to defend axiom (i). Only what Professor Meade has called 'an excess of philosophy' could provoke objections to it; for, in the face of the fact that commodity bundles do exist and that individuals do choose between them, it is hard even to give meaning to the contrary statement that the binary relation, P, does not exist. The most extreme supposition that all choices are made at random is not contrary to our axiom.

† Continuity and monotonicity together imply the existence of indifference classes as we shall see.

Axiom (ii) is of a very different order. We require in addition:
(ii) that the relation P should be transitive; that is, x^0Px^1
and x^1Px^2 together imply x^0Px^2.

There is no reason, of course, to suppose that, in general, a
logical relationship must be transitive, for it is easy to suggest
meaningful examples which are not. On the other hand, as soon
as we associate P with the process of choosing we begin to think
of transitivity as a condition of *consistency* of choice, i.e. rational
choice. Against this we have to recognize at least two general
circumstances in which it might be possible to reconcile intransitivity of the choice relation with rational behaviour. The first
of these can arise if the *reasons* for choosing x^0 rather than x^1
are in any way connected with the actual conditions under
which the alternatives are presented. The second may occur in
practice if time or uncertainty is involved. The first case is
different in principle from the second.

Consider an example. Suppose an individual is faced with a
choice between a large apple and a small one. He chooses the
small one because he does not wish to be thought greedy.
Suppose now that, on another occasion, he is offered the choice
between a small apple and a rather larger pear. This time he is
not bound by the fear of being thought greedy since he feels
that any onlooker will imagine simply that he dislikes apples;
the pear therefore is taken. When the choice is between the
large apple (larger than the pear), and the pear, again there
might be no fear of being thought greedy. The large apple could
be chosen. Thus we have the pear preferred to the small apple,
the small apple preferred to the large apple, but the large apple
preferred to the pear. This is an intransitive relationship but
the chooser is perfectly rational. Moreover, he may be quite
consistent in his behaviour in the sense that he will always act
the same way in the same circumstances.

It is clear that we cannot infer transitivity simply from the
fact that the P relation describes a rational choice process. On
the other hand, it will be fairly safe to say that as long as choices
are presented under ordinary market conditions such conditions
will *not* be a factor influencing the ordering in the usual case.

As with most assumptions in economics it might be possible to find individual exceptions—e.g. the consumer who has some social relationship with the owner of the corner shop—but in dealing with aggregates, as we shall be, the broad generalization is a valuable first approximation. We do not hesitate to make the statement 'snow is falling' even though it is always possible to find single flakes floating upwards.

The second case where apparent intransitivity of the P relation might be encountered in practice has often been discussed but is not in fact true intransitivity. It could well be that a consumer chooses x^0 rather than x^1, and x^1 rather than x^2, but later chooses x^2 rather than x^0, simply because he has changed his mind. This can be interpreted as meaning that an ordering exists but that, at some moment of time, there is a change in the ordering of the various pairs so as to give the appearance of intransitivity to the observer. Evidently apparent intransitivity of this kind is most likely to arise where there is a high degree of uncertainty or ignorance. It may also occur if the time period is so short that the consumer is influenced in choices for the current period by particular choices made in the previous period. For example, it is sometimes argued that the current preference as between, say, ice cream or a cup of tea, may well depend on how many cups of tea have been consumed in the preceding half hour.

Clearly objections to the transitivity assumption based upon this second class of cases amount to no more than a contention that the choice relation might not be sufficiently stable over time to justify attempts to measure the parameters connected with it. It would be out of place therefore to argue the point here. We shall return to it at a later stage. In the meantime it is sufficient to point out that facts which suggest instability of the preference ordering do not constitute evidence of intransitivity even though they may give rise to observations which are consistent with intransitivity. It is recognized, of course, that, if no experiment can be devised capable of distinguishing between instability and intransitivity, then any conceptual distinction is valueless. But this is hardly the case, for the individual actually choosing must be aware of the difference even if the independent observer is not.

We conclude that axiom (ii) is virtually synonymous with the two assumptions (a) that the consumer is rational, and (b) that his ordering principles are independent of the way in which opportunities for choosing occur. The reader should note also that we are still not committed to any supposition that commodity bundles are ordered according to their want satisfying power. Many other principles may be involved.

Axioms (i) and (ii) together totally order the whole set, S, of commodity bundles. By this we mean simply that for any bundle x^0 we can always divide the whole set S, or any subset of S, into two groups, those that come before x^0 or are equal to x^0 in the ordering, and the remainder. We have something which is very close to a 'utility' function but is not yet it. What we need is a continuous, order-preserving, function $u(x)$ such that $u(x^0) \geq u(x^1)$ if and only if x^0 is ordered before, or on the same level as, x^1. The fact that a total ordering exists does not by any means imply that an order-preserving function can be constructed.

Economists who have not been conditioned by repeated failure of their intuition to a degree of scepticism approaching that of the mathematician may be surprised that the existence of an ordering is not the same thing as the existence of what has come to be called an 'ordinal' utility function. It seems desirable therefore to quote an example due to Debreu.† This example will help also in our assessment of the significance of axiom (iii), which it will be necessary to introduce below.

Consider the simple case where two goods only exist: x_1 and x_2. Commodity bundles may now be represented as points in a plane (see Fig. 1). Suppose now that the consumer orders such bundles lexicographically; that is $x^0 P x^1$ if the bundle x^0 contains $x_1^0 > x_1^1$ contained in the bundle x^1. If $x_1^0 = x_1^1$ then $x^0 P x^1$ if and only if $x_2^0 > x_2^1$. In other words good one takes precedence over good two just as letter a in a dictionary takes precedence over letter b, whatever the following letters.

† Cf. G. Debreu, 'Representation of a Preference Ordering by a Numerical Function', *Decision Processes*, edited by Thrall, Coombs, and Davis.

Such an ordering gives rise to the situation represented in Fig. 1: x^0 is evidently ordered before x^1 since the bundle x^0 contains more of the dominant good one. x^2, on the other hand, is ordered before x^0 for, although both x^2 and x^0 contain equal amounts of the dominant good, x^2 contains more of good two.

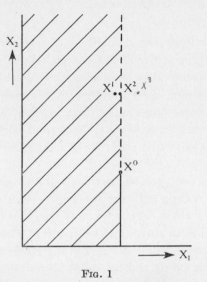

FIG. 1

In fact x^0 is ordered before any bundle in the shaded area *excluding* that part of the boundary represented by the broken line but *including* that part of the boundary represented by the continuous line. It is impossible to draw a boundary line separating those bundles which are ordered after x^0 and those bundles which are ordered equal to x^0 or before.

Clearly also as x^1 approaches x^2 the ordering of x^1 must remain less than x^0 so long as x^1 continues to be within the shaded area, however close x^1 is to x^2; and it may be made to approach x^2 as close as we like. On the other hand, x^2 itself is ordered above x^0.

It will scarcely surprise the reader to learn that the lexicographical ordering of Fig. 1 cannot be represented by a numerical function continuous in x. On the other hand, it is not immediately obvious, although it is true,† that such an ordering cannot

† For a proof see G. Debreu, loc. cit., n. 5.

uncountability.

be represented by any kind of numerical function whatever, whether continuous or not. The proof of this will not be repeated here since it has little intuitive appeal and is scarcely relevant. We content ourselves with the statement of axiom (iii) which is sufficient to ensure that it will be possible to construct a continuous order-preserving function.

Axiom (iii) requires:

(iii) that the ordering defined by the transitive relation P should be continuous in x. Loosely speaking this means no more than that two commodity bundles with *almost* the same content must take positions close together in the ordering. Or, more rigorously, however close in the ordering the bundle x^0 is to the bundle x^2, it must be possible to 'surround' the bundle x^2 with other bundles sufficiently like it to be even closer in the ordering than x^0.

It is easy to see that the lexicographical ordering of Fig. 1 does not meet axiom (iii); for the points x^1 and x^2 define very similar bundles which do not lie close together in the ordering.† It is not possible to surround the point x^2 with bundles which lie closer in the ordering than x^0; for any circle with x^2 as centre must include a point in the shaded area however small its radius.

sphere not include any close bundles that lie closer than x^0.

In conventional mathematical language axiom (iii) assumes: (*a*) that for any bundle x^0 contained in the set, S, of all bundles, the subset, S^0, consisting of all bundles x in S such that xPx^0, is an open set; and (*b*) that for any bundle x^0 contained in the set, S, of all bundles the subset, S_0, consisting of all bundles x in S such that x^0Px, is an open set.‡ For all practical purposes, and in the present context, this statement is equivalent to the less precise formulation above. It is quoted in the more rigorous terminology only so that it may be recognized as the sufficient condition given by Debreu§ for the existence of a continuous,

† Similar in the sense that they contain almost the same quantities of identical goods.

‡ For an exact definition of an open set cf. E. M. Patterson, *Topology*, pp. 27–30.

§ Loc. cit., theorem II, p. 163. Again we do not attempt to state the proof since it adds little to our intuitive understanding of the problem.

real, order-preserving function. The reader who understands the meaning of an open set will see at once that the set of all bundles, x, in Fig. 1 which are 'preferred' to x^0 is neither open nor closed and accordingly the Debreu conditions are not met.

In the discussion so far of axiom (iii) an attempt has been made to steer the narrow course between the Scylla of incorrect inference and the Charybdis of unnecessary rigour. Even so it is still possible that anxiety to avoid statements not strictly true has led the writer somewhat into the whirlpool. Accordingly we append by way of explanation some further very loose comments.

Axiom (iii) is an axiom of continuity. It would be most unfortunate, however, if the impression were given, because of this, that the whole of demand theory as we know it rests upon some kind of belief that commodities are purely divisible to an infinite degree. Such a belief is already too commonly held, examples of indivisible goods being referred to with appropriate 'humorous' comment upon the consequences of attempting to chop them up. The case of electric-light globes is one providing all the scope necessary for a suitable display of wit. In this connexion the following points should be noted.

First, the possibility of constructing an order-preserving function does not depend directly on the assumption of continuity. On the contrary the difficulty arises, in part, precisely because we want to consider all conceivable quantities, x. Remarkably enough, if we were to introduce into the example of Fig. 1 the kind of discontinuity consequent upon the indivisibility of electric-light globes, so that the continuous plane x_1, x_2 breaks up into a set of distinct and separate points, then an order-preserving function could be constructed despite the lexicographical ordering.

This may easily be seen as follows. Imagine a third dimension u in Fig. 1 and suppose that on each admissible point in the plane x_1, x_2 we erect a flagpole, the height of each flagpole being determined by the ordering of the point on which it is set up. In other words, on the least 'preferred' point we have a one-foot pole, on the next a two-foot pole, and so on. The height of each pole then measures along the u axis the value of a function u of bundles x^0, x^1, etc., which is order-preserving. Such a construction is always possible as long as the number of admissible commodity bundles is countable.† It is only when we try to make the number of flagpoles very great indeed that we run into difficulty with the lexicographical ordering. Evidently, from the point of view of practical economics, the real restriction is contained in a condition of regularity implicit in the assumption of continuity in x of the function u, namely, however close $u(x^0)$ is to $u(x^2)$ we can always choose some $u(x^1)$ at least as close by making x^1 sufficiently like x^2. This condition could easily be imposed on the flagpole function by saying simply, that if the difference between the x^0 pole and the x^2 pole is one foot, then x^2 must be ringed by flagpoles which differ from the x^2 pole by plus or minus one foot. The lexicographical ordering is thereby excluded even in the discrete case.

In accepting such a restriction, however, we do approach the notion of indifference; for we thereby imply that the two identical pots of jam which figure in our earlier example must be equal in the ordering. Indeed if all derivatives of the continuous function, u, which by axiom (iii) can be constructed, exist and are finite and non zero, then an indifference curve can be drawn through any point. For taking u as a constant u^0 we have a relation $x_1 = \psi(x_2)$ linking all points which are equal in the ordering. Axiom (iii) is in fact used to establish the existence of indifference curves in a different context later.

In view of this powerful consequence of axiom (iii) and in view of past arguments about the meaning of indifference we consider for a moment, from an empirical point of view, what would be implied by its rejection. To reject axiom (iii) would be to claim the following possibility. Let x^0 be some commodity bundle and $(x^0 + \Delta x)$ be some different bundle whose general element x_i differs from the corresponding element in x^0 by an amount Δx_i. Let the bundles be chosen such that

$$x^0 P(x^0 + \Delta x).$$

† For a suitable explanation of the idea of countability cf. Birkhoff and MacLane, *A Survey of Modern Algebra*, p. 358. It is assumed that the set S to be ordered includes only finite commodity bundles.

It *might* now be true that we can find some other bundle (x^0+dx) such that $$(x^0+\Delta x)P(x^0+dx)$$ *however small the differences dx.*

Now we will argue later, from our definition of a quantity x, that this can be varied by very fine amounts in practice. We could therefore choose dx so small that empirically (x^0+dx) is scarcely distinguishable from x^0, whereas the quantities Δx must be distinguishable by the original choice of $$x^0P(x^0+\Delta x).$$ We have therefore a situation where the giving up of Δx receiving nothing in exchange yields a bundle x^0 which is put higher in the ordering, whilst the giving up of Δx in exchange for a bundle dx yields a bundle hardly distinguishable from x^0 which is placed lower in the ordering. Looked at this way it does not seem reasonable to reject axiom (iii).

The second fact to be emphasized in regard to the assumption of perfect divisibility of commodities is, that given the kind of regularity discussed above, a continuous function, based on perfect divisibility, will always give an approximation to a discrete real situation, sufficiently close for all practical purposes. If it were really true that the facts require us to think in terms of discrete bundles of commodities two choices would be open. We could succumb to the prevailing trend and develop all the familiar results in terms of finite algebra.† Alternatively we might accept a smooth model as a first approximation to the truth and regard all of our results as such.

On the other hand, neither alternative need be followed if we reject the indivisible commodity premise. The case for a continuous function need not rest on any kind of compromise. This point is very relevant to the problem of consumer durables which it seems appropriate to consider now.

Clearly the question whether a commodity is indivisible or not is one which cannot even be put until we define precisely how it is to be measured, distinguishing carefully between stocks

† Professor P. A. Samuelson goes a long way in this direction; see *The Foundations of Economic Analysis*, pp. 107–13. Professor J. R. Hicks also employs techniques essentially similar with explicit reference to discrete bundles; see *A Revision of Demand Theory*.

and flows. We have so far put off saying what we mean by a commodity bundle, x, beyond the fact that it is a set of quantities consumed in a time period. This is necessarily an ambiguous notion when some goods are, by their very nature, used up in a single act of consumption, whilst others have a definite 'life' period. Some attempt must be made to give it precision.

In the case of single use goods the quantity x^0 must be thought of as a flow per unit of time. We have to recognize, however, that in practice it is not an even flow, as for example the flow of water through a pipe. We may consume on the average fifty-two pounds of sugar per annum, which can be expressed as one pound per week, or approximately one ten-thousandth of a pound per minute; and from the point of view of defining a choice function, x (sugar), may mean any of these three equivalent things. But when we express x as a flow per minute, we do not thereby imply that individuals make a practice of swallowing a grain of sugar every minute. Evidently where the flow is uneven we have to distinguish between the time period used to describe the flow and the minimum time period required to take an accurate observation of the rate of flow.

Put this way we see at once that the fact that it is the common practice to buy sugar in one-pound bags does not in any way inhibit the consumer from making adjustments in his rate of consumption which are very fine indeed. There can be no objection in the case of single use goods to the use of the continuity assumption.

The comments above put us in a position also to meet an objection noted earlier in our discussion of the transitivity axiom. The claim that the choice between an ice-cream and a cup of tea is likely to be influenced by the number of cups of tea consumed in the previous half hour is at bottom no more than a claim that, because consumption flows are uneven, a relatively long minimum time period will be required in practice to determine its averge rate. The theory of demand attempts to explain the average rate of flow only.†

† For the purpose of computing elasticities it is assumed in later chapters of this book that the most suitable time period for taking observations is one

It may well be, of course, that at some future date a more satisfactory dynamic theory of demand will be developed capable of explaining, not only the relationship between price, expenditure, and the average rate of flow of consumption, but also the incidence and interrelationships of irregularities. For the present, however, we content ourselves with the more limited objective calling only for the simpler concepts. If it should prove, following attempts to take measurements, that the average rate of flow is as unstable and unpredictable as we fear the irregularities in the flow might be, then a new theory must be sought. But this point in our investigations can hardly be said to have been reached as yet.

The case of durable goods is not essentially different even though it is tempting to suppose that it is. The quantity bundle, x^0, must measure a *flow*, i.e. the amount used up per unit of time; it cannot represent the *stock* of durable goods *in use* during the period as we might think at first sight. This is best made clear by an example.

Consider the celebrated electric-light globe. An individual may own a house provided with two lamp sockets, in which case two possibilities are open to him. Either he can maintain a stock of two globes in use or, since he lives alone, he need only keep one globe in use transferring it from room to room as occasion arises. Neglecting the element of inconvenience the amount of lighting provided *per unit of time* is the same by either procedure. The two alternatives would be equal in the consumer's ordering. Thus if x^0 measures stock in use we have the two bundles x (globes) $= 2$ and x (globes) $= 1$ equal in the preference ordering, which, besides being obvious nonsense, is in contradiction with the regularity axiom (iii).

On the other hand, if we define x^0 as the quantity used up per unit of time, we recognize at once that there is no contradiction, for, on the average, electric-light globes have the same given life in use. A single globe transferred from room to room will

year, largely because of seasonal movement in the consumption of some commodities. Seasonal movements, of course, are an example of an unevenness of flow which we already have a theory to explain.

have an actual life of only one-half the average life of two separate globes in the circumstances described. Evidently, in any one time period, the quantity of light globe used up is the same in both cases so that axiom (iii) is satisfied.

The problem of measuring the quantity of a durable good used up per unit of time is clearly not a simple one. Nevertheless, 'quantity used up' remains an operational concept and in making any economic choice involving durables the individual will naturally attempt to assess it. The case above shows that one of the elements determining any particular quantity, x^0, is the length of life in use of the assets included, another being the intended time in use per unit of time. In fact if l is the life in use of a globe and t is the number of hours per week it is burned then t/l might crudely be said to be the quantity used up per week of a single globe. But this is far from being the end of the matter; for in most cases there will be a measure of quantity in the ordinary sense also involved. If the stock of globes in use is say q, then the quantity used up per week is clearly qt/l. Moreover, the meaning of q may not always be as obvious as in the case of light globes. For example, a 10-cubic-foot refrigerator provides a greater quantity of refrigerating space than a 4-cubic-foot refrigerator, and a concert grand is in some sense more piano than a baby grand.

Two points emerge from this discussion. The first is that at least two elements of quantity used up are directly under the control of the consumer, namely q and t. And it is hard to think of an example where these are not continuous to a degree sufficient to justify the assumption of divisibility of x^0. We cannot divide a light globe but we can adjust the number of hours per week we burn it. Moreover, it is a general rule of economic life that, wherever there is an indivisibility preventing individuals from consuming exactly the commodity bundle they want to consume, there is usually an entrepreneur ready to exploit this disequilibrium to his own profit. There are countless examples of this to be seen everywhere, and we need only cite miniature motor-cars and launderettes to encourage the reader to recognize them.

Secondly, we have to face the fact that the formula qt/l is not the final answer to the problem of measuring x^0. The difficulties may well vary from commodity to commodity. The rules which should govern our thinking are, however, fairly straightforward. The money spent on durable goods is unambiguous. The price tag is also unambiguous. Any definition of quantity must be consistent with the condition that price times quantity equals money spent. We have also to be sure that elements used to define quantity, e.g. q, t, and l, are in principle meaningful and measurable. Later we shall return to the problem and extend the idea of quantity used up per unit of time in accordance with these rules.

In the meantime our object has been to introduce the elementary formula qt/l and to show how this adds plausibility to the continuity assumption.

1.2. Properties of the 'utility' function

The three axioms of section 1.1 are intended to make quite clear what is implied by the assumption that the consumer's attitude to commodities can be described by a continuous order-preserving function u. This function for want of a better term, we shall henceforth call a utility function. No doubt to many readers it will appear that the whole of section 1.1 has been something of a storm in a tea-cup, and this is a view with which the writer has a good deal of sympathy. To those more interested in economics than in logic or mathematics there is no particular virtue in attempting to distinguish between an axiom and an empirical hypothesis; nor will a simple hypothesis necessarily appear more attractive than a more complex one. The only criterion by which a hypothesis can properly be judged is its power to explain the facts. If logic and mathematics become an end in themselves rather than a means to an end, then we are no longer discussing economics. It is from this point of view that both section 1.1 and the present section have been written; for we have taken care at each step to defend what we have called 'axioms' as if they were empirical hypotheses, which indeed in the present context they are.

Against the storm in a tea-cup view, however, it is as well to recognize that the breaking down of the utility function hypothesis into simpler components does in itself offer opportunities for testing it against the facts not otherwise immediately obvious. In particular we find ourselves, on the evidence of introspection, better able to meet what might be called para-psychological objections to the idea that individuals in some way mentally measure the amount of satisfaction derived from a bundle of goods. In this connexion we notice especially that, if one order-preserving (utility) function u can be constructed, then so can an infinity of them; for *any* monotonically increasing function of u must also be order-preserving. In other words if

$$F(u^0) \geqq F(u^1)$$

whenever $u^0 \geqq u^1$, which is always the case when F is a single-valued increasing function of u (e.g. u^2), then $F(u)$ is a utility function just as u is. Evidently no idea of measurement of any kind is implied by the work so far. With this in mind we shall, from time to time, show that results holding for u hold equally for any $F(u)$.

Another important conclusion follows directly from the work of section 1.1. Because, by construction, the utility function orders bundles as they would be chosen, then in any situation the consumer must be trying to maximize his utility function. This is not an assumption but a *consequence* of assumptions already made.

In this connexion we comment upon the suggestion sometimes put forward that many individuals ignore the prices of minor items in allocating their expenditure. There may be reasons for this which make good sense and we shall point to possible explanations at a later stage. In the meantime, however, it is worth noting that if we accept this price indifference as ordinary then we contradict the hypothesis of section 1.1; for it is hardly possible to maximize a function subject to constraints without looking at the constraints.

We now proceed, even more in the spirit of the empirical economist, to introduce and defend hypotheses which impose further restrictions on the form of the utility function u. The first needs little justification. It is:

(i) Monotonicity of u. This means that when any commodity bundle, x^0, contains more of at least one commodity than another bundle, x^1, without at the same time containing less of any other commodity, then x^0 will rank at least equal to x^1 in the consumer's ordering. Accordingly $u(x^0) \geqq u(x^1)$ when $x^0 \geq x^1$, where $x^0 \geq x^1$ means $x_i^0 \in$ (being a member of) $x^0 \geqq x_i^1 \in x^1$ for all i, $x^0 \neq x^1$.

In practical terms hypothesis (i) merely implies that, given the opportunity, individuals will choose more of a good rather than less. On the other hand, it is not impossible that a point of satiation may be reached where the consumer would be indifferent between a large quantity of a good and an even larger one. Our definition of monotonicity of the utility function admits of this possibility. It does not, however, leave room for the case where too much becomes a nuisance. This limitation will not trouble us, however, for monotonicity everywhere is not essential to the results which follow. We assume it only because the logic of the theory later suggests that we need be concerned only with areas of the function, u, where it is an increasing or constant function of x.

It is worth noting also that hypothesis (i), together with the continuity assumption of 1.1, implies that indifference curves must exist. There has been some dispute among economists on this point† although once again the issues raised may be felt to have little practical importance. Indeed those who reject the concept of an indifference curve do so on the very ground (perhaps inadmissible) that no observable behaviour can establish its existence or otherwise. Clearly if the observation of consumer behaviour cannot establish the existence of points of indifference then whether they exist or not cannot affect behaviour.

On the other hand, it is intuitively obvious that on the assumptions of monotonicity and continuity indifference points must exist. For given any commodity bundle x^0 we can always

† Cf. I. M. D. Little, *A Critique of Welfare Economics*.

find some other bundle x^1 higher in the ordering by including more of all goods. Again we can find a third bundle λx^1 lower in the ordering than x^0 by making λ small enough. λx^1, for example, may contain one-half or one-quarter of all the goods in x^1, the proportion of each good being the same. Ordinary notions of continuity now suggest that by varying λ continuously we can also find some $\lambda^1 x^1$ equal in the ordering to x^0. In other words, $\lambda^1 x^1$ and x^0 are points of indifference.†

We next assume:

(ii) Quasi-convexity of u. Geometrically this is the familiar condition that indifference hyper surfaces should be convex to the origin. That is, the set of all commodity bundles x such that $u(x)$ is greater than or equal to any given value of u (say u^0) must be a convex set.‡

Probably it is wrong to give this statement the status of a hypothesis for it virtually follows from the axioms of 1.1. We have in fact already seen that, by our definition of u, the consumer who actually makes a choice must be attempting to maximize u. And we are to be concerned with a theory about choices made in the market under the constraints imposed by prices and a limited money income. It follows that market choices must represent positions of maximum u subject to budget constraints. But it is well known and we shall later confirm that for such positions of 'equilibrium' to exist at all u must be quasi-convex in the equilibrium region.

In other words, given the axioms of 1.1, either u is quasi-

† More formally we might say: Consider the set, S^1, of all commodity bundles λx^1, where λ is any real non-negative number and x^1 is arbitrarily chosen from the set, S, of all bundles. S^1 must be identical with the union of two subsets of itself namely $[x \in S^1 : u(x^0) \geqq u(x)]$ and $[x \in S^1 : u(x) \geqq u(x^0)]$ where x^0 is any arbitrarily chosen bundle in S but not in S^1. Suppose one of the subsets defined is not closed, then it must possess a limit point not included in it. Such a limit point if it existed would also be a limit point of a similarly defined subset of the set S of all bundles and again cannot be a member of the larger subset. Thus one of the subsets $[x \in S : u(x) \geqq u(x^0)]$ and $[x \in S : u(x^0) \geqq u(x)]$ cannot be closed. But this is impossible by axiom (iii). It follows that both subsets must contain a common limit point x^1. Therefore $u(x^1) \geqq u(x^0)$ and $u(x^0) \geqq u(x^1)$ or $u(x^1) = u(x^0)$ so that two points of indifference exist.

‡ This means that, if two bundles x^0 and x^1 are both in the set, any weighted average of them is also in the set.

convex or some very odd behaviour would be observed in the
market. This can be made clear in two dimensions by an
elementary geometrical argument. The difficulties which arise
are no different in principle in the more general case.

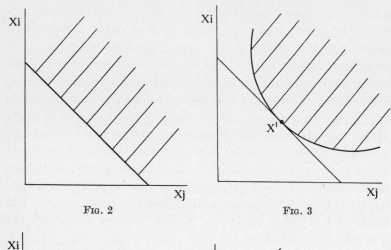

FIG. 2   FIG. 3

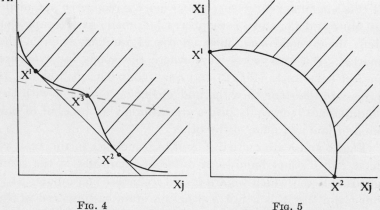

FIG. 4   FIG. 5

The shaded areas in Figs. 2–5 represent the set of all commodity bundles of two goods i and j such that $u(x)$ is greater
than or equal to a given constant. The boundaries of the shaded
areas therefore are 'indifference' curves. In Figs. 2 and 3 u is
quasi-convex, in Figs. 4 and 5 it is not.

When a consumer makes a choice under market conditions he takes prices and total spending as given. He is therefore constrained by a budget line as in Fig. 3. He must choose that commodity bundle on the budget line (e.g. x^1, Fig. 3) which maximizes u. In Fig. 3 it is perfectly clear that x^1 alone maximizes u. In Figs. 4 and 5, however, we have a possible budget line which could leave the consumer undecided between two commodity bundles x^1 and x^2 giving equal satisfaction. It is clear that such a situation can always occur whenever u is not quasi-convex as in Figs. 4 and 5. In fact 5 is a specialization of 4.

Evidently cases 4 and 5 would be immediately recognizable in practice if they arose. The consumer, being unable to make up his mind between two possible bundles, would be forced to choose at random. This is contrary to experience. To rule out 4 and 5 we have to appeal to the facts of the market and claim that consumers are not normally forced to the point where they have to choose at random, except perhaps between, say, two kinds of jam. This brings us to Fig. 2 which illustrates the exception.

It is a common experience that when i is raspberry jam made by Mutt and Co. and j is raspberry jam made by a competitor Jeff, then we do sometimes choose at random, even in the market. But this is the case where the goods involved are perfect substitutes (Fig. 2) and quasi-convexity still holds. If prices are the same then the budget line is coincident with the 'indifference' curve. If prices are different we take all of one kind of jam and none of the other.

Figs. 4 and 5 are quite different in principle. In this case we have two distinct bundles of different quantities of the same goods between which we are forced to choose at random. It is our claim that this is not a situation often encountered in the market. As long as goods i and j are distinguishable it appears that most consumers can settle fairly readily on a unique pattern of expenditure.

It is emphasized again that we are not arguing that it is impossible to find bundles between which we should be forced to choose at random if no prices or income constraints were involved. Indeed we have already proved the contrary. What we are arguing is that when a choice x^0 is made *in the market* it is our usual experience that any other bundle which we rank equal to x^0 in our ordering costs more than x^0. In short the housewife goes to the market with a fairly certain idea of what on the average it is 'best' for her to buy.

We notice also that Figs. 4 and 5 imply that there is some combination of goods i and j (e.g. x^3 Fig. 4) which would *never* be bought at *any* set of prices. This again is contrary to experience, which suggests that changing relative prices induces a fairly smooth transition from one pattern of spending to another, rather than a leap from x^2 to x^1 as in Fig. 4. For the individual, of course, a leap is common experience when a change is made from Mutt's jam to Jeff's following a price change. But this can be explained in terms of perfect substitutability as in Fig. 2.

One other argument might be used. It is sometimes said, on the evidence of introspection, that, the more we have of any good relative to a second good, the more of it we should be willing to give up in exchange for one unit of the second good. This is consistent with Fig. 3 but inconsistent with Figs. 4 and 5.

Finally we state hypothesis three:

(iii) The function u is assumed to be twice differentiable.

This smoothness postulate is introduced as a matter of convenience only. It would almost certainly be possible to say all that appears below entirely in terms of finite mathematics. For various reasons, however, this has not been attempted.

We shall not, on the other hand, exclude from the discussion interesting and practically important cases where the optimum position is a boundary optimum, e.g. as could be the case in Fig. 2 above, when prices are such that the consumer takes all of one kind of jam and none of the other.

Nor shall we hesitate to relax the assumption that the derivatives of u are continuous if the occasion calls for it. In a later chapter, for example, we shall consider the possibility of complete complementarity where, in certain regions, indifference surfaces degenerate into points or have a 'corner' in at least one direction. Thus it is claimed there is no loss of generality in our chosen approach.

We are now in a position to set out the principal results of the theory of demand. Before turning to this, however, further comment seems called for on the meaning of a commodity bundle x^0. We have discussed at length the difficulties connected with the measurement of quantity, but we have not yet defined a commodity. It is worth reminding ourselves that it is not simply a matter of convenience whether we choose to distinguish, as separate commodities, say, knives and spoons, or whether we lump the two together into a composite good called 'cutlery'. There exist in the world, as a matter of fact, certain basic goods which are separately identifiable as long as their prices can in principle vary independently of the price of *all* other goods.†

Even though it is sometimes convenient, for practical reasons, to aggregate basic goods into groups, it must be remembered that there is nothing in the theory of demand to suggest that such a procedure is valid in general. In some cases the error involved may be small, in others aggregation could give utterly misleading results. The problem in general is difficult and only partially soluble. It will concern us later.

In the meantime, in what follows a commodity bundle x^0 must be taken to mean a bundle of basic goods. To decide whether a particular good, i, is basic or not we look for a second good j whose price is so bound up with the price of i that the two must in all circumstances vary proportionately. If no such good j exists then i is basic. If j does exist then i and j can be combined and the combined good is basic.‡

† This is one of the very few points on which the present writer finds himself not wholly in agreement with Professor P. A. Samuelson, who argues in *The Foundations of Economic Analysis* (p. 130) that 'even if we confine our attention to what is ordinarily called a commodity, such as "wheat", we find ourselves dealing with a composite commodity made up of winter wheat, spring wheat, of varying grades. Each of these in turn is a composite of heterogeneous components, and so forth in infinite regression.' The regression is not quite infinite and we have proposed in the text a satisfactory working rule by which to identify a basic good.

‡ The statement that goods whose prices vary proportionately can be treated as one good, is so obvious intuitively that a proof is scarcely needed,

→1.3. On long- and short-run saving

So far we have established that, on our assumptions, consumer behaviour must reflect the consequences of attempts to maximize a utility function u (as defined in sections 1.1 and 1.2), subject to certain constraints. We now examine the nature of the constraints.

First we notice that the price p_i of the ith individual good is unambiguously known as soon as the unit of quantity, q_i, is decided upon. Here we use q_i as in section 1.2 to mean a physical quantity as most conveniently measured. The reader is reminded that q_i might be very different from x_i which is the quantity used up in the time period.

We now define
$$C_n = \sum_i p_i x_i. \qquad\qquad 1.3 \text{ (i)}$$

C_n is 'notional' money spending in the time period. The existence of consumer durables makes it necessary to distinguish carefully between C_n and the *actual* money C_a spent on purchases in the time period.

1.3 (i) is described as a definition of C_n. Such a definition, however, cannot be any more precise than the not very satisfactory definition of x_i given in section 1.2. On the other hand, 1.3 (i) suggests the possibility that we might be able to give a more exact meaning to 'quantity used up' by some new definition of C_n and we shall discover this to be the case.

Spending is identically income less saving, and income is a fairly well established, measurable, entity. Most of the difficulties are in fact associated with the notion of saving. To begin with we separate two motives for saving which might be

even if we had already assembled the necessary apparatus to give it; for we can easily define the unit of quantity of the composite commodity as £'s worth at base year prices and there can never be any price index number problem as long as the prices of all elements vary proportionately. Moreover, 'price' multiplied by 'quantity' of the composite commodity will always be the same as total expenditure on all the elements.

The reader who very properly doubts intuitive argument is invited to take each of the results of section 1.4 (below) in turn and to test whether they hold for a composite good $\bar{x} \equiv \sum p_i x_i$ given that the ratio of all p_i is invariant. Proofs are simple and direct.

A more general approach to the problem is set out in P. A. Samuelson, *The Foundations of Economic Analysis*, p. 141.

called short run and long run. Short-run saving or dis-saving is designed to meet irregularities in the flow of payments for durable consumer goods and will be explained later. Long-run saving, on the other hand, is a much more complex phenomenon governed by a variety of forces.

It is not intended, at this point, to try to develop a theory of long-run saving.† We may mention, however, some of the possible determinants of additions to long-run saving per time period. Essentially the consumer wishes to enjoy the fruits of his whole life's labour at a rate different from that at which he earns income. He may even wish to leave some part of his wealth to be spent after his death by dependants or others. In any time period, therefore, he must consider his stock of wealth, the rate of interest, expected future prices, and expected earnings.

It follows that in so far as current spending is influenced by the factors noted they should appear in any function purporting to define current consumption of the ith good. The alternative might be to include long-run saving itself (or, what we shall claim amounts to the same thing, C_n) directly in the demand function as an independent variable. In fact the main purpose of Chapter 2 will be to identify the circumstances in which this is a valid procedure. For the moment we anticipate the results of Chapter 2 by assuming that it is.

In other words we shall develop a theory of demand to explain how *current* demand in a given time period is determined, given current prices and overall current *notional* spending. We shall not attempt to explain what determines current notional spending but we shall define it carefully and argue that it is an operational concept. Under ideal conditions it could be directly measured and parameters associated with it computed.

What we have called short-run saving is not really saving at all but the operation of lending to self to finance the purchase of durable consumer goods. In principle the consumer is acting as his own hire-purchase company. An example will make clear the various distinctions. Suppose that the consumer has a stock

† There is a very considerable literature on this subject. A suitable reference would be *A Theory of the Consumption Function* by Milton Friedman.

of wealth of £1,000 which he wishes to leave to his children. He might use the money as follows without diminishing his stock of wealth. He buys a car for £1,000 paying himself an annual hire charge appropriately calculated. The hire charge is invested as paid. At any moment of time the consumer's total assets will be valued at £1,000. Additions to long-run saving are zero. Total *notional* expenditure C_n is the same as annual income. Actual annual expenditure C_a is income less the hire charge which is 'short run saved'. In the year in which the car wears out and is replaced, actual expenditure will, of course, be greater than income so that, on the average over the years, actual expenditure and notional expenditure are the same.

If the consumer's stock of wealth is zero and he borrows from a hire-purchase company, the principles are precisely the same. On the other hand, it should be remembered that, in practice, hire-purchase companies lay down rigid rules regarding repayment, which impose limitations on the hirer's freedom to determine the 'life' of the asset for the purpose of computing the hire charge. This merely reflects the fact already noted, that useful life depends on t, the number of hours in use per unit of time, as well as l, the technical life. Hire-purchase companies cannot control t but the consumer can. In practice, therefore, the consumer who buys on hire purchase must be thought of as borrowing, partly from the finance company and partly from himself in a somewhat complicated pattern.

C_n can now be precisely defined. If r is the rate of interest, then the hire charge for q units of a durable item of price p is the equivalent payment per unit of time, p', such that

$$\int_0^{l/t} p'e^{-rl/t}\, d(l/t) = qp,$$

or
$$p' = \frac{rpq}{1-e^{-rl/t}}. \qquad \text{1.3 (ii)}\dagger$$

† The present value has been written in the exponential (continuous) form $e^{-rl/t}$ so that we might avoid the tedious summation of a geometric series of the type
$$\sum_{T=0}^{l-1} p'(1+r)^{-T} \quad (T = \text{time}).$$
The principle is precisely the same and the difference negligible for small r.

In words, we choose an equivalent payment such that the present (discounted) value of the whole series of payments over the life of the asset is equal to present price. l/t is, of course, the actual life of the asset whose technical life is l and whose owner intends to use it for one tth of each time period. Summing all equivalent payments in any time period we obtain a definition of C_n, namely

$$C_n = \sum_i p_i \frac{rq_i}{1 - e^{-rl_i/l_i}}. \qquad \text{1.3 (iii)}$$

Comparing 1.3 (i) and 1.3 (iii) yields the more exact definition of quantity used up which we seek

$$x_i = \frac{rq_i}{1 - e^{-rl_i/l_i}}. \qquad \text{1.3 (iv)}$$

At first sight this may appear a somewhat odd definition of a quantity; but it is not by any means illogical. If there were no rate of interest 1.3 (iv) would reduce to $t_i q_i/l_i$ which is the common-sense definition of quantity used up previously given. The fact that the rate of interest does appear as part of x_i reminds us of something we may tend otherwise to forget, namely that when we buy a durable asset *we cannot escape buying at the same time a loan service*. As long as r is positive 1.3 (iv) is greater than $t_i q_i/l_i$, the addition to $t_i q_i/l_i$ being a measure of the quantity of loan service complementary to the purchase.

If the loan service happens to be provided by the purchaser of the durable good himself, this merely disguises, but does not alter, the fact that it *has* been provided. By deducting q_i from 1.3 (iv) we could obtain explicitly a measure of the quantity of loan service at price p_i, namely

$$\frac{q_i(r - 1 + e^{-rl_i/l_i})}{1 - e^{-rl_i/l_i}}.$$

But this is of little interest; for we have here an example of two goods (asset and loan service) whose prices p_i are always the same. They may therefore be treated as one good alone by the rule already noted in 1.2; and we shall proceed in this way.

From this point on we develop our theory strictly in terms of quantities x_i as defined in 1.3 (iv). The budget constraint will be written as in 1.3 (i) which is equivalent to 1.3 (iv). Of course, actual expenditure C_a in the time period is usually more easily observed than the notional expenditure C_n. Nevertheless, given the age distribution of assets, intentions regarding their use, and the rate of interest, C_n can be computed from a knowledge of C_a. Moreover, estimation of C_a in the aggregate is not without its practical difficulties in view of the existence of second-hand markets.

In the empirical work of later chapters lack of information makes it necessary to devise approximate methods or to introduce assumptions not strictly consistent with the theory. Nevertheless, it is contended here, firstly that a precise theory is necessary to an understanding of our aims, and secondly, that no such theory is possible except on the lines outlined above.

Accordingly, in what follows, when we distinguish between income and consumption, we use the symbols y and C. C means C_n. Where we do not distinguish between income and consumption we use the symbol y to mean C_n, y being a more familiar notation. The concept of income as opposed to spending is dropped after the discussion in Chapter 2 for reasons which will be given in that chapter. This means that, contrary to the more usual practice, we think of current consumption of any commodity as dependent upon all prices and *total spending*, rather than current *income*, and the computations of later chapters are consistent with this definition. Thus, except in Chapter 2, we shall write $y \equiv \sum p_i x_i$ where p_i and x_i have meanings as in 1.3 (i). This is the budget constraint.

1.4. The principal results

The following treatment will be very brief since most of the work of this section is well known.†

In a position of consumer equilibrium the function u is maximized subject to the budget constraint $\sum p_i x_i - y = 0$.

† Cf., for example, P. A. Samuelson, *The Foundations of Economic Analysis*, chap. v.

This is equivalent to maximizing the Lagrangian expression

$$u - \lambda\left(\sum p_i x_i - y \right) = 0$$

given p's and y as parameters.†

Necessary conditions for a maximum are therefore

$$u_i - \lambda p_i = 0 \quad (i = 1, 2, ..., n) \qquad \text{1.4 (i)}$$

where u_i is the partial derivative of u with respect to the ith good. u_i will be referred to as the marginal utility of the ith good. 1.4 (i) implies

$$u_i / u_j = p_i / p_j,$$

a condition which is sometimes stated in words as follows: 'The marginal utilities of all goods must be proportional, in equilibrium, to their prices.'

The λ of 1.4 (i) is often called the marginal utility of money and this is a useful and intuitively acceptable name for it. On the other hand, λ must not be thought of as a measurable magnitude, at least on the basis of the present theory. This much is obvious from the work of earlier sections; for we have been at pains to show that u is an arbitrary order-preserving function which can just as well be replaced by any $F(u)$. In this case 1.4 (i) would read

$$F' u_i - \lambda p_i = 0 \qquad \text{1.4 (ii)}$$

where F' is the derivative of F with respect to u.

Dividing throughout by F' yields a result identical with 1.4 (i) except that λ is replaced by λ/F'. This may be interpreted simply as meaning that 1.4 (i) stands whatever the order-preserving function chosen but that λ depends on the choice of function. We shall show in due course that behaviour is invariant under changes in the marginal utility of money so that no experiment can determine λ.

In spite of the fact, however, that the name 'marginal utility of money' must not be taken to imply, *a priori*, that some kind of measure can be attached to subjective feelings about the usefulness of money, the term is convenient: for p_i of 1.4 (i) has a money dimension giving λp_i a utility dimension similar to u_i. Thus 1.4 (i) can be interpreted as meaning that the ith good

† Cf. R. G. D. Allen, *Mathematical Analysis for Economists*, p. 366.

will be bought up to the point where the marginal utility of the last unit purchased is equal to the marginal utility of the money given up for it. There is no reason at all why we should not think of 1.4 (i) in these common-sense terms.

It is also common practice to illustrate the equilibrium 1.4 (i) as a point of tangency between a budget line or hyper-plane determined by the equation

$$\sum_i p_i x_i / p_j = y/p_j$$

and some one indifference hyper-surface defined by $u = $ constant, in the manner of the diagrams Figs. 2–5 in section 1.2. Clearly the slope of the budget line is $-p_i/p_j$ and the slope of the indifference curve is $-u_i/u_j$, so that tangency is equivalent to 1.4 (i). The reader may find it convenient later in this book to have the geometrical picture in mind.

Finally, on the subject of utility maximizing conditions, we notice that, to be sure of being able to attain a point of equality as in 1.4 (i), the function u_i must be continuous. In general this is ensured by our assumption that u is twice differentiable. There are, however, at least three cases where this assumption might appear to be too restrictive. The first occurs where it is suspected that there may exist an attainable point of satiation, i.e. where a small increment of some one good has no effect whatever upon the position in the consumer's ordering of the commodity bundle concerned. In other words, a point where $u_i = 0$.

Evidently as long as p_i is greater than zero and u_i is continuous then 1.4 (i) ensures that the consumer will never choose a commodity bundle containing sufficient of any good to attain a satiation point (unless, of course, demand for all goods is satiated and $\lambda = 0$). Moreover, nothing in the experiments described in later chapters in any way contradicts this conclusion, which implies that responses in consumption to price changes can never be zero for any good.† On the other hand, it

† Where there is high complementarity in consumption between one good and all others, and where a very small proportion of total income is spent on that good, price response could be very small. But it cannot reach zero unless demand is completely satisfied. See Chapter 4 below.

has been argued on the basis of introspection that, in practice, consumers do in fact choose bundles which completely satiate their demand for some items. Alternatively it is claimed that certain small purchases are commonly made without any regard whatever to prices, a view which is considered in greater detail in section 1.7. Such behaviour, if it occurred, would not be inconsistent with the hypothesis that discontinuities exist in the function u_i, in which case 1.4 (i) must be replaced by the inequality

$$u_i \geqq \lambda p_i. \qquad\qquad 1.4 \text{ (iii)}$$

Thus, if u_i takes values, say five and zero, in the region of the same point then the same commodity bundle will be chosen for all λp_i between five and zero.

Against the idea of attainable points of satiation, however, it is worth noting that there are plausible alternative explanations of price-ignoring behaviour. Efficient purchasing cannot be undertaken without sacrifice in terms of personal 'toil and trouble'. Sometimes we may feel that fine adjustment of purchases to small price changes which may have occurred is just not worth the effort. This possibility seems the more likely the higher is real income; and such a view again is confirmed by objective evidence. In practice the toil and trouble effect might show up as a time lag in adjustment to price changes.

In short, when we recognize that points of satiation necessarily imply a discontinuity in u_i (or u), it appears much less likely that they should be attainable, particularly in the face of the arguments of section 1.2 which claim that all x_i are continuously variable, and having in view alternative explanations of price ignoring behaviour. Nevertheless, we recognize the possibility.

The second and more interesting reason why 1.4 (i) may take the form of an inequality is due to the possibility of complete complementarity. Two goods i and j may be so related that they are always taken in fixed proportions. We have a situation in which a small increase in i makes no difference to the ordering of the bundle simply because there is no corresponding change in j. But a small change in i and j together, in the right proportion, would make a change in the ordering. Thus u_i is zero and

u_j is zero so that once again 1.4 (i) becomes the inequality 1.4 (iii). The indifference curve has a sharp corner and tangency to a budget plane is meaningless. A wide range of relative prices gives the same choice of commodity bundle.

In a sense complementarity is very like satiation; for given a certain amount of good i, the 'utility' of j increases steadily up to the point where i and j are in their complementary proportions, whereas beyond that point marginal utility suddenly becomes zero; i.e. the function

$$u_j(x_j, x_i^0) \quad (x_i^0 = \text{constant})$$

has a discontinuity. The demand for j, given i, is satiated at a certain point. This kind of want satiation does not present the same logical difficulties as satiation without complementarity. We shall consider complementarity at length in Chapter 3.

The third case where the equality 1.4 (i) may not be attainable is that where the maximum is a border maximum, i.e. where all of one good and nothing of another is taken. It may be that nowhere on the budget plane is u_i sufficiently great in relation to λp_i to attain the equality 1.4 (i). If there were only two goods we might then have

$$\frac{u_j}{u_i} > \frac{p_j}{p_i}$$

with no i bought. This possibility is normally irrelevant since it disappears if we exclude from the system any good which is not taken. On the other hand, it may be important when we come to deal with group demand or when the excluded commodity is on the margin of being included. In any case 1.4 (iii) remains a necessary condition for a maximum.

This seems a suitable point at which to make it clear once again that when we make use of the necessary condition for a maximum in the form 1.4 (i) we do so because it is the more usual case, or a good approximation to it. The exceptional cases will be dealt with as and when occasion arises.

In passing it is worth noting also that, although the assumption of a quasi-convex utility function ensures that the equilibrium defined by 1.4 (i) is unique, it does not imply diminishing marginal utility everywhere; i.e. it is not necessary that u_i (given all x_j, $j \neq i$) should be a continuously diminishing function of x_i. It may well be, for example, that the 'marginal utility' of a set of golf clubs remains very low until their owner practices with them sufficiently often to maintain a certain minimum level of skill in their use. This possibility is allowed for by our insistence that it is only indifference curves which are convex and not the utility function itself. A proof of uniqueness of equilibrium on the weaker condition is scarcely needed in view of the discussion in section 1.2.†

The n equations 1.4 (i), together with the budget constraint, may now be solved for the n commodity demands, x_i, and the marginal utility of money, λ, in terms of prices, p_i, and spending y. The fact that λ can be expressed as a function of the observable p's and y does not contradict the argument above showing that λ cannot be measured; for the form of the λ function will depend on the choice of utility function. On the other hand, it is easy to see that this is not true of demand functions, for writing 1.4 (i) in the form

$$u_i/u_j = p_i/p_j \qquad \text{1.4 (iv)}$$

we see that we have $n-1$ equations which together with the budget constraint make n equations which do not depend on the choice of utility function. These equations yield demand equations which are in turn independent of the choice of utility function. It is clear also that, when we put the budget equation in the form

$$\sum_i \frac{p_i x_i}{p_j} = \frac{y}{p_j}$$

the n prices and y can be treated as $n-1$ price ratios and y/p_i. In view of the form of 1.4 (iv) it follows that demand equations must be homogeneous of order zero. The doubling of prices and *spending* must leave the quantities consumed unchanged. By

---

† A convex u would imply that the determinant $|u_{ij}|$ is the discriminant of a negative definite quadratic form. The weaker condition requires only that the bordered determinant

$$\begin{vmatrix} 0 & u_i \\ u_j & u_{ij} \end{vmatrix}$$

should be the discriminant of a negative semi-definite quadratic form.

Euler's theorem† therefore we have the result

$$\sum_j p_j \frac{\partial x_i}{\partial p_j} + y \frac{\partial x_i}{\partial y} = 0,$$

or

$$\sum_j \frac{p_j}{x_i} \frac{\partial x_i}{\partial p_j} = -\frac{y}{x_i} \frac{\partial x_i}{\partial y}.$$ 1.4 (v)

The logarithmic derivatives

$$\frac{p_j}{x_i} \frac{\partial x_i}{\partial p_j}$$

are usually called elasticities or cross elasticities of demand and will be written E_{ij}. The expression on the right-hand side of 1.4 (v) is the logarithmic derivative of the demand function with respect to spending. This spending derivative is sometimes loosely called income elasticity in the work that follows, in the same spirit in which y is used interchangeably with C_n. Thus we may put 1.4 (v) into words as follows: 'The sum of elasticities and cross elasticities of demand for any good with respect to prices is equal to minus the income elasticity.'

An analogous result to 1.4 (v) can be obtained as follows. By definition:

$$\sum p_i x_i = y.$$

Differentiating with respect to p_j yields:

$$\sum_i p_i \frac{\partial x_i}{\partial p_j} = -x_j,$$ 1.4 (vi)

or

$$\sum_i \frac{x_i}{x_j} E_{ij} = -1.$$ 1.4 (vii)

Consider now any change, dp_j, in the jth price. Clearly there is a sense in which the consumer can be compensated for this change; for, if we award him a sum of money equal to $x_j\, dp_j$, he is free to buy precisely the same bundle of commodities as in his original position. The fact that he may not wish to buy the original bundle in face of the new prices does not alter the fact that he cannot make himself significantly better off by a change; for any small move in the region of equilibrium leaves the consumer equally well off, by definition of equilibrium.

† Cf. R. G. D. Allen, *Mathematical Analysis for Economists*, p. 319.

Suppose that we do in fact award the consumer a money compensation of $x_j \, dp_j$. The extra expenditure allocated to the ith good will be

$$p_i \frac{\partial x_i}{\partial y} (x_j \, dp_j)$$

and the sum of all allocations must be equal to $x_j \, dp_j$. Thus

$$\sum_i p_i \frac{\partial x_i}{\partial y} (x_j \, dp_j) = x_j \, dp_j$$

or
$$\sum_i p_i \frac{\partial x_i}{\partial y} x_j = x_j. \qquad \text{1.4 (viii)}$$

We could, of course, have written this down straight away from the fact that differentiating the budget equation by y gives

$$\sum_i p_i \frac{\partial x_i}{\partial y} = 1. \qquad \text{1.4 (ix)}$$

Adding 1.4 (viii) to 1.4 (vi) we get

$$\sum_i p_i \left[\frac{\partial x_i}{\partial p_j} + x_j \frac{\partial x_i}{\partial y} \right] = 0.$$

The bracketed expressions are known to economists as 'substitution effects' and they measure the rate of change in consumption of the ith good with respect to changes in the jth price *when money compensation is given*. Substitution effects are written σ_{ij} in the work that follows. The result

$$\sum_i p_i \sigma_{ij} = 0 \qquad \text{1.4 (x)}$$

has been used with great effect in the theory of international trade.

The logic of the expression compensation is further underlined when we recall that
$$p_i = u_i / \lambda$$

by the equilibrium condition. Thus 1.4 (x) can be written

$$\sum_i u_i \sigma_{ij} = 0.$$

This confirms that the value of the utility function remains unchanged when compensation is paid, following a price rise, sufficient to enable the consumer to buy his originally chosen bundle of goods. That the original bundle is not chosen although it could be, is evident from the fact that all σ_{ij} are not normally zero.

From the definition of σ_{ij} it follows that the partial derivatives of every demand equation are made up of two terms as follows:

$$\frac{\partial x_i}{\partial p_j} = -x_j\frac{\partial x_i}{\partial y} + \sigma_{ij}. \qquad 1.4\ (\text{xi})$$

The possibility of breaking up price responses into two parts in this way has again been found to be of great value in the theory of international trade. It plays a key role also in the later work of this book. The term $-x_j\,(\partial x_i/\partial y)$ has been given the name 'income effect'. It will be noticed that it measures the change in demand for the ith good due to the loss in real wealth incurred by the rise in the jth price.

It is sometimes convenient to convert 1.4 (xi) into elasticity form and write

$$E_{ij} = -C_i x_j/x_i + p_i \sigma_{ij}/x_i$$

where C_i is called the marginal propensity to consume the ith good. C_i is in fact the proportion of unit increase in money income which would be spent on the ith good, all prices remaining unchanged.

An analogous result to 1.4 (x) can be obtained directly from 1.4 (v) by breaking up the price response into its two parts as follows:

$$\sum_j \frac{p_j}{x_i}\left(-x_j\frac{\partial x_i}{\partial y} + \sigma_{ij}\right) = -\frac{y}{x_i}\frac{\partial x_i}{\partial y}.$$

Summing and using the budget identity $\sum_j p_j x_j = y$ yields

$$\sum_j p_j \sigma_{ij} = 0, \qquad 1.4\ (\text{xii})$$

1.4 (x) and 1.4 (xii) would clearly be the same if σ_{ij} were identically equal to σ_{ji}. But this is not yet established. To prove it calls for a great deal more work.

In this connexion it is worth pausing for a moment to reflect that all of the restrictions on demand functions so far identified could have been obtained directly from two simple assumptions:

(a) that the demand for any commodity is dependent on prices and total spending, and

(b) that doubling prices and money spending leaves demand unchanged.

The reader may be tempted to wonder why it is considered so necessary to show that a utility function can be constructed.

The answer is that the symmetry of substitution effects (i.e. $\sigma_{ij} = \sigma_{ji}$) is a direct consequence of the transitivity of the preference relation, P, of section 1.1. In other words, symmetry implies the existence of an order-preserving function. Whatever approach to demand theory we favour (cf. section 1.6 below), we must either at some stage introduce the transitivity assumption (or its equivalent) or do without symmetry. And it will later become clear that the symmetry restriction, if it is empirically justified, not only suggests valuable qualitative conclusions but can be of crucial importance to econometricians. It is in fact a cornerstone of later work in this book. The elaborate analysis of the foundations of utility theory, with which this chapter began, was designed to justify, on strictly empirical grounds, the claim that the symmetry hypothesis is at least worth testing, and to show that, until the matter is settled one way or another, there are good reasons for accepting as valid any consequences of the assumption.

There are various ways of proving symmetry, some more elegant than others. We choose the straightforward method, which, although somewhat tedious, provides, in the opinion of the writer, the greatest insight into the theory. We begin by differentiating the budget identity and the n equations

$$u_i - \lambda p_i = 0 \quad (i = 1, 2, ..., n)$$

partially with respect to p_j. This yields $n+1$ equations as follows:

$$\sum_i p_i \frac{\partial x_i}{\partial p_j} = -x_j,$$

$$-p_k \frac{\partial \lambda}{\partial p_j} + \sum_i u_{ki} \frac{\partial x_i}{\partial p_j} = 0 \quad (k = 1, 2, ..., n; \; k \neq j),$$

$$-p_j \frac{\partial \lambda}{\partial p_j} + \sum_i u_{ji} \frac{\partial x_i}{\partial p_j} = \lambda. \qquad \qquad 1.4 \text{ (xiii)}$$

Before attempting to solve for $\partial x_i / \partial p_j$ we remind ourselves that

u can equally be any arbitrary function of u, $F(u)$. In such a case u_{ij} above is replaced by $F''u_i u_j + F'u_{ij}$ where F' and F'' are the first and second derivatives of $F(u)$. Consider now the bordered determinant

$$\begin{vmatrix} 0 & p_j \\ p_i & F''u_i u_j + F'u_{ij} \end{vmatrix}.$$

Using the fact that $F'u_j = \lambda p_j$ it is clear that this determinant, or any minor including a row or column of p's can be written without terms in F'', as under

$$\begin{vmatrix} 0 & p_j \\ p_i & F'u_{ij} \end{vmatrix}$$

for multiplying the p row or column by $u_j F''\lambda/F'$ and deducting from the jth row or column eliminates terms involving F''.

Evidently also, solutions for $\partial x_i/\partial p_j$ taken from 1.4 (xiii) will appear as the ratio of pairs of determinants of the reducible kind. By dividing top and bottom of these ratios by λ, or by F', where appropriate, all p_i become u_i and all F' disappear. This simply confirms what we previously proved, namely, that demand functions are independent of our choice of F. Thus we are (so long as we remember that λ is *not* a constant) free to choose a utility function u such that λ is unity at the equilibrium point under consideration. Accordingly we put $p_i = u_i$ in equilibrium.

The solution for $\partial x_i/\partial p_j$ taken from 1.4 (xiii) may now be written:

$$\frac{\partial x_i}{\partial p_j} = -x_j \frac{\Delta_i}{\Delta} + \frac{\Delta_{ji}}{\Delta} \qquad \text{1.4 (xiv)}$$

where Δ is the bordered determinant

$$\begin{vmatrix} 0 & u_i \\ u_j & u_{ji} \end{vmatrix}$$

that is, the so-called Hessian determinant of the utility function u bordered by u_i. Δ_i is the co-factor of the element u_i in Δ and Δ_{ji} is the co-factor of the element u_{ji}. It is true also that as long as u exists and is continuous, with continuous partial derivatives, Δ is symmetric, i.e. $u_{ij} = u_{ji}$, the order of differentiation not affecting the value of the second derivative.

The two terms of 1.4 (xiv) can easily be shown to be the income and substitution effect respectively of $\partial x_i/\partial p_j$; for if the equations of equilibrium and the budget equations are differentiated with respect to spending, y, instead of p_j, the solution for $\partial x_i/\partial y$ turns out to be Δ_i/Δ. Thus

$$\frac{\Delta_{ji}}{\Delta} = \sigma_{ji}$$

and the symmetry of Δ ensures that

$$\sigma_{ij} = \sigma_{ji} \qquad\qquad 1.4 \text{ (xv)}$$

which is our fundamental result.

We now develop certain conditions of sign which can be imposed on σ_{ij}. These are a consequence of the quasi-convexity of u, or more properly of the fact that u is maximized. A very simple proof is available based on the uniqueness of the maximum.

Suppose the consumer at prices p^0 chooses a commodity bundle x^0. It follows from the uniqueness of the maximum of u, subject to constraint, that the relation $x^0 P x^1$ holds for any x^1 meeting the condition:

$$(p^0, x^0) \geqq (p^0, x^1) \quad \left(\text{where } (p^0, x^0) = \text{ the inner product } \sum_i p_i^0 x_i^0\right),$$

that is, for any x^1 which could have been bought for the same or less money than x^0 with prices p^0. If it were not so x^1 would have been chosen rather than x^0.

Again since $x^0 P x^1$ it follows that, for any set of prices p^1, and spending, at which x^1 is chosen it must be true that

$$(p^1, x^0) > (p^1, x^1).$$

That is, x^0 must be unattainable at prices p^1 and spending (p^1, x^1), otherwise x^0 would be taken contrary to hypothesis.

Thus writing dx for $x^0 - x^1$ we have

$$(p^0, dx) \geqq 0$$

implies

$$(p^1, dx) > 0$$

or

$$\{(p^0 - dp), dx\} > 0.$$

In the special case where the changes dx leave the consumer on the same budget line, i.e. where $(p^0, dx) = 0$ we have therefore the condition

$$(dp, dx) < 0$$

or, writing this inner product in full,

$$\sum_i dp_i \, dx_i < 0. \qquad \text{1.4 (xvi)}$$

In order now to avoid the approximation involved in the use of differentials consider arbitrary total derivatives dx_i/dp_k.

Any single
$$\frac{dx_i}{dp_k} = \sum_j \frac{\partial x_i}{\partial p_j} \frac{dp_j}{dp_k} + \frac{\partial x_i}{\partial y} \frac{dy}{dp_k}.$$

And, by definition,
$$y \equiv \sum p_i x_i$$

so that
$$\frac{dy}{dp_k} = \sum_i p_i \frac{dx_i}{dp_k} + \sum_i x_i \frac{dp_i}{dp_k}.$$

Moreover, in the special case where $\sum_i p_i \dfrac{dx_i}{dp_k} = 0$

$$\frac{dy}{dp_k} = \sum_i x_i \frac{dp_i}{dp_k},$$

thus the general dx_i/dp_k may be written

$$\frac{dx_i}{dp_k} = \sum_j \frac{\partial x_i}{\partial p_j} \frac{dp_j}{dp_k} + \sum_j x_j \frac{\partial x_i}{\partial y} \frac{dp_j}{dp_k} = \sum_j \sigma_{ij} \frac{dp_j}{dp_k}.$$

But 1.4 (xvi) implies that

$$\sum_i \frac{dp_i}{dp_k} \frac{dx_i}{dp_k} < 0,$$

from which it follows that 1.4 (xvi) is equivalent to

$$\sum_i \sum_j \sigma_{ij} \frac{dp_i}{dp_k} \frac{dp_j}{dp_k} < 0. \qquad \text{1.4 (xvii)}$$

Consider now for a moment whether there is any restriction imposed on the values which the dp_i/dp_k's of 1.4 (xvii) might take, bearing in mind that the rates of change dx_i/dp_k leave the rate of change of utility at zero. We have already seen that any price change whatever can be compensated for by giving the consumer an income sufficient to buy his old commodity bundle at the new price. Similarly any set of price changes may be compensated. At first sight, therefore, it would appear that the dp_i/dp_k's are unrestricted. One case is, however, inadmissible. In stating the original conditions from which 1.4 (xvii) was derived it was tacitly assumed that x^0 and x^1 are different bundles when p^0 and p^1 are different prices. But we have earlier seen that demand functions are homogeneous of order zero in prices and spending, so that x^0 and x^1 could be identical bundles if p^1 simply doubled or trebled all the prices of p^0. If we wish to include the case where the dp_i/dp_k's are equal to the ratios p_i/p_k we have to include the case where

$$p^1 x^0 = p^1 x^1$$

and all dx_i/dp_k are zero. Thus we write

$$\sum_i \sum_j \sigma_{ij} \frac{dp_i}{dp_k} \frac{dp_j}{dp_k} \leqq 0 \qquad \text{1.4 (xviii)}$$

instead of 1.4 (xvii) in order that it should be true for *all* dp_i/dp_k's. If 1.4 (xviii) holds for all dp_i/dp_k's it follows that the determinant $|\sigma_{ij}|$ must be the discriminant of a negative semi-definite quadratic form.† Accordingly we have the following conditions:

$$\sigma_{ii} < 0,$$

$$\begin{vmatrix} \sigma_{ii} & \sigma_{ij} \\ \sigma_{ji} & \sigma_{jj} \end{vmatrix} > 0,$$

$$\begin{vmatrix} \sigma_{ii} & \sigma_{ij} & \sigma_{ik} \\ \sigma_{ji} & \sigma_{jj} & \sigma_{jk} \\ \sigma_{ki} & \sigma_{kj} & \sigma_{kk} \end{vmatrix} < 0, \qquad \text{1.4 (xix)}$$

and so on, with the final nth order determinant *equal* to zero. That the final nth order determinant is zero follows in any case from 1.4 (xii) since there can be no solution to the homogeneous equations

$$\sum_j \sigma_{ij} p_j = 0 \quad (i = 1, 2, ..., n)$$

unless the determinant $|\sigma_{ij}|$ is zero.

It will be helpful for later work if we look at the conditions 1.4 (xix) from a slightly different point of view. In order to be sure that the equilibrium conditions 1.4 (i) define a maximum

---

† Cf. R. G. D. Allen, *Mathematical Analysis for Economists*, p. 485 ff.

value of u, subject to the budget constraint, it is necessary that the bordered Hessian determinant of u

$$\begin{vmatrix} 0 & u_i \\ u_j & u_{ij} \end{vmatrix}$$

should be the discriminant of a negative definite quadratic form.†
By Jacobi's theorem on the minors of the adjugate determinant,‡ it follows that, if $|\Delta_{ij}^r|$ is any rth order minor of the determinant $|\Delta_{ij}|$ (which is the adjugate of the bordered Hessian determinant of u), then

$$|\Delta_{ij}^r| = |u_{ij}^{n-r}| \times |\Delta|^{r-1}$$

where $|u_{ij}^{n-r}|$ is the complementary minor of $|\Delta_{ij}^r|$ in the bordered Hessian determinant of u. Hence

$$|\sigma_{ij}^r| = |\Delta_{ij}^r|/|\Delta|^r = |u_{ij}^{n-r}|/|\Delta|. \qquad 1.4\ (\text{xx})$$

From this result and the fact that the bordered Hessian determinant of u is the discriminant of a negative definite form, the conditions 1.4 (xix) follow at once.

Equations (i), (v), (vii), (ix), (x), (xii), (xv), (xix), and the relation (xx) of this section summarize all of the generally recognized restrictions upon demand functions. Simple though they may appear, a remarkable edifice of economic theory has been constructed upon them as a base. In later pages we shall suggest specializations which imply further restrictions of wide applicability.

1.5. The planning view

Physicists have recently suggested that there may exist an unseen anti-universe, composed of anti-matter, which is in some sense a mirror image of the matter of which we are conscious. On a somewhat less grandiose scale it is open to economists to show that an anti-demand theory is possible which is a mirror image of that set out in section 1.4. The argument that demand theory is two-faced in this way comes strongly out of Professor J. R. Hicks's *Revision of Demand Theory*, and the work of this

† Cf. P. A. Samuelson, *The Foundations of Economic Analysis*, pp. 362 and ff.
‡ Cf. W. L. Ferrar, *Algebra*, theorem 18, p. 57.

section was born of the writer's attempt to grasp Professor Hicks's meaning. It is proper to confess, however, to some degree of uncertainty as to whether this attempt has been successful or not.

First it is clear that although we have concentrated so far upon demand equations, i.e. upon x_i and λ expressed as functions of p's and y, we could equally well write down price equations, i.e. p_i and λ expressed as functions of x's and y.† This might be called the economic planner's view; for the planner asks what price he must set to clear the market of planned output. In the free economy, on the other hand, the chief concern is to know the quantity which can be sold at a given price.

In fact the planning equations are much more easily written than the demand equations, for they stem straight from the equilibrium conditions

$$\lambda p_i = u_i \quad (i = 1, 2, ..., n).$$

To eliminate λ we recall that

$$\sum_i p_i x_i = y = \sum_i u_i x_i / \lambda.$$

Hence
$$p_i = \frac{y u_i}{\sum_i u_i x_i} \quad (i = 1, 2, ..., n) \qquad 1.5 \text{ (i)}$$

and
$$\lambda = \frac{\sum_i u_i x_i}{y}. \qquad 1.5 \text{ (ii)}$$

As before we have the budget equation

$$\sum_i x_i p_i = y$$

which on differentiation with respect to x_j yields

$$\sum_i x_i \frac{\partial p_i}{\partial x_j} = -p_j, \qquad 1.5 \text{ (iii)}$$

the exact analogue of 1.4 (vi).

The price equations, unlike the demand equations, are not

---

† Strictly speaking, of course, the exact mirror image would be the system which expresses all p's and y as functions of x's and λ. But such a system could have little empirical interest; for the partial derivative $\partial p_i / \partial x_j$ *with* λ *constant* is evidently dependent on the choice of utility index.

homogeneous of order zero in y and x, but they are homogeneous of order one in y. Hence

$$p_i = y \frac{\partial p_i}{\partial y},$$

or
$$\frac{\partial p_i}{\partial y} = \frac{p_i}{y} = \frac{u_i}{\sum_i u_i x_i}. \qquad 1.5\ (\text{iv})$$

This result bears a close affinity to 1.4 (v). It tells us in fact that

$$\sum_i x_i \frac{\partial p_i}{\partial y} = 1 \qquad\qquad 1.5\ (\text{v})$$

which is the mirror image of 1.4 (ix).

Following the procedure of section 1.4 we now look for the corresponding entity to the income compensation $x_j dp_j$. By analogy this should be $p_j dx_j$ and, surprisingly, this has a sensible economic interpretation very relevant to planning propositions. Of course, $p_j dx_j$ is not a compensation in the ordinary sense. On the contrary the consumer who has been given an extra dx_j units of the jth good, with no diminution in any other, will not require compensation; indeed quite the reverse. Nevertheless, we recognize $p_j dx_j$ as the amount of extra income, y, which would enable the consumer to buy his old pattern of goods *plus* the extra dx_j units of j at the old prices. He will not *want* to buy this without some adjustment of prices, however; and these adjustments are defined by the 'compensated' response.

There are many instances where the creation of extra goods, without diminution of any other, automatically generates the income to buy them; and we might very well be interested in the new price pattern required to clear the market after such a change. Still in the spirit of the mirror image, we choose the symbol, v, for this price 'substitution' effect. That is, v_{ij} is the change in the price of the ith good required to clear the market of unit increase in the jth commodity, when total spending is increased by the market value of the increased production.

Thus we can write

$$\frac{\partial p_i}{\partial x_j} = -p_j \frac{\partial p_i}{\partial y} + v_{ij}, \qquad\qquad 1.5\ (\text{vi})$$

which is the precise analogue of 1.4 (xi). $\partial p_i/\partial x_j$ is the 'uncompensated' derivative of the price equation. Compensation by an amount p_j will change the price p_i by $p_j\partial p_i/\partial y$ leaving a residual v_{ij}.

Furthermore, from 1.5 (iii) and 1.5 (vi) we have

$$\sum_i x_i v_{ij} - p_j \sum_i x_i \frac{\partial p_i}{\partial y} = -p_j,$$

which in view of 1.5 (v) implies

$$\sum_i x_i v_{ij} = 0, \qquad\qquad 1.5 \text{ (vii)}$$

the analogue of 1.4 (x).

Remarkably enough in the 'planning' view it is the income effect which is symmetric and not the substitution effect. Thus

$$-p_j\frac{\partial p_i}{\partial y} = -\frac{p_j p_i}{y}\ (\text{by } 1.5\ (\text{iv})) = -\frac{p_i p_j}{y} = -p_i\frac{\partial p_j}{\partial y}.$$

$$1.5 \text{ (viii)}$$

That $$v_{ij} \neq v_{ji}$$

in general is easily seen by differentiating 1.5 (i) directly with respect to x_j. This yields

$$\frac{\partial p_i}{\partial x_j} = \left[\frac{y u_{ij}}{\sum\limits_i u_i x_i} - \frac{u_i y \sum\limits_i u_{ij} x_i}{\left(\sum\limits_i u_i x_i\right)^2}\right] - \frac{y u_j u_i}{\left(\sum\limits_i u_i x_i\right)^2}. \qquad 1.5 \text{ (ix)}$$

The final term of 1.5 (ix) is clearly income effect since

$$\frac{p_i p_j}{y} = \frac{u_i u_j}{y\lambda^2} = \frac{y u_i u_j}{\left(\sum u_i x_i\right)^2} \quad (\text{by } 1.5\ (\text{ii})).$$

The term in the square brackets (1.5 (ix)) is therefore v_{ij} which is evidently not symmetric unless special restrictions are imposed on the utility function.

Consider now whether conditions of sign parallel to those of 1.4 (xix) can be imposed upon the partials $\partial p_i/\partial x_j$ and/or the price substitution effects v_{ij}. First let us suppose that the utility function is homogeneous of order one, so that doubling the quantities of all goods doubles the value of u. u_i is then homogeneous of order zero in x's, which implies (by Euler's theorem) that $\sum_j u_{ij} x_j$ is zero. Thus the second term of 1.5 (ix) vanishes,

$$v_{ij} = v_{ji},$$

and incidentally
$$\frac{\partial p_i}{\partial x_j} = \frac{\partial p_j}{\partial x_i}.$$

Evidently homogeneity is a sufficient condition for symmetry in a strong sense.

We recall also that u_{ii} is negative on the 'normal' assumption of diminishing marginal utility; and the income effect is certainly negative. Thus both v_{ii} and $\partial p_i/\partial x_i$ are negative if the utility function is homogeneous of order one. v_{ij} tends to be negative if i and j are substitutes and positive if they are complementary. This contention is based on an intuitive marginal utility argument, which suggests that the marginal utility of good i is decreased by the award of an increment of a substitute, and increased by an increment of any good which is useless without a corresponding quantity of good i itself. If v_{ij} is negative then $\partial p_i/\partial x_j$ is surely negative in the homogeneous case. If v_{ij} is positive then $\partial p_i/\partial x_j$ is of uncertain sign.

In general, when u is not homogeneous, a case may be made for sign rules as for homogeneity, based on the argument that the second term of 1.5 (ix) is likely to be small relative to the others. Such an argument can be sustained for broad classifications of commodities where the marginal propensity to consume each composite good tends not to differ too much from the average, i.e. when

$$\frac{\partial x_i}{\partial y} \frac{y}{x_i}$$

is not very different from unity. In other cases very little can be said about sign.

Remarkably enough, however, a quite general condition restricts the sign of bordered determinants of partials of order two and upward in the spirit of 1.4 (xix). Consider the determinant

$$\begin{vmatrix} 0 & p_j \\ p_i & \dfrac{\partial p_i}{\partial x_j} \end{vmatrix} \equiv \begin{vmatrix} 0 & p_j \\ p_i & u_{ij}/\lambda - \dfrac{\partial \lambda}{\partial x_j} u_i/\lambda^2 \end{vmatrix}.$$

This may easily be reduced (by multiplying column one by

$$\frac{\partial\lambda/\partial x_j}{\lambda}$$

and deducting from column j) to:

$$\frac{1}{\lambda^r}\begin{vmatrix} 0 & u_j \\ u_i & u_{ij} \end{vmatrix}$$

which, since λ is necessarily positive, alternates in sign with order. Thus, corresponding to 1.4 (xix) we have

$$\begin{vmatrix} 0 & p_i & p_j \\ p_i & \dfrac{\partial p_i}{\partial x_i} & \dfrac{\partial p_i}{\partial x_j} \\ p_j & \dfrac{\partial p_j}{\partial x_i} & \dfrac{\partial p_j}{\partial x_j} \end{vmatrix} > 0,$$

$$\begin{vmatrix} 0 & p_i & p_j & p_k \\ p_i & \dfrac{\partial p_i}{\partial x_i} & \dfrac{\partial p_i}{\partial x_j} & \dfrac{\partial p_i}{\partial x_k} \\ p_j & \dfrac{\partial p_j}{\partial x_i} & \dfrac{\partial p_j}{\partial x_j} & \dfrac{\partial p_j}{\partial x_k} \\ p_k & \dfrac{\partial p_k}{\partial x_i} & \dfrac{\partial p_k}{\partial x_j} & \dfrac{\partial p_k}{\partial x_k} \end{vmatrix} < 0, \qquad 1.5\text{ (x)}$$

and so on.

Moreover, it is clear from the form of 1.5 (ix) that we could similarly reduce the bordered determinant

$$\begin{vmatrix} 0 & p_j \\ p_i & v_{ij} \end{vmatrix}. \qquad 1.5\text{ (xi)}$$

In fact each bordered determinant of type 1.5 (xi), of order two and above, takes the same value as the corresponding determinant in 1.5 (x). They possess, therefore, similar properties of sign. It should be noted that none of these determinants are symmetrical as they stand even though they are reducible to a symmetric form.

It is not clear whether all, or any, of the above results were in Professor Hicks's mind as he wrote *A Revision of Demand*

Theory. This is because he works all the time in terms of a 'money' commodity which possesses a utility in its own right.

Nevertheless, he was able to propound the following theorem. 'The change in the price of [the ith good] resulting from a unit change in the quantity of [the jth good] equals the change in the price of [j] resulting from unit change in the quantity of [i] —the quantities of all other commodities than money being kept constant in each case and the quantity of money being adjusted so as to maintain indifference.'†

Evidently this does not mean, in our notation, $v_{ij} = v_{ji}$; for we have just proved this proposition false in general. Moreover, on our definition of money, the whole notion of compensation by money 'so as to maintain indifference' is impossible if the quantity of all commodities consumed is to remain constant; for we have defined u as a function of goods consumed alone, and not of the money spent. From the demand equation point of view, y compensates only by making it possible to buy more goods; but on the planning view, changing y, holding x's constant, merely changes p's, leaving utility unchanged.

On the other hand, we have already noted the set of $n-1$ equations

$$\frac{p_i}{p_k} = \frac{u_i}{u_k} \quad (i = 1, 2, ..., n; \; i \neq k) \qquad \text{1.5 (xii)}$$

which come straight from the equilibrium conditions 1.4 (i). If the kth good is thought of as a *numéraire* (money) commodity whose price p_k is always unity, then we have in effect the remaining $n-1$ prices as functions of all x_i and the quantity of the money commodity x_k. It is now possible to interpret Professor Hicks's theorem as meaning

$$\frac{\partial(p_i/p_k)}{\partial x_j} - \frac{u_j}{u_k} \frac{\partial(p_i/p_k)}{\partial x_k} = \frac{\partial(p_j/p_k)}{\partial x_i} - \frac{u_i}{u_k} \frac{\partial(p_j/p_k)}{\partial x_k}. \qquad \text{1.5 (xiii)}$$

The second term in each case is a compensation term strictly as described by Professor Hicks; for suppose the quantity of good j consumed is changed by unit amount, the amount dx_k

† J. R. Hicks, *A Revision of Demand Theory*, p. 155.

of the money good, k, to be taken away to maintain indifference is u_j/u_k. For then

$$u_j - \left(\frac{u_j}{u_k}\right)u_k = d(u) = 0, \qquad 1.5 \text{ (xiv)}$$

which means no change in utility.

That 1.5 (xiii) must hold can be shown in a straightforward way by differentiating 1.5 (xii) by x_j subject to the side relation $u_j + u_k (dx_k/dx_j) = 0$ which is 1.5 (xiv). Thus we obtain

$$\frac{\partial(p_i/p_k)}{\partial x_j} - \frac{u_j}{u_k} \frac{\partial(p_i/p_k)}{\partial x_k} = \frac{u_{ij}}{u_k} - \frac{u_i}{u_k^2}u_{kj} - \frac{u_j}{u_k}\frac{u_{ik}}{u_k} + \frac{u_j}{u_k}\frac{u_i}{u_k^2}u_{kk},$$

which is symmetric in i and j. Thus 1.5 (xiii) is proved.

It may well be that the importance of this and other 'planning' theorems has been overlooked in the literature; for that of Professor Hicks is the only mention known to the present writer, and even Professor Hicks's explicit treatment is confined to a development of 1.5 (xiii). On the other hand, it is possible to imagine practical problems to which the planning theorems immediately apply.

Suppose, for example, marginal costs are proportional to prices as under competition. A shift of resources from the production of good k to production of good i gives precisely the compensated change of 1.5 (xiii). For, by definition of marginal cost ($= mc$), £1 worth of resources transferred to the production of good i, creates $1/mc_i$ units of i and diminishes output of k by $1/mc_k$ units. The consequent change in the price of good j, given k as *numéraire*, will be

$$\frac{\partial(p_j/p_k)}{\partial x_i} - \frac{mc_i}{mc_k} \frac{\partial(p_j/p_k)}{\partial x_k}$$

which, when mc is proportional to price and price is proportional to marginal utility, is exactly the right-hand side of 1.5 (xiii).

Accordingly, if we were considering the alternatives of shifting resources from use k, either to use i, or to use j, we have in 1.5 (xiii) a relevant theorem relating two of the changes in relative prices necessary to clear the market of the new production.

1.6. Revealed preference

It would be wrong to conclude this account of the basic theory of demand without some reference to what has come to be known as the 'revealed preference' approach. The point of view taken in this section is also very relevant to the work of Chapter 3.

Historically the idea of a utility function was based upon a hedonistic, introspective view of the want satisfying power of commodities. It seemed reasonable to begin from the assumption that the consumer can, in some sense, measure within himself this want satisfying power and accordingly 'knows', and is able to maximize, his own utility function. This is a straightforward way of looking at the matter which is not without value in some contexts. On the other hand, controversy has raged, and in one form or another still rages, on the subject of whether, and in what sense, utility can be measured; or, what amounts to the same thing, whether it is ever proper to define the idea of preference in other than purely behavioural terms. Thus it is often said that 'x^0 is preferred to x^1' can only mean that x^0 will always be chosen whenever x^0 and x^1 are offered. This being so, demand theory is no more than an attempt to explain market behaviour in terms of a utility function which can only be defined in terms of that same market behaviour.

Fortunately, in the present context, there is no need to contribute to the already extensive debate on this subject; for it has recently come to be realized that, so far as the theory of market behaviour is concerned, we do not need utility in its original sense. The reader will already understand that, although the utility function of 1.2 was developed on a purely behavioural basis, we have nevertheless been able to deduce meaningful empirical restrictions on demand functions which are useful and can, in principle, be tested. The argument is not in any way circular.

This does not mean that there are no contexts in which the concept of the hedonistic utility function might be useful. On the contrary, every wage-fixing tribunal, every judge, and every finance minister considering the imposition of a tax, is constantly required not only to think in terms of such utility, but to attach a measure of some kind to it. Moreover, it is one of the functions of economists to try to separate arguments which involve ideas of utility and justice into that part which concerns economic efficiency only and that part which calls for a value judgement. It is simply our good fortune that, in the present book, we are primarily concerned with the description and measurement of market behaviour which, as it turns out, leaves us free to dispense entirely with any concept of welfare.

The reason why, despite our behavioural definition of utility, we are nevertheless able to deduce meaningful theorems about market behaviour is very simple. The clue lies in the word 'market'. The existence of an ordering of commodity bundles was inferred from our knowledge of the fact that individuals can choose, whether there are price and income constraints or not. From this we were able to deduce certain empirical consequences for choices made under market conditions. We have no reason to expect this to lead to circular argument.

We are grateful for the pioneering work done by revealed preference theorists who rightly perceived that the much criticized 'measurable' utility is not necessary to a purely behavioural theory. Nevertheless, it may be that a little too much of the old approach was rejected, with the result that relatively easy things become difficult.

What was rejected in the first instance is all that we suspect about the individual's capacity to choose where there are no price and income constraints, i.e. precisely the part that gives us our meaningful theorems in the work above. It is not surprising therefore that, in these circumstances, it became necessary to introduce an 'axiom of revealed preference' before any theory could be developed. Nor is it surprising that the rationale of the axiom of revealed preference is exactly the rejected part of the basic hypothesis of this book.

The starting-point of revealed preference theorists lies in the observation that under market conditions the individual can choose a unique commodity bundle. This gives demand functions, i.e. a vector value function relating every commodity bundle to prices and spending, written

$$x = f(p, y). \qquad \qquad 1.6 \text{ (i)}$$

By definition of y, this function is also subject to the budget condition

$$(p, x) = y \quad \text{or, in the notation of 1.4,} \quad \sum p_i x_i = y.$$

The mere observation that the consumer, when faced with a set of prices, can and does select, with some degree of certainty, a particular commodity bundle, evidently implies the results 1.4 ((vi), (ix), (x), (xi)); but none of these conditions *per se* imposes any empirical restriction on the form of 1.6 (i). All apply to any function whatsoever.

At this point it is usual to assume that the function 1.6 (i) possesses an inverse. In other words, given any commodity bundle x^0 and some y^0, there is a unique set of prices p^0 which will just induce the consumer to buy x^0. This again accords with our empirically derived ideas of a market. Even so we are still without any useful restriction on the form of the demand function. No further progress is possible.

The attempt was made, therefore, to work backwards and to infer the existence of a quasi-utility function from the fact that individuals choose in the market. In other words, does a u exist such that

$$\lambda p_i = u_i \quad (i = 1, 2, ..., n). \qquad \qquad 1.6 \text{ (ii)}$$

One thing is certain. The inverse of 1.6 (i) will give us p_i as a function of all x's and y, and there are good empirical reasons for suspecting this function to be homogeneous of order one in y. p_i/y is a function of x's alone. Thus if we write the differential equation

$$\sum p_i \, dx_i = 0 \qquad \qquad 1.6 \text{ (iii)}$$

we can, by multiplication by an appropriate factor, eliminate y. It follows therefore from 1.6 (ii) that any solution of 1.6 (iii) must be a solution also of the differential equation

$$\sum u_i \, dx_i = 0$$

and will therefore be a utility function determined up to a monotonic transformation $F(u)$. That u, if it exists, is not fully determined is no more than we should expect from our earlier argument that behaviour is independent of λ.

Unfortunately we know that for the vast majority of functions of the type 1.6 (i) no solution will exist for the differential equation 1.6 (iii). For a solution to exist certain integrability conditions must be fulfilled, which in themselves constitute restrictions on the demand function. These restrictions are in fact precisely equivalent to the symmetry conditions 1.4 (xv). Evidently we cannot prove symmetry from the mere observation that market equilibrium exists. We need a utility function as was earlier explained (p. 52). No detailed account of the 'integrability' problem is given at this point since the matter is taken up again in Chapter 3, where it is of crucial importance to the theory of community demand there developed. We cannot assume that a utility function exists for a community. Nor can we assume a preference relation.

We notice, moreover, that we should be no more than one step forward even if it could be shown that the integrability conditions were always met by the demand function 1.6 (i). We should have symmetry but we should not have the sign conditions 1.4 (xix), without which the greater part of economic theory could not exist. To establish the sign conditions it is necessary to assume, in one way or another, that market equilibrium maximizes u, or, if u does not exist, that marginal rates of substitution diminish.† Again we come back to this problem in Chapter 3 in connexion with community demand theory.

In order to be able to impose the required sign restrictions, revealed preference theorists introduced, at this point, an axiom of revealed preference. This supposes that if, under market conditions, x^0 is chosen when x^1 *could* have been chosen then x^1 will *never* be chosen under market conditions in which x^0 could be chosen. Thus if

$$(p^0, x^0) \geqq (p^0, x^1) \quad (x^0 \neq x^1),$$

† This is really the assumption that an 'indifference' curve exists between every pair of commodities (all other commodity quantities constant), and that such a curve is convex to the origin. Cf. R. G. D. Allen, *Mathematical Analysis for Economists*, pp. 512 ff.

then we say that x^0 is revealed preferred to x^1, and we write $x^0 R x^1$. The amount of money required to buy x^1 at prices p^0 is less than or equal to the sum spent on x^0, so that x^1 could have been chosen. The revealed preference axiom simply says that

$$\text{if} \quad x^0 R x^1 \quad \text{then} \quad \overline{x^1 R x^0}. \qquad \qquad 1.6 \text{ (iv)}$$

Evidently this assumption is inspired by preconceived notions regarding the principles upon which consumers choose in the market. To illustrate this consider an apparent nonsense alternative. Suppose that the consumer has in mind a complete ordering exactly as in 1.1, but that he chooses always the lowest commodity bundle on his list, subject to the condition that a given sum of money, y, is spent. This would yield a demand equation indistinguishable from 1.6 (i) but would, in general, imply restrictions contrary to the revealed preference axiom. In Chapter 3 we shall see that, in extreme cases, precisely this situation is possible with community demand equations.

In short the axiom 1.6 (iv) postulates something very like the preference relation of section 1.1. Indeed if we consider all possible sets of prices and income, and hence (by the assumption that 1.6 (i) possesses an inverse) all possible commodity bundles, we have a binary relation on all commodity bundles; for either $x^0 R x^1$ or $\overline{x^0 R x^1}$ for all x. And the revealed preference axiom assumes that $x^0 R x^1$ implies $\overline{x^1 R x^0}$, which is the first condition for the existence of a total ordering of all bundles.† If it could be shown that the relation R is also transitive, R would be exactly equivalent to the relation P of section 1.1.

Moreover, the asymmetry of the relation R, which is the revealed preference axiom, is precisely the condition used in section 1.4 (p. 54) to impose restrictions on the sign of substitution effects. If we avoid speaking of the substitution effects as movement around an indifference curve and set the condition $(p, dx) = 0$ in its place, it is clear, from the work of 1.4, that the transitivity of R is not required to prove the sign conditions 1.4 (xix). Without transitivity, however, the substitution effect

† Cf. G. Debreu, 'Representation of a Preference Ordering', *Decision Processes*, edited by Thrall, Coombs, and Davis.

loses much of its meaning, as does the whole notion of income compensation.

It will not surprise the reader, however, that we can prove the sign conditions apparently without transitivity and without assuming the existence of a total ordering of commodity bundles; for we have already seen, from 1.4, that the uniqueness of market equilibrium, combined with what amounts to a definition of the relation R, implies convexity of the order-preserving function. On the other hand, this may be something of an illusion for we now have available an argument of Professor H. Uzawa† which makes it clear that, on certain conditions of continuity of the demand function, 1.6 (i), the 'weak' axiom of revealed preference quoted is a sufficient condition for the transitivity of R, and hence the existence of an ordering exactly as in 1.1.

In the ordinary way a logical relation can be asymmetric without being transitive, i.e. it does not follow from the condition, $x^0 R x^1$ implies $\overline{x^1 R x^0}$, that $x^0 R x^1$ and $x^1 R x^2$ implies $x^0 R x^2$. It is easy to see, however, that, in the narrow context of the present problem, the two properties of R are closely related; for both characterize what might be called consistency of behaviour. Indeed in the special case where there are only two commodities a very simple geometrical argument is all that is needed to prove Uzawa's theorem.‡ On the other hand, the most general proof is complex and adds little to our intuitive understanding. It will not therefore be repeated here. The important point is that we now understand R and P to be equivalent.

Historically the necessity of establishing the transitivity of the R relation proved a difficult stumbling-block. The first solution to the problem was suggested by H. S. Houthakker§ who proposed a 'strong' axiom of revealed preference as follows. The relation $x^0 R^* x^s$ is said to exist whenever $s-1$ commodity

---

† 'Preference and Rational Choice in the Theory of Consumption', *Mathematical Methods in the Social Sciences* (1959), Stanford University Press.

‡ Cf. S. Karlin, *Mathematical Methods and Theory in Games, Programming and Economics*, vol. 1, p. 270. Cf. also J. R. Hicks, *A Revision of Demand Theory*, pp. 53–54.

§ 'Revealed Preference and the Utility Function', *Economica*, xviii, pp. 159–74.

bundles can be found such that x^0Rx^1, x^1Rx^2,..., $x^{s-1}Rx^s$. The strong axiom requires that the relation R^* should be asymmetric.

The reason for the introduction of the R^* relation is simply that R^* is transitive by definition; for if $x^0R^*x^1$ and $x^1R^*x^2$ then all bundles between x^0 and x^1, x^1 itself, and all bundles between x^1 and x^2, form a sequence, s, of bundles sufficient to ensure $x^0R^*x^2$.

Given the asymmetry and transitivity of R^*, Professor Houthakker showed that the differential equation 1.6 (iii) is integrable and a utility function can be found. More recently P. Newman† has treated the same problem by similar methods, but rather more neatly, with a view to establishing the existence of a total ordering from the assumption of the asymmetry of R^*. His results confirm that the relation R^* is, on the assumption of its asymmetry, precisely equivalent to the relation P of section 1.1 above. Professor Uzawa's work shows simply that, on reasonable assumptions, the relations R and R^* are in fact equivalent, and equivalent to P. The assumptions of the revealed-preference approach also imply continuity, convexity, and monotonicity as in 1.2.

In short, although revealed-preference theorists pioneered a more objective approach to demand theory, which absolves economists from the necessity of tedious debate with philosophers,‡ it now seems that the more direct approach of sections 1.1 and 1.2 gains in simplicity without any of the disadvantages associated with the hedonistic view of utility. Just as it was necessary to assume transitivity of the relation P, so, in the revealed preference approach, it is necessary to assume what amounts to transitivity of the relation R. Neither the weak hypothesis nor the strong hypothesis, both of which we now understand imply transitivity, have any greater intuitive appeal

---

† 'Complete Ordering and Revealed Preference', *Review of Economic Studies*, Feb. 1960.

‡ e.g. Mr. Newman (loc. cit., para. 35) continues to be worried as to whether any class of bundles equal in the consumer's ordering (i.e. such that $\overline{x^1R^*x^2}$ and $\overline{x^2R^*x^1}$ for all pairs of bundles x) should be called an 'equivalence' class or an 'indifference' class, despite the fact that his own approach is deliberately designed to reduce the issue to one of mere semantics.

than the direct assumption of transitivity itself; and both call for long and tedious proofs to establish the desired results.

1.7. On price consciousness

Almost all that we think we know about economic behaviour is based upon the theory of demand set out above. Indeed the greater number of the 'laws' of economics are particular applications of that part of 1.4 (xix) which asserts that σ_{ii} is negative or, what amounts to the same thing, that the lower the price of a good the greater the demand for it. Fortunately this central result is fairly well established on straightforward empirical grounds; for many attempts have been made to measure σ_{ii} for various goods by statistical analysis of time series. And whatever may be thought in general about the accuracy of the numerical results obtained, a sufficient percentage of negative values have emerged to justify at least the qualitative conclusion.

On the other hand, symmetry of substitution effects and higher than first-order conditions on sign can scarcely be said to have been tested to the point where it is proper to speak of these uniformities as 'laws' of demand. And yet they are coming to play a part in economic theory which may in the end prove to be crucial.† For this reason no scrap of empirical evidence should be neglected, and for the same reason we have, at each stage of the argument, emphasized the empirical content of the various hypotheses introduced.

In this spirit it has seemed useful to draw attention at this point to a most interesting survey recently undertaken with the object of testing in a novel way the utility maximizing assumption.‡ Evidently it is impossible to maximize utility subject to prices and a budget constraint without studying prices. In a general way it is well known that consumers are deeply conscious of what might be called the general level of prices, but this by itself does not imply very much regarding the principles of allocation of expenditure between goods. On the other hand, strong evidence of an awareness on the part of consumers of the

† Cf. below, Chapter 3.
‡ 'On the Price Consciousness of Consumers', André Gabor and C. W. J. Granger, *Applied Statistics*, vol. x, no. 3, 1961.

individual prices of separate commodities would suggest that such prices do play a part in determining the allocation, as well as the overall level of consumer expenditure.

With this in mind Gabor and Granger organized a survey in which housewives were asked to name, from memory, the prices of food and other items recently purchased. Part of the results of this survey are set out in Tables 1.7.1 and 1.7.2 below. Table 1.7.1 requires little explanation, being simply a tabulation of the number of items purchased, by place of purchase (either co-operative society or elsewhere), and by social groups A to E. Social groups correspond roughly to incomes earned with A the wealthy and E the poor.

TABLE 1.7.1

	Place of Purchase					
	Co-operative society		Grocer, etc.		All	
Social group	No.†	Per cent‡	No.	Per cent	No.	Per cent
A	..	..	120	63·3	120	63·3
B	32	87·5	331	64·4	363	66·4
C	360	80·3	1163	81·0	1523	80·8
D	1110	85·9	1785	85·3	2895	85·5
E	132	72·0	243	84·8	375	80·3
All	1634	83·6	3642	81·2	5276	82·0

† No. = number of purchases.
‡ Per cent = percentage of prices named.

In view of the fact that failure to name a price may mean simply that it was considered at the time but later forgotten, whilst ability to name a price *must* mean that it was considered, the overall figure of 82 per cent prices named is remarkable. Indeed, it is rather more than even the most enthusiastic believer in the 'economic man' would be likely to guess. The inverse correlation between wealth and price consciousness might be thought to lend support also to an argument already put forward in section 1.4. Some effort is involved in the process of utility maximization. If income is high, and hence marginal utility low, and if the item purchased is small, the gain due to careful consideration of price may be worth less than the cost in terms of effort.

Table 1.7.2 gives a breakdown of the same information by commodity.

The considerable variation of the percentage of prices named between commodities is of interest. Already in section 1.4 we have suggested that price might be irrelevant to the problem of

TABLE 1.7.2

	Place of Purchase					
	Co-operative society		Grocer, etc.		All	
Commodity	No.†	Per cent‡	No.	Per cent	No.	Per cent
Tea	145	96·6	231	93·5	376	94·7
Eggs	111	96·4	296	92·2	407	93·4
Sausages.	37	83·8	244	91·8	281	90·7
Margarine	97	86·6	167	90·4	264	89·0
Potatoes.	59	88·1	320	88·8	379	88·7
Coffee	50	94·0	120	85·8	170	88·2
Bacon	89	83·1	271	84·5	360	84·2
Butter	133	84·2	273	83·5	406	83·7
Jam and marmalade . .	86	86·0	162	80·2	248	82·3
Cheese	98	76·5	263	81·4	361	80·1
Washing powders and detergents	166	88·0	356	74·7	522	78·9
Sugar	152	80·9	273	76·6	425	78·1
Soap	118	74·6	211	71·6	329	72·6
Breakfast cereal . . .	143	81·1	200	62·0	343	70·0
Flour	150	64·8	255	61·6	405	62·7
All	1634	83·6	3642	81·2	5276	82·0

† No. = number of purchases.   ‡ Per cent = percentage of prices named.

allocation where there is complete satiation or high complementarity. The reader is invited to consider whether such items as soap, flour, or cheese might not, for some consumers, fall into these categories.

To sum up we claim that even if no further evidence were forthcoming there remain good reasons, both subjective and objective, for accepting the theory set out above. This would be so even if qualitative macro-economic predictions of the kind economists customarily attempt did not, in so far as they are successful, further confirm the value of our ideas. In succeeding chapters we shall advance the work farther, comment upon its usefulness, and show how still more testing might be undertaken.

SAVINGS

2.1. Introductory comments

FROM the remarks of section 1.3 it will be clear that, so far, we have evaded the problem of long-run saving rather than solved it. There is nothing in the work of Chapter 1 which would in any way help in the analysis of statistics of saving and spending in the aggregate. We have a theory which tells us how notional consumption, C_n (henceforth written without the subscript n and without the qualifying adjective 'notional'), will be allocated among commodities, given prices. But there is nothing to suggest how we might predict C itself; nor do we know what parameters we should seek to measure.

More than this, we shall discover that there exist very special problems connected with saving, the nature of which will become clear as we proceed. It is possible to point to facts which cast serious doubt upon the validity of all the work up to this point. Indeed the purpose of the present chapter is not so much to set up a definitive theory of saving as to attempt to rescue the theory of demand from what might appear to be a critical dilemma. Any theory of saving which emerges in the process should be regarded as a by-product the full implications of which have not been thoroughly explored.

Demand theory as ordinarily set out assumes implicitly that *all* income, y, is spent on consumption. In other words, y is identically equal to C. Since we have a theory of production to explain how y is determined, it follows that C is independently known. Alternatively, saving can be thought of as a commodity just like any other. Either way it is possible to avoid any explicit mention of the subject.

In fact, of course, C is not independently known, given y. Moreover, the determination of C is intimately bound up with the choice of the commodity bundle for current consumption, for saving is designed to augment future consumption and simply reflects the intertemporal facet of the process of allocating expenditure.

Probably the assumption that C and y are identical is a good first approximation, provided we are looking only at demand for a single good. On the other hand, certain of the less obvious results of demand theory have now developed into rather more than a mathematical curiosity, and find their place in arguments put forward in support of actual policy. They appear, moreover, in general equilibrium contexts, where all commodities are assumed to be aggregated into two or three goods, and where saving itself plays a big role in the discussion. A particular example will be referred to later.

In cases such as this economists have tended, with certain notable exceptions and with varying degrees of uncertainty, to follow one or other of two lines. Money saving is regarded either as a residual so that,

$$s = y - \sum p_i x_i, \qquad\qquad 2.1\ (i)$$

i.e. saving is the difference between income and expenditure; or some x, say x_j, is specifically defined as saving, in which case

$$y = \sum p_i x_i \qquad\qquad 2.1\ (ii)$$

in the usual way.

The first of these treatments is correct as far as it goes but it does not provide us with any *explanation* of the way in which the choice between saving and spending is made. We shall come back to this point. That the second approach can be quite misleading is evident as soon as we begin to ask questions about the nature of demand equations. It is valid only in so far as 2.1 (ii) can be regarded as simply an alternative way of writing 2.1 (i).

It is easy to see intuitively that the demand equation for money saving cannot have the same properties as the demand equation for any good and must therefore be separately considered. For, in the simple case where the individual has no accumulated titles to wealth to begin with, the doubling of all prices and income will leave the real situation unchanged. The consumer will buy precisely what he had planned to buy before the change but he will save twice as much in money terms. The quantity of the ith good and money saving are both functions of prices and income, but doubling prices and income will double money saving whilst leaving consumption of the ith good unchanged. Mathematically the demand equation for the ith good will be homogeneous of order zero whilst the demand equation for saving will be homogeneous of order one.

At this point some readers may feel that the lost symmetry can easily be restored by defining x_j as real, rather than money, saving; and it seems likely that writers who favour approach two have this thought in mind. Clearly in the example above real saving remains unchanged in exactly the same way as consumption.

Unfortunately this still leaves us with no answer to the question, in what units should real saving be measured. It is circular argument to assert that real saving is merely money saving deflated by a suitable price index; for what is a suitable price index depends upon the solution of the very problem we are trying to evade—namely, what are the effects of price changes on money saving?

Of course, the difference we have noted in the order of homogeneity of the saving and demand equations is in itself unimportant. It is a symptom rather than a cause and is introduced only to draw attention to the fact that a non-trivial problem exists. In fact there is no reason to suppose that either consumption demand equations or the savings equation will be homogeneous† at all in the general case where there exist accumulated titles to wealth, the money value of which does not double with the doubling of all prices. If the doubling of prices reduces the purchasing power of accumulated wealth, savings may be more than doubled in an effort to replace losses. Thus money spent cannot be doubled even though income is.

The basic difficulty is one which has been commented on many

† We are here assuming that demand equations are expressed as functions of prices and y and not prices and C.

times before. The utility derived from consumption comes
directly from the goods consumed. The utility from saving
comes partly from interest earned, partly from the satisfaction
that the power to command wealth for its own sake gives, and
partly from goods which it is intended to purchase in the future.
Clearly, therefore, on at least two counts, possibly three, the
utility derived from saving depends on expected future prices,
which will in all probability be related to current prices.

Traditional demand theory supposes that the current period's
income will be laid out in such a way as to maximize a utility
which depends solely upon the quantities $x_1,..., x_n$ of goods consumed. But we have now shown that, if some current income is
to be put to saving, the utility function to be maximized must
depend also on expected future prices, the rate of interest, and
on titles to wealth accumulated in past periods. In symbols we
write

$$u = u(x_1,..., x_n, q_1,..., q_n, r, s, w), \qquad 2.1 \text{ (iii)}$$

where q_i is the expected future price of good i, r is the rate of
interest, and w is wealth accumulated in past periods. The
current period's money saving, s, is distinguished from w since
it can be varied at will by the consumer so as to maximize
satisfaction. w, on the other hand, is given, being the actual
wealth in hand at the moment the choice is made.

We now see even more clearly why the introduction of saving
makes more than a trivial difference to utility analysis. For it is
no longer possible to show, by means of indifference surfaces and
a budget plane, how consumption will change following changes
in the prices of the goods x_i. As long as expected future prices,
q_i, and r and w are given we can, of course, draw indifference
surfaces in the usual textbook manner. We can also draw a
budget plane connecting all combinations of the x's and s possible
with a given income y. And, as before, the point of tangency
between the indifference surface and the budget plane will define
the consumer's choice. The difficulty is that, as soon as we change
any price p_i to observe the effect on consumption, the corresponding expected future price q_i will, in general, change also and hence
the whole indifference map with it. We have in fact three effects:

an income effect, a substitution effect, and an effect due to the change in the position of the indifference map itself.

Mathematically, however, we may proceed exactly as before, maximizing the function u subject to the constraint imposed by the fact that money income is given, i.e. subject to the constraint

$$y = s + \sum p_i x_i. \qquad \text{2.1 (iv)}$$

We have only to remember that we now have to deal with changes in utility due to changes in expected future prices as well as to changes in the x_i's. In other words, there is a marginal utility of expected future prices as well as a marginal utility for every good. In section 2.2 we shall set out an analysis on these lines. In the meantime consider the preliminaries to such an analysis.

Maximizing the modified function u, 2.1 (iii), subject to the constraint 2.1 (iv) yields, by the method of Lagrange multipliers, $n+1$ equations, where n is the number of goods. These are

$$u_i = \lambda p_i \quad (i = 1, 2, ..., n),$$

$$u_s = \lambda. \qquad \text{2.1 (v)}$$

q's, r, and w are, of course, taken to be parameters, given and constant throughout the maximizing process. They are elements beyond the control of the consumer at the moment of making his choice.

The first n equations of 2.1 (v) are familiar from Chapter 1, and show simply that the marginal utilities of all goods must, in equilibrium, be proportional to prices. The u_i have precisely the meaning of Chapter 1. The last equation is the additional equation needed to determine the choice between saving and consumption. It indicates that saving will be carried to the point where its marginal utility is equal to the marginal utility of money, i.e. to the proportionality factor, λ.

It is important to recognize that *all* of these $n+1$ equations *and* equation 2.1 (iv) are needed to be able to express the $n+2$ variables x_i, s, λ as functions of the parameters p_i, q_i, r, and w. We have already commented upon the shortcomings of the approach in which s is treated simply as a residual. It is now clear that s must be known before any of the x_i can be determined, so that s itself can never be determined solely from equation 2.1 (iv).

This simple fact gives rise to difficulties which are not at all easy to understand or to overcome. For purposes of illustration, therefore, we digress for a moment to consider an approach to the problem devised by Professor J. E. Meade in the course of his work in the field of international trade. In effect Professor Meade proceeds as follows. Suppose that s is known and that we know also the way in which s depends on prices and money income. The equation $u_s = \lambda$ is then no longer required, although, of course, our prior knowledge is not necessarily inconsistent with it. We can now solve for all x_i, in terms of our parameters and s, from the n equations $u_i = \lambda p_i$ and 2.1 (iv). If in addition we write 2.1 (iv) as

$$C = \sum p_i x_i$$

it appears that we can proceed exactly as in Chapter 1.

We must, of course, redefine elasticity of demand, as in Chapter 1, to mean the response to a price change with *consumption* constant rather than *income* constant. But this seems to present no special difficulty for we can always write

$$\frac{dx_i}{dp_i} = \frac{\partial x_i}{\partial p_i} + \frac{\partial x_i}{\partial C}\frac{\partial C}{\partial p_i},$$

i.e. the *total* rate of change of x_i with respect to changes in the price p_i is equal to that part, $\partial x_i/\partial p_i$, which would occur if C were held constant plus the rate of change of x_i with respect to a change in consumption (prices constant), multiplied by the rate of change of consumption due to the change in p_i (money income constant).

Moreover, since $C = y - s$ and y is held constant,

$$\frac{\partial C}{\partial p_i} = -\frac{\partial s}{\partial p_i},$$

so that $\qquad\qquad \dfrac{dx_i}{dp_i} = \dfrac{\partial x_i}{\partial p_i} - \dfrac{\partial x_i}{\partial C}\dfrac{\partial s}{\partial p_i}.$ \hfill 2.1 (vi)

It might now appear that, because we have kept y constant, the total derivative 2.1 (vi) is in fact equivalent to the partial derivative of the demand equation expressed in terms of y rather than C.

Moreover, if we could assume that the work of Chapter 1 continues to be valid in this new view, the partial derivative $\partial x_i/\partial p_i$ of 2.1 (vi) can be split up into income and substitution effects as before, as long as we take care only to put C for y wherever it occurs. That is, it is supposed that we can write

$$\frac{dx_i}{dp_i} = -x_i\frac{\partial x_i}{\partial C} + \sigma_{ii} - \frac{\partial x_i}{\partial C}\frac{\partial s}{\partial p_i} = -\left(x_i + \frac{\partial s}{\partial p_i}\right)\frac{\partial x_i}{\partial C} + \sigma_{ii}.$$

If it is further assumed with Professor Meade that $\partial s/\partial p_i = 0$ we have, apparently, a neat and convenient substitution and income effect. The substitution effect has the desirable symmetric property. The only difference is that the income effect is equal in magnitude to the proportion of an increase in *consumption* which would be spent on x_i rather than the proportion of an increase in *income*.

Using the fact that $\qquad y = C + s,$

or $$\frac{\partial y}{\partial C} = 1 + \frac{\partial s}{\partial y}\frac{\partial y}{\partial C} = \frac{1}{1 - \partial s/\partial y},$$

we can also write

$$\frac{dx_i}{dp_i} = -\frac{1}{1-h}\left(x_i + \frac{\partial s}{\partial p_i}\right)\frac{\partial x_i}{\partial y} + \sigma_{ii} \qquad\qquad 2.1\ (\text{vii})$$

where h is the marginal propensity to save $\partial s/\partial y$. In this form the modification due to saving seems to be quite clear.

Unfortunately, the work of Chapter 1 is not valid unless a further assumption is made. Consider the new utility function 2.1 (iii). Total utility depends, in general, upon future prices, q. Any change in price, p_i, will automatically change q_i and will therefore change both the shape and position of every indifference surface. The argument of Chapter 1, on the other hand, depends upon the implicit assumption that utility is independent of price.

In this connexion it is as well to remind ourselves that we cannot escape the difficulty by assuming expected future prices to be independent of current prices. Or rather we could do so, but not with any semblance of realism; for to assume that

expected future prices are independent of current prices is to
assume that the consumer expects every price change to be
temporary.

To validate the work of Chapter 1 we need to impose some
condition on the form of u. A sufficient condition would, of
course, be complete independence between utility from consumption and utility from saving; this is equivalent to saying
that s, r, and q's do not appear in the utility function, so that
Chapter 1 stands. On the other hand, few economists would
wish to claim that the possession of greater titles to wealth
would have no effect at all upon the satisfaction derived from
current consumption. Such a claim clearly contradicts the basic
hypothesis of diminishing marginal utility.

Fortunately, as we shall see later from the mathematics, a
weaker assumption is also sufficient. If it can be accepted that
an increase in wealth will not affect the *relative* marginal utilities
of goods in current consumption, then the result 2.1 (vii) stil
holds. To put it another way, we suppose that the knowledge
that a higher standard of living can be enjoyed in the future
does not affect the way in which any *given* current expenditure
is distributed now. We should not lose sight of the fact, however,
that the certainty that, in ten years, when we retire, we shall be
able to afford a world tour may very well induce us to take a
short holiday this year in England rather than in Europe. The
difference in cost may be spent on other current luxuries. In
this case 2.1 (vii) might not hold, since the division into income
and substitution effects is no longer valid.

It may be as well to make it clear now that the greater part
of the work of this book is based upon the 'weak' assumption
of the previous paragraph. The reader who perseveres to the
final chapters will come to recognize also that this assumption
is equivalent to what is later called 'neutral want association'
between future and current goods. The boundary between
future and current wants is delimited by what has been referred
to in the literature as a 'marked gap in the chain of substitutes',
a concept which is clearly of much more general applicability
than fully independent utilities.

2.2. Long-run saving

So far we have made a number of assertions, based largely on intuitive argument, and pointed to certain difficulties. We shall now develop the most general theory of demand with saving and show how the work of Chapter 1 may be justified. Alternatives will be presented. As this can be done with only slight modifications to methods already outlined, only the briefest sketch of the proof will be given. Equations 2.1 (iv) and 2.1 (v) can be differentiated partially with respect to p_i to give

$$\sum p_j \frac{\partial x_j}{\partial p_i} + \frac{\partial s}{\partial p_i} = -x_i$$

$$-p_i \frac{\partial \lambda}{\partial p_i} + \sum u_{ij} \frac{\partial x_j}{\partial p_i} + u_{is} \frac{\partial s}{\partial p_i} = \lambda - u_{iq_i} \frac{\partial q_i}{\partial p_i}$$

$$-p_k \frac{\partial \lambda}{\partial p_i} + \sum u_{kj} \frac{\partial x_j}{\partial p_i} + u_{ks} \frac{\partial s}{\partial p_i} = -u_{kq_i} \frac{\partial q_i}{\partial p_i} \quad \begin{array}{l}(k = 1, 2, ..., n; \\ k \neq i)\end{array}$$

and

$$-\frac{\partial \lambda}{\partial p_i} + \sum u_{sj} \frac{\partial x_j}{\partial p_i} + u_{ss} \frac{\partial s}{\partial p_i} = -u_{sq_i} \frac{\partial q_i}{\partial p_i}.$$

u_{kq_i} is the rate of change of marginal utility of the kth good with respect to a change in the expected future price q_i. $\partial q_i/\partial p_i$ is the reaction of the expected future price to a current price change. From this point, to avoid continually writing the extra term, we assume that current prices and expected future prices are always the same so that

$$\frac{\partial q_i}{\partial p_i} = 1.$$

We have also assumed throughout that a change in the current price of any good will have no effect at all on any expected future price other than its own.

The matrix of coefficients on the left can be seen to form the familiar bordered Hessian determinant of the utility function u. Solution for any $\partial x_j/\partial p_i$ yields three terms which turn out to be:

(i) The usual income effect $-x_i(\partial x_j/\partial y)$. This may be confirmed by differentiating the original equations partially with respect to y, solving for $\partial x_j/\partial y$ and comparing with term one.

(ii) A substitution effect σ_{ji} possessing the symmetric property. This follows from the symmetry of the bordered Hessian determinant.

(iii) A sum of terms of the type $-u_{kq_i}(\Delta_{kj}/\Delta)$ where Δ_{kj} is the co-factor of the element u_{kj} in the Hessian determinant Δ. The meaning of the sum of terms (iii) can be easily seen. If we differentiate our original equations partially with respect to q_i rather than p_i we have a set of equations as above, except that $\partial x_j/\partial p_i$'s become $\partial x_j/\partial q_i$'s, and the $-x_i$ and λ on the right-hand side disappear. Solving for $\partial x_j/\partial q_i$ we obtain precisely the sum of terms (iii).

It follows that the general partial derivative of demand equations, when these are expressed in terms of p's and income, y, may be written

$$\frac{\partial x_j}{\partial p_i} = -x_i\frac{\partial x_j}{\partial y} + \sigma_{ji} + \frac{\partial x_j}{\partial q_i}. \qquad 2.2 \text{ (i)}$$

The last term is the change which would result in the consumption of the jth good following unit rise in the expected future price of the ith good, assuming all current prices and all expected prices other than q_i remain constant.

This result may be compared with that obtained earlier, namely

$$\frac{dx_j}{dp_i} = -x_i\frac{\partial x_j}{\partial C} + \sigma_{ji} - \frac{\partial x_j}{\partial C}\frac{\partial s}{\partial p_i}.$$

For two reasons it must *not* be inferred that by subtraction we can now write

$$\frac{\partial x_j}{\partial q_i} = x_i\left(\frac{\partial x_j}{\partial y} - \frac{\partial x_j}{\partial C}\right) - \frac{\partial x_j}{\partial C}\frac{\partial s}{\partial p_i} = \left(-\frac{1}{1-h}\frac{\partial s}{\partial p_i} - \frac{h}{1-h}x_i\right)\frac{\partial x_j}{\partial y}.$$

First, equation 2.2 (i) is quite general whereas the earlier result depends on assumptions regarding the form of the utility function. Secondly, the two σ_{ji} are not the same. In 2.1 (vii) σ_{ji} does not contain any element of substitution into money saving whereas in 2.2 (i) it does. To maintain the distinction we shall therefore write the substitution effect in 2.2 (i) as $[\sigma_{ji}]_s$.

A property of the term $\partial x_j/\partial q_i$ should also be noted. Since

$$\sum p_i x_i + s = y$$

we have
$$\sum p_j \frac{\partial x_j}{\partial q_i} + \frac{\partial s}{\partial q_i} = 0. \qquad 2.2 \text{ (ii)}$$

Multiplication by λ yields

$$\sum u_j \frac{\partial x_j}{\partial q_i} + \lambda \frac{\partial s}{\partial q_i} = 0.$$

Thus the changes in the disbursement of a given income, induced by an increase in one expected future price, do not in themselves imply any change in total utility. This is, of course, the characteristic property of the substitution effect $[\sigma_{ji}]_s$ for evidently

$$\sum p_j [\sigma_{ji}]_s + [\sigma_{si}]_s = 0 \qquad 2.2 \text{ (iii)}$$

and accordingly $\quad \sum u_j [\sigma_{ji}]_s + \lambda [\sigma_{si}]_s = 0.$

This tempts us to add together the two effects $[\sigma_{ji}]_s$ and $\partial x_j / \partial q_i$ calling the whole σ_{ji}^*. Thus σ_{ji}^* clearly has the property

$$\sum_j p_j \sigma_{ji}^* = 0.$$

Moreover, we can now write the partial derivative 2.2 (i) in the familiar form

$$\frac{\partial x_j}{\partial p_i} = -x_i \frac{\partial x_j}{\partial y} + \sigma_{ji}^*. \qquad 2.2 \text{ (iv)}$$

Unfortunately this procedure loses us almost everything of value in the theory of demand; for it is easy to show

(i) that $\qquad \sigma_{ji}^* \neq \sigma_{ij}^*$

and (ii) that, in general, no conditions of sign can be imposed on any σ_{ji}^* or any determinant made up of elements σ_{ji}^*. The reader will easily see why this is so if the substitution effect of 2.2 (i) is written out in full in determinant form. In fact

$$\sigma_{ji}^* = \Delta^{-1} \begin{vmatrix} 0 & \cdot & p_i & \cdot & 0 & \cdot & 1 \\ \cdot & \cdot & \cdot & \cdot & \cdot & \cdot & \cdot \\ p_i & \cdot & u_{ii} & \cdot & \lambda - u_{iq_i} & \cdot & u_{is} \\ \cdot & \cdot & \cdot & \cdot & \cdot & \cdot & \cdot \\ p_j & \cdot & \cdot & \cdot & -u_{jq_i} & \cdot & u_{js} \\ \cdot & \cdot & \cdot & \cdot & \cdot & \cdot & \cdot \\ 1 & \cdot & \cdot & \cdot & -u_{sq_i} & \cdot & u_{ss} \end{vmatrix} \quad 2.2 \text{ (v)}$$

This is clearly not symmetric, nor can it be represented as proportional to any co-factor of the bordered Hessian determinant,

Δ, of the utility function. No use can be made of the fact that Δ is the discriminant of a negative definite form, even though we know this to be the case. Equilibrium is a constrained maximum of u but this does not help us to identify conditions of sign on the determinant $|\sigma_{ji}^*|$ as in 1.4 (xix).

Again we notice that although

$$-x_i \frac{\partial x_j}{\partial y}$$

of 2.2 (iv) appears as income effect, as in section 1.4, x_i is no longer the compensating variation. If we change a price p_i by an amount dp_i the consumer will not be fully compensated by giving him a sum of money $x_i dp_i$. It is true that this sum of money would enable him to buy exactly what he bought before and to save, in money terms, what he saved before. But it would not compensate him for the loss in the real purchasing power of current saving and accumulated wealth.

The thoroughly confusing nature of the whole problem becomes even more apparent when we remind ourselves that, although $x_i dp_i$ is insufficient to compensate, none the less the 'utility' change of the sum of all substitution effects remains zero as before (cf. 2.2 (ii)). The explanation of this paradox lies in the fact that utility is changed not only by the change in all variables x and s but also by changes in parameters q. It is true that if price i rises by an amount dp_i and income is increased by $x_i dp_i$ the utility changes due to changes in x and s sum to zero. But the change dp_i implies also a change dq_i which changes utility by

$$\frac{\partial u}{\partial q_i} \frac{dq_i}{dp_i} dp_i$$

or, on our assumption that prices once changed are not expected to change again, by

$$\frac{\partial u}{\partial q_i} dp_i$$

which in money terms will be

$$\frac{1}{\lambda} \frac{\partial u}{\partial q_i} dp_i < 0. \qquad\qquad \text{2.2 (vi)}$$

It is reasonable to assume that the sign of $\partial u / \partial q_i$ will always be

negative, yielding the inequality 2.2 (vi); for a rise in expected
future prices means that accumulated saving will buy less, so
that given money wealth yields less satisfaction. Certain conclusions can be derived from 2.2 (vi) as we shall see.

Evidently the *total* amount of money required to compensate
for a price rise dp_i will be

$$\left(x_i - \frac{1}{\lambda}\frac{\partial u}{\partial q_i}\right) dp_i \qquad\qquad 2.2\ \text{(vii)}$$

which must always be positive and greater than $x_i\, dp_i$. Only if
there is no saving or wealth holding do we find that 2.2 (vii)
reduces to $x_i\, dp_i$.

In view of this we could, if we chose, define income effect as
income compensation multiplied by minus $\partial x_i/\partial y$ and substitution effect as the remainder. But this is unlikely to be at all
useful since both terms would then contain non-measurable
entities, and neither term would have any of the properties that
have been found so valuable.

Geometrically we can think of the compensation $x_i\, dp_i$ as
carrying the consumer back to the same indifference surface.
But because of the change in q_i this indifference surface will
represent a lower level of satisfaction by the amount $(\partial u/\partial q_i)\, dp_i$.
There will also have been a slight adjustment in the *shape* of the
indifference surface, but the secondary adjustment of the x's
and s due to this will have no effect on total utility.

The reader who is alarmed at this apparent complete collapse
of the whole of demand theory, due simply to the introduction
of long-run saving in a realistic way, is reminded that most of
the more obvious conclusions of economic theory are based upon
nothing more subtle than the belief that demand curves slope
downward to the right. And to re-establish this we need only
show that $\partial x_i/\partial q_i$ of 2.2 (i) is negative; for when $i = j$ the first
two terms of 2.2 (i) are bound to be negative. Indeed we need
only show that $\partial x_i/\partial q_i$ is not large enough to outweigh the effect
of the first two terms.

A fully general proof of this is not possible, for the required
condition is evidently a restriction on the form of the utility

function. On the other hand, ruling out the possibility of speculative purchasing for stock, it seems hardly likely that the expectation of a rise in the price of a commodity, with its consequent loss in the real value of money wealth, will induce persons to buy more of the same commodity *currently*. Clearly it is only the more subtle results of demand theory which are in danger.

In order to defend these we shall now proceed to show how, on the assumption already described, namely that future consumption is 'neutrally want associated' with current consumption, all of the results of Chapter 1 can be reinstated as they stand, and some further restrictions on the form of the long-run savings function can be identified. It is claimed, moreover, that the assumption that the future pattern of spending is not greatly affected by the current pattern is sufficiently realistic to justify any *qualitative* conclusion which may emerge. Whether or not quantitative results are equally valid (e.g. the symmetry of substitution effects) is a matter for empirical test. It is in fact indirectly tested in the work of later chapters.

As the question is of some importance, and as it is taken up again later in a different context, the reader is especially asked to notice at this point that the neutral want association assumption does not mean that we can write separate utility functions for current consumption and for saving and wealth, although the converse is true. Neutral want association is not the same as independence but there is some affinity which we shall need to investigate at length.

We now state our utility restrictions in mathematical terms. Our assumption in fact requires

$$\frac{\partial(u_i/u_j)}{\partial q_i} = \frac{\partial(u_i/u_j)}{\partial s} = 0,$$

or

$$\left. \begin{array}{l} u_{iq_i} = \alpha u_i = \beta p_i \\ u_{jq_i} = \alpha u_j = \beta p_j \\ u_{is} = \alpha' u_i = \beta' p_i \\ u_{js} = \alpha' u_j = \beta' p_j \end{array} \right\}. \qquad \text{2.2 (viii)}$$

It is convenient to begin by proving two lemmas consequent

upon 2.2 (viii). These are

$$\frac{\partial x_j}{\partial q_i} = -\frac{\partial s}{\partial q_i}\frac{\partial x_j}{\partial y}\left(\frac{1}{1-h}\right), \qquad \text{2.2 (ix)}$$

where $h = \partial s/\partial y$, and

$$[\sigma_{ji}]_s - \sigma_{ji} = -[\sigma_{si}]_s\frac{\partial x_j}{\partial y}\left(\frac{1}{1-h}\right), \qquad \text{2.2 (x)}$$

where σ_{ji} is obtained the same way as $[\sigma_{ji}]_s$, except that total money spending is held constant instead of income. That is, we differentiate the equilibrium equations 2.1 (iv) and 2.1 (v) partially with respect to p_i, this time assuming that the consumer is not free to vary s. Thus σ_{ji} has the same meaning as in 2.1 (vii), i.e. it contains no substitution into or out of s.

The common sense of these two lemmas is as follows. The left-hand side of 2.2 (ix) is the third term of the partial $\partial x_j/\partial p_i$ as in 2.2 (i). $\partial s/\partial q_i$ is the change in saving due to the rise in the expected future price q_i. 2.2 (ix) simply says that this change in saving will be allocated to current expenditure proportionately to income responses, $\partial x_j/\partial y$. 2.2 (x) says precisely the same thing about the substitution part, $[\sigma_{si}]_s$ of the partial $\partial s/\partial p_i$. The left-hand side of 2.2 (x) is that part of total substitution into good j which has come from substitution out of saving.

2.2 (ix) is proved in a straightforward way by differentiating the equilibrium equations 2.1 (iv) and 2.1 (v) successively with respect to q_i and y, and solving for $\partial s/\partial q_i$, $\partial x_j/\partial y$, and $h = \partial s/\partial y$. The conditions 2.2 (viii) make it possible to eliminate all elements u_{iqi} except u_{sqi} by multiplying column one of the determinants in the various solutions by β and subtracting. Thus we have

$$\frac{\partial s}{\partial q_i} = -(u_{sqi}+\beta)\Delta_{ss}/\Delta,$$

$$\frac{\partial x_j}{\partial y} = \Delta_j/\Delta,$$

$$h = \Delta_1/\Delta,$$

where Δ_{ss}, Δ_j, and Δ_1 are respectively the co-factors of the elements u_{ss}, p_j, and 0 of the bordered Hessian determinant of the utility function Δ.

We notice also that, on the conditions 2.2 (viii),

$$\Delta - \Delta_1 = \Delta_{ss}(u_{ss} - \beta') \qquad \qquad 2.2 \text{ (xi)}$$

and $\qquad \qquad \Delta_{sj} = \Delta_j/(u_{ss} - \beta').$

From these results 2.2 (ix) may easily be seen to be an identity.

Turning now to 2.2 (x) we remind ourselves that

$$\sum_j p_j[\sigma_{ji}]_s + [\sigma_{si}]_s = 0$$

and $\qquad \qquad \sum_j p_j \sigma_{ji} = 0,$

so that $\qquad \sum_j p_j([\sigma_{ji}]_s - \sigma_{ji}) = -[\sigma_{si}]_s.$

Thus we confirm that all terms like the left-hand side of 2.2 (x) do in fact sum to the total substitution out of saving which is the amount to be allocated.

The full proof of 2.2 (x) is rather more tedious than that for 2.2 (ix) but the method follows the same lines. The expression obtained for σ_{ji} is similar to that for $[\sigma_{ji}]_s$ except that the determinants in both numerator and denominator of the former are without the final column and row, $1,\ldots, u_{sj},\ldots, u_{ss}$. Writing the full Hessian determinant of the utility function for the moment as Δ^* and the corresponding reduced determinant as Δ, we recognize from 2.2 (xi) that

$$\Delta^* - h\Delta^* = \Delta(u_{ss} - \beta')$$

since in the new notation $\Delta \equiv \Delta_{ss}^*$. This relation facilitates the reduction of the left-hand side of 2.2 (x). When the conditions 2.2 (viii) are applied to the right-hand side also, 2.2 (x) can be seen to be an identity.

The two lemmas 2.2 (ix) and 2.2 (x) suggest two new ways in which the partial derivative of the demand function $\partial x_j/\partial p_i$ may be written. First, for easy reference we repeat the result 2.2 (i)

$$\frac{\partial x_j}{\partial p_i} = -x_i \frac{\partial x_j}{\partial y} + [\sigma_{ji}]_s + \frac{\partial x_j}{\partial q_i}.$$

From lemma 2.2 (ix) we now see that it is possible to take the term $\partial x_j/\partial q_i$ into the income effect and write

$$\frac{\partial x_j}{\partial p_i} = -\left(x_i + \frac{1}{1-h}\frac{\partial s}{\partial q_i}\right)\frac{\partial x_j}{\partial y} + [\sigma_{ji}]_s. \qquad 2.2 \text{ (xii)}$$

We now have a substitution effect obeying all the rules of sign and symmetry, and an income effect which can be shown to be negative in the usual way. It is easy to see in fact that $\partial s/\partial q_i$ must be positive, for we have already shown our solution for this to be

$$\frac{\partial s}{\partial q_i} = -(u_{sq_i}+\beta)\Delta_{ss}/\Delta.$$

And on our assumptions 2.2 (viii) all u_{iq_i} must have the same sign, which will be positive; for increasing q_i reduces real well-being which increases marginal utilities. Hence β is positive. Similarly u_{sq_i} will be positive since decreasing the value of real saving will increase the marginal utility of saving. Again Δ_{ss}/Δ will be negative by the usual stability argument. Hence $\partial s/\partial q_i$ is positive. We notice in passing that in view of 2.2 (ix) a positive $\partial s/\partial q_i$ implies a negative $\partial x_j/\partial q_i$, a result which we have already anticipated on intuitive grounds and which can be applied directly to the form 2.2 (i).

Finally, in connexion with 2.2 (xii), it is important to recognize that this form does not apply to the partial $\partial s/\partial p_i$; for 2.2 (ix) makes nonsense in this case. In fact all that we can write for $\partial s/\partial p_i$ is

$$\frac{\partial s}{\partial p_i} = -x_i\frac{\partial s}{\partial y}+[\sigma_{si}]_s+\frac{\partial s}{\partial q_i} \qquad \text{2.2 (xiii)}$$

which is 2.2 (i). It may sometimes be convenient, however, to apply to this the conclusion that $\partial s/\partial q_i$ is positive.

The second possible form of the general partial $\partial x_j/\partial p_i$ on the neutral want association assumption is obtained by substituting 2.2 (xiii) into 2.2 (xii), making use of lemma 2.2 (x). Thus we obtain

$$\frac{\partial x_j}{\partial p_i} = -\frac{1}{1-h}\left(x_i+\frac{\partial s}{\partial p_i}\right)\frac{\partial x_j}{\partial y}+\sigma_{ji}. \qquad \text{2.2 (xiv)}$$

This is equivalent to 2.1 (vii) and it is this result which justifies all of the work of Chapter 1, as explained in section 2.1. It is easy in fact to see that dropping the term $\partial s/\partial p_i$ is now precisely equivalent to writing the demand function in terms of consumption C rather than income, y, a practice which will be continued in later chapters.

Again in passing it is worth noting that, when we come to deal with the community as a whole, the theory of saving as we have set it out can, in some contexts, lose much of its meaning. For community consumption may include government consumption, and budget surpluses or deficits are not determined by considerations of utility maximization. On the contrary, as long as policy is designed to maintain full employment and balanced overseas payments, total consumption will be held equal to total production whatever happens to prices. Anything the individual is induced to do, in accordance with the principles set out above, the government will deliberately offset. Thus there is a positive advantage in writing demand equations as functions of consumption rather than the sum of personal incomes. Indeed this procedure was found to be unavoidable by the present writer when attempting to deal with a problem in international trade.†

2.3. Conclusions

In view of the somewhat tedious nature of the argument of section 2.2 it seems desirable to summarize the more important results before continuing. These are:

(i) That, in the most general case, when saving is explicitly treated, a new term appears added to the traditional income and substitution effect of the demand response to price changes, so that

$$\frac{\partial x_j}{\partial p_i} = -x_i \frac{\partial x_j}{\partial y} + [\sigma_{ji}]_s + \frac{\partial x_j}{\partial q_i}.$$

It is impossible with certainty to attach a sign to $\partial x_j / \partial q_i$ although there is a strong supposition that it will normally be negative.

$\partial x_j / \partial q_i$ may, of course, be included at will, either in the income effect or in the substitution effect, but nothing is gained thereby; for by so doing we simply disguise all of the useful properties of the term to which it is added.

(ii) On the assumption that the gain or loss of titles to wealth does not affect the *shape* of the function measuring utility from

† Cf. 'The Problem of the Balance of Payments', *International Economic Review*, Jan. 1961.

current consumption, but only the level of satisfaction obtained, it is possible to write the partial $\partial x_j/\partial p_i$ in either of two alternative ways. These are

$$(a) \quad \frac{\partial x_j}{\partial p_i} = -\left(x_i + \frac{1}{1-h}\frac{\partial s}{\partial q_i}\right)\frac{\partial x_j}{\partial y} + [\sigma_{ji}]_s$$

and $$(b) \quad \frac{\partial x_j}{\partial p_i} = -\frac{1}{1-h}\left(x_i + \frac{\partial s}{\partial p_i}\right)\frac{\partial x_j}{\partial y} + \sigma_{ji}.$$

In case (a) the sign of $\partial s/\partial q_i$ is known to be positive. In case (b) the sign of $\partial s/\partial p_i$ is not known. In both cases (a) and (b) $\partial s/\partial p_i$ must be written

$$\frac{\partial s}{\partial p_i} = -x_i\frac{\partial s}{\partial y} + [\sigma_{si}]_s + \frac{\partial s}{\partial q_i}.$$

Both σ_{ji} and $[\sigma_{ji}]_s$ have at all times the familiar sign and symmetry properties. The former exclude substitution into saving but the latter include it.

It may be added that the savings function can be expected to be homogeneous of order one in prices, income, and wealth holding w, assuming that future prices are expected to remain equal to current prices. Thus

$$\sum_j p_j\frac{\partial s}{\partial p_j} + y\frac{\partial s}{\partial y} + w\frac{\partial s}{\partial w} = s. \qquad 2.3 \ (i)$$

From this it is sometimes possible to infer something about the sign of $\partial s/\partial p_i$ (cf. section 2.5).

(iii) If demand is written as a function of consumption instead of income, then the partial $\partial x_j/\partial p_i$ may be written in the usual way and has all the familiar properties *provided only that the assumption in* (ii) *holds*.

(iv) In no case does the coefficient of $\partial x_j/\partial y$ measure the true income compensating variation. In particular a sum of money $x_i\,dp_i$ is never sufficient to compensate for a price rise dp_i whenever there is saving or accumulated titles to wealth.

2.4. A possible alternative

At this point we refer to an approach to the savings problem pioneered by Dr. C. E. V. Leser.[†]

† 'The Consumer's Demand for Money', *Econometrica*, vol. ii, 1943.

What follows goes somewhat beyond the point to which Dr. Leser carried the argument, but the principle is the same. In the view of the present writer Dr. Leser's approach, although it is more restrictive and in many ways less helpful, does give a better insight into the nature of the difficulty which we have to face.

It could be assumed that the individual at the moment of saving makes a plan of future as well as current expenditure and that all utility from current income and accumulated wealth stems from that plan. That is, the consumer maximizes a function

$$u = u(x_1,...,x_n, z_1,...,z_n)$$

where z_i is the intended *future* consumption and x_i the current consumption of the ith good. The budget constraint will be

$$y+w = \sum p_i x_i + \sum q_i z_i$$

where w is, as before, wealth accumulated to date.

If this is worked through on the usual lines we find that the Marshallian partial now breaks down into two income effects and two substitution effects in a way similar to, but not precisely the same as in Dr. Leser's modified equation (loc. cit.).

We have in fact

$$\frac{\partial x_j}{\partial p_i} = -x_i \frac{\partial x_j}{\partial y} - z_i \frac{\partial x_j}{\partial y} + \sigma_{xj\,pi} + \sigma_{xj\,qi}. \qquad \text{2.4 (i)}$$

This is a much more intuitively acceptable result than any so far obtained. We have a substitution and income effect due to the current price change and a similar substitution and income effect due to the expected future price change. (x_i+z_i) is now in a sense a true income-compensating variation but we have a serious difficulty. For whilst an increase in income of that amount would completely compensate for losses in utility from consumption and wealth accumulated to date, it does not take into account the loss of purchasing power of *future* savings. The income effect also involves a term z_i, the intended future consumption of the good. This is a difficult entity to measure even if the consumer could be said to be fully conscious of it.

Again the substitution part $(\sigma_{xj\,pi} + \sigma_{xj\,qi})$ does not have the symmetric properties we would like, for the substitution part of $\partial x_i / \partial p_j$ will be $(\sigma_{xi\,pj} + \sigma_{xi\,qj})$ and whilst $\sigma_{xj\,pi}$ and $\sigma_{xi\,pj}$ are equal, $\sigma_{xj\,qi}$ and $\sigma_{xi\,qj}$ are not.

We could, of course, go on to develop expressions for the savings partials $\partial s / \partial p_i$, since saving to date is merely the total of intended expenditure on goods z. But because of the difficulties already noted this will not lead to results which seem likely to be useful in any way. The method is introduced only for the sake of completeness and because the intuitively plausible result 2.4 (i) serves to confirm the more general argument above.

2.5. Applications

Apart from its importance in the justification of later work, section 2.2 is not without immediate applications. The reader is reminded that the sign of the entity $\partial s / \partial p_i$, as it appears in certain macro-economic models, has, in the past, been the centre of considerable debate and may be again in the future. Whenever it is supposed that currency depreciation will be allowed to have some effect upon the general level of employment, the change in money saving due to the rise in the price of importables (i.e. $\partial s / \partial p_i$) becomes a crucial factor to be considered.

Professor J. E. Meade, throughout his monumental work *The Theory of International Economic Policy*, implicitly assumes that $\partial s / \partial p_i$ can be taken to be zero. Professor H. G. Johnson has very properly drawn attention to Professor Meade's assumption,[†] at the same time arguing that, if there is no 'substitution' effect, $\partial s / \partial p_i$ will always be negative. More precisely Professor A. C. Harberger[‡] puts

$$\frac{\partial s}{\partial p_i} = - x_i \frac{\partial s}{\partial y}.$$

Mr. A. C. L. Day, on the other hand, takes the view that 'substitution' out of consumption into saving could be large enough to

---

[†] In a review of Vol. I entitled 'The Taxonomic Approach to Economic Policy', *Economic Journal*, vol. lxi, Dec. 1951.

[‡] 'Currency Depreciation, Income and the Balance of Trade', *Journal of Political Economy*, vol. 58, 1950.

turn $\partial s/\partial p_i$ positive.† Finally, Mr. J. Spraos argues that nothing in fact can be said on the matter.‡

This list of quoted opinions is not intended to be complete.§ Rather it is selected simply to show that of the four views conceivably possible, four have in fact been taken. Moreover, throughout the debate the words 'income effect' and 'substitution effect' have been freely used in regard to saving, as if these were the only two terms to be considered, the only concession to the peculiar status of 'saving' in the hierarchy of 'goods' being the interpolation from time to time of the adjective 'real'.

No criticism of any of the writers referred to is intended, for, in the absence of a properly worked-out theory of demand with saving, little more than informed speculation is possible. And indeed this is precisely the point of the present section. The reader is invited to judge whether the following extract, taken from a contribution by the present writer to the debate referred to above, could ever have been written were it not for the fortunate circumstance that he had before him at the time the analysis of section 2.2. We quote:

'It seems important to draw attention to the fact that as between real consumption and real saving there is no *a priori* reason to suppose that devaluation will bring about any relative price change at all. The cost of real saving will have been affected in much the same way as the cost of consumption. Mr. Day explains that the stream of satisfaction from consumer goods and the stream of satisfaction derived from interest on bonds are substitutes. This is unquestionably true, but no substitution will actually take place until relative prices have changed. Devaluation will increase the cost of consumption but in so doing it will reduce *pari passu* the purchasing power of both money saving and the stream of interest, and hence reduce their real value.

'Of course, if the pattern of current expenditure is different

† 'Relative Price, Expenditure and the Trade Balance', *Economica*, vol. xxi, 1954.

‡ 'Consumers' Behaviour and the Conditions for Exchange Stability', *Economica*, May 1955.

§ Cf. J. Spraos, loc. cit., for a suitable review of the literature.

from the intended pattern of expenditure out of past saving
and interest streams, there may be some relative price change.
But it should be noted that unless we know these expenditure
patterns it is impossible to say whether the substitution will be
into or out of real saving. Now Mr. Spraos, in criticizing Mr. Day
(pp. 143–4), speaks of substitutability and complementarity in
this connexion, as if the phenomenon were something to do
with the shape of an indifference surface drawn between imports,
exports, and utility from saving. But utility from saving has
no meaning independent of the prices of imports and exports
and any attempt to give it one by means of some arbitrarily
chosen price index must either be restrictive or question begging.

'Two conclusions emerge. The first is that there are much
stronger grounds for arguing in favour of a zero substitution
effect than any of the writers under review have consciously
realized. (There is in fact a close affinity between this assumption and the randomness assumption introduced below.) The
second is that even if we did admit the possibility of a substitution effect we do not know whether the price of utility from
consumption has increased or decreased relatively, without a
knowledge of the patterns of current and intended expenditure
both of which will in any event have changed as a result of the
devaluation.

'In passing it is worth noting that the money substitution
required to achieve any given real substitution must (because
of the price change) be greater than the real substitution valued
in money terms. . . .

'The question of what is substitution effect and what is not, is,
however, not important in the present context except in so far
as it has been used to throw light on the probable value of $\partial s/\partial p$.
It is easy to show without reference to this question at all that
both Professor Harberger's and Mr. Day's formulae rest upon
assumptions equivalent to saying that the marginal propensity
to save is unity. Arguing that x is the compensating variation
and that substitution will be negligible, Professor Harberger
puts $\partial s/\partial p$ equal to $-xh$, where h is the marginal propensity to
save and x is the quantity of imports. Write money saving as

a function of all prices and money income y as under:

$$s = s(p_1,..., p_n, y).$$

Now it is usually accepted that doubling all prices and doubling money income should in fact double saving and this for the moment will be assumed. (The consequences of not assuming it are of some importance and will be considered later.) By Euler's theorem, therefore, it follows that:

$$s = \sum_1^n p_i \frac{\partial s}{\partial p_i} + y \frac{\partial s}{\partial y}. \qquad 2.5 \text{ (i)}$$

Following Professor Harberger we substitute $-hx_i$ for $\partial s/\partial p_i$ (x_i = quantity taken of the ith good) and h for $\partial s/\partial y$. Hence:

$$s = h\left(-\sum_1^n p_i x_i + y\right). \qquad 2.5 \text{ (ii)}$$

But the terms inside the bracket represent simply money income less consumption, therefore

$$s = hs$$

or $$h = 1.$$

Mr. Day's formula implies the same thing also since he has simply added a substitution effect to Professor Harberger's income effect.

'The importance of this procedure lies not so much in the fact that it shows up the weakness of Professor Harberger's assumptions, as in the use to which 2.5 (i) may be put in an attempt to say something which will throw light on the probable limits of magnitude of $\partial s/\partial p_i$, for from 2.5 (i) above we see that

$$\sum p_i \frac{\partial s}{\partial p_i} = s - hy$$

and this will be zero if the average propensity to consume is equal to the marginal propensity to consume.

'At this point it is convenient to raise again the question of homogeneity in prices and income of the savings function since 2.5 (i) depends upon this. Mr. Spraos suggests that Professor Harberger's and Mr. Day's assumptions would be justified if there were money illusion, the existence of which would, of course, invalidate the homogeneity hypothesis. I do not, however, share Mr. Spraos's view that the "special variety of money illusion" here required is a "not implausible" variety. For it requires that the individual should appreciate the significance of his loss in real income from consumption and adjust savings accordingly, but that at the same time he should fail to note the loss in the purchasing power of these savings. This seems inconsistent and unlikely behaviour on the part of consumers. More likely is the complete failure to adjust money saving at all, i.e. zero $\partial s/\partial p$; and if this is the case the whole point of the discussion is lost.

'On the other hand, if we do away with money illusion we should do so completely and take into account not only the loss in the real value of current saving but also the loss in the purchasing power of all accumulated titles to wealth expressed in money terms. Doubling all prices will, of course, double the money value of tangible assets, but it will not double the value of bonds and cash. If we wish to maintain homogeneity we must include a new variable w to represent cash and bonds. Doubling prices and income will not double money saving unless we double also the money value of bonds and cash held. Thus we obtain

$$\sum p_i \frac{\partial s}{\partial p_i} = s - hy - w\frac{\partial s}{\partial w}. \qquad \text{2.5 (iii)}$$

Bearing in mind that we are talking of a community we should expect the bonds part of w to cancel out since every loan must be someone's debt. On the other hand, the government is scarcely likely to wish to adjust its budgetary policy to changes in the purchasing power of the national debt so that cash plus the national debt should represent a reasonable estimate of w. $\partial s/\partial w$ must be expected to be negative since a rise in the purchasing power of wealth holdings will normally induce a reduction in current saving. Hence $\sum p_i(\partial s/\partial p_i)$ will be greater than $s-hy$.

'Now $\partial s/\partial p$ in the case of devaluation means in fact $\partial s/\partial k$ where k is the rate of exchange and

$$\frac{\partial s}{\partial k} dk = \sum_1^r \frac{\partial s}{\partial p_i} dp_i \quad (r = \text{number of goods imported}).$$

Moreover, the price changes dp will bear the same proportion to prices as dk bears to k, for a percentage change in the rate of exchange leads to the same percentage change in prices. Hence

$$\frac{\partial s}{\partial k} = \frac{1}{k} \sum_1^r \frac{\partial s}{\partial p_i} p_i.$$

And if those goods which enter into imports are randomly selected *vis-à-vis* the values of the $p_i(\partial s/\partial p_i)$, which seems not unlikely, then $\partial s/\partial k$ will be numerically less than $s - hy - w(\partial s/\partial w)$ (from 2.5 (iii)).

'This formula seems likely to be of value in helping to set limits on the size of $\partial s/\partial k$, particularly as the entities involved are (relatively) easy to calculate or guess at from national income statistics.

'As a rough example which may help to give some idea of the magnitudes involved, let us suppose that the money value of bonds falls by an amount dw. Suppose further, that the average individual has half his saving life to replace his lost assets, that his preferences are such that he divides his loss equally between saving and consumption, and that he holds half of his life savings in bonds or cash. His money savings will increase by an amount equal to $\frac{1}{4}s$ multiplied by the proportionate fall in the money value of his bonds.

'Thus
$$\tfrac{1}{4}s\frac{dw}{w} = -\frac{\partial s}{\partial w}\, dw,$$

i.e.
$$s - hy - w\frac{\partial s}{\partial w} = 1\tfrac{1}{4}s - hy.$$

In this case $\partial s/\partial k$ would be zero if the marginal propensity to save were 25 per cent greater than the average propensity to save. . . .'

3

COMMUNITY-DEMAND THEORY

3.1. An aggregation problem

WE now have at our disposal a well-developed theory of consumer demand for the individual, but not for the community
as a whole. On the other hand, applications of demand theory
are, in the nature of things, almost always confined to cases
where the relevant variables measure the aggregate consumption
of many individuals. For example, it is often found convenient
to represent the market-preference pattern of a country by
means of a system of curves analogous to the constant utility
(indifference) curves of the individual. Alternatively, helpful
results have been obtained, particularly in the field of international trade, by separating aggregate demand price responses
into income and substitution effects, which are then supposed
to obey the same rules of sign and symmetry known to hold in
the case of the individual.† If these practices cannot be justified
a great deal might be lost.

Unfortunately, attempts so far made to create a consistent
theory of community demand have served only to emphasize
that, in the most general case, the properties of individual
demand functions do *not* hold in the aggregate and that accordingly nothing resembling the familiar indifference curve can be
drawn for a group.‡ Examples are easily constructed to show
that all of the rules may be broken.

On the other hand, it would seem, and it is the purpose of this
chapter to show, that many of the difficulties are more apparent
than real. Only very weak assumptions are needed to reinstate
most of the familiar results. And even where they cannot be

† Cf. J. E. Meade, *The Theory of International Economic Policy*. vols. i
and ii.
‡ Cf. J. R. Hicks, *A Revision of Demand Theory*, chap. vi.

reinstated it is not hard to prove, that in a general way, only a negligible error is involved in assuming that they can.

For purposes of exposition we begin, in section 3.2, with the simple case of two commodities only, where a community-behaviour function (analogous to the individual utility function but with only limited welfare significance) can be developed at once. It is emphasized thereby that failure of the celebrated consistency tests† or their equivalent, the 'axioms of revealed preference', can be due as much to wrongly shaped community-behaviour functions as to the fact that no community-behaviour function exists. General conditions necessary for a properly convex behaviour function are identified and it is argued that the concave case is not likely to be any more significant in practice than the possibility of a positively sloped demand curve, often referred to as the Giffen paradox.

In section 3.3 we turn to the n commodity case. It is shown that the general condition for the existence of a community-behaviour function (the integrability condition) is in fact a condition on the shapes of individual Engel curves.‡ In order to demonstrate that the known characteristics of Engel curves do not impart any bias toward non-integrability a form of function is proposed which is over-sufficient to ensure integrability. It is noted that the function proposed has very similar properties to the logarithmic function claimed by Wold and Juréen§ to give a very good fit to empirical data. Finally it is shown that for a community of many individuals any error involved in assuming integrability must be very small relative

† Cf. J. R. Hicks, loc. cit., chap. vi; cf. also Chapter 1, section 6 above.

‡ Engel curves are curves which trace out the set of commodity bundles which would be chosen as overall expenditure increases, with prices held constant. In other words, it is the set of curves defined by the demand function

$$x = f(p_0\, y)$$

for every given p_0. Intuition suggests that these will not be straight lines. On the contrary the elasticities

$$\frac{\partial x_i}{\partial y}\frac{y}{x_i}$$

will be greater than unity for luxury goods where the marginal propensity to consume exceeds the average and less than unity for necessaries where the opposite is likely to be true.

§ H. Wold and L. Juréen, *Demand Analysis*, chap. i.

to the magnitude of income effects, and hence to the magnitude of elasticities in general.

In the course of the work attention is drawn to the fact that many of the difficulties of aggregation are due to the impossibility of giving a meaning to the idea of utility when applied to a group. If this were not so, an alternative definition of a market-preference function would be available and perhaps more useful. As things are, however, the alternative definition gives rise to non-operational concepts and must therefore be discarded. It has seemed desirable to comment on this and other matters related to welfare economics in a final section.

3.2. The two-commodity case

We begin by noticing an important difference between the demand function for an individual and the demand function for the community as a whole. Individual demand is dependent on price and money income; community demand, on the other hand, is dependent, not only upon price and community income, but also upon the way in which that income is distributed among the individuals within the group. Before we can proceed farther there is need to consider the most satisfactory way to meet this new difficulty.

To some extent, of course, the distribution of money incomes depends upon prices, and if this relationship were exact no problem would arise; for as long as income shares are always precisely determined by the price structure, the aggregate demand equation can always (by substitution) be written as a function of prices and aggregate spending alone. A price elasticity of demand for the community could be defined which would be, in principle, consistent and measurable and which would embody any income redistribution effect.

Unfortunately, price influences on income distribution operate more through commodity supply functions and are only indirectly connected with demand. Furthermore, income redistribution can occur for reasons quite unconnected with price changes. It would seem better, therefore, to define the community behaviour (or market preference) functions as of a *given* income distribution, supposing that the function as a whole shifts with every change in the proportion of national income accruing to each individual.

There is nothing approximate in this choice of procedure. All that is implied is that, in any particular problem in which it is proposed to make use of the results below, we have to consider whether an income redistribution is likely to have taken place or not. If it has, we must add to the total change in consumption of the ith commodity a term which we might write

$$\sum_r \left(\frac{\partial x_i}{\partial y}\right)_r \left(\frac{dy}{Y}\right)_r,$$ 3.2 (i)

where $(\partial x_i/\partial y)_r$ is the rth consumer's rate of change of demand for the ith good in response to own income changes (prices constant), and $(dy/Y)_r$ is the share of income redistribution accruing to him. Evidently

$$\sum_r \left(\frac{dy}{Y}\right)_r = 0$$

since national income is merely redistributed. The expression 3.2 (i) therefore will be zero provided there is no correlation between the individual's marginal propensity to consume the ith good and his share of the redistribution.

Put this way it becomes clear that, far from being a mere expedient, there is a positive advantage in our choice of definitions; for there are many problems in which it will be not unreasonable to assume that redistribution effects are zero. Non-zero redistribution effects will occur only if there is a bias favouring either the rich or the poor, or, perhaps, a particular class of persons likely to have special market preferences. Moreover, by defining a behaviour function which excludes redistribution effects, we shall have succeeded in maintaining the sharp traditional distinction between the theory of demand and the theory of supply.

The foregoing remarks may also be taken to be an introduction to a further observation of some importance. Certain writers, in pursuit of a community theory of demand and/or consequent propositions in welfare economics, have sought to give meaning to the notion of a social welfare function in every way equivalent and not simply analogous, to the utility function of the individual. If this were possible there would be no difference between the theory of demand for the individual and the theory of demand for the group. All theorems would follow at once and by the usual direct proofs.

In this case the defined social welfare function would imply, among other things, a particular distribution of money incomes associated with every conceivable set of prices and national income. Once again we should be able to write aggregate consumption as a function of prices and national income alone. It must be clear to the reader, however, that, unless we could be sure that the income distribution implied by the social welfare function chosen is actually and always attained in practice, we could never, even in principle, observe and measure the aggregate demand elasticities defined by the theory. We have in fact a typical example of a non-operational concept. In the course of discussion of the welfare significance of the behaviour function developed in this chapter, it has seemed worth while to expand upon the point just made and to refer to a particular example (cf. section 4).

We turn now to the actual construction of the community behaviour function. The procedure is, in the first instance, analogous to the 'revealed preference approach' to individual demand theory of Chapter 1, section 6. Given any money national income, its distribution R, and a set of prices, individual demand, and hence aggregate demand, for all commodities is determined. In other words, assuming R given throughout, we have, just as in the revealed preference approach to individual demand theory, a national budget line defining income and, for two goods only, the price ratio between them. The community will choose one single set of commodities represented by a point on the budget line.

To put it the other way round, given any collection of goods, there is one and only one price ratio which will just clear the market for any given distribution of national income between individuals. Thus for every point on a diagram (see points A

and B, Fig. 6 below) representing quantities consumed of each of two goods, there is a corresponding slope (price ratio). What we have to prove is:

(a) *Integrability*, i.e. that the fragments of the budget line, defining the price ratio corresponding to every possible collection of commodities taken, all fit together to form market preference curves, and that they do not lie in haphazard fashion. This gives an answer to the question: Does the market preference (behaviour) function exist?† and

(b) *Maximization*. Even if the integrability condition is met we must still show that the resulting behaviour function is maximized subject to the national budget constraint. It follows from the way that our market preference curves are constructed that, given any budget constraint line, equilibrium is defined by the point of tangency with some market preference curve. That is to say we know before we begin that equilibrium must be a minimum or a maximum. We have only to determine which it is. In short we have to prove convexity of the market preference function.

In the case of individual demand theory we either assume both (a) and (b) by supposing that the consumer maximizes a utility function, or we appeal to 'consistency tests' or the axiom of revealed preference. As explained in Chapter 1, the axiom of revealed preference takes it to be self-evident, first that if an individual in one situation chooses x^0 rather than x^1 and in another chooses x^1, then in the second situation x^0 is not available. This we have equated with consistency of choice. Secondly, it is supposed that x^0 is not available *because it is too expensive*. The two halves of the axiom of revealed preference should be carefully noted for they correspond exactly to (a) and (b). The one implies integrability;‡ the other, convexity.

† Cf. P. A. Samuelson, 'The Problem of Integrability in Utility Theory', *Economica*, pp. 344 ff., 1950.

‡ Strictly speaking the relationship R between x^0 and x^1, defined by the 'weak' axiom of revealed preference, is not by itself sufficient for integrability. We require also that the relationship R should be transitive. But this is implied by the weak axiom under certain conditions of regularity. Cf. Chapter 1, section 6.

In practice, economists who favour the revealed preference approach very seldom distinguish between the two parts of the revealed preference axiom. It is hardly ever recognized that it would be perfectly possible to have consistency of choice (part 1 of the axiom) at the same time supposing that x^0 is unattainable because it is too cheap, or for some other arbitrary reason. In this case we should be able to prove that a 'utility' function exists (integrability), but we might be driven to suppose that the consumer attempts to minimize rather than maximize it.†️ In framing consistency tests or the revealed preference axiom it has always been implicitly assumed that the individual can, if he chooses, spend less than his income and that by spending his whole income he will gain a greater satisfaction. This is, of course, perfectly reasonable, but we have now to recognize that when consistency tests are so framed they may fail *either* because the utility function does not exist *or* because it is concave rather than convex.

The crucial importance of all this lies in the fact that, for the community as a whole, we have no longer any reason, based on introspection, to suppose that consistency tests should be framed as for the individual. We do *not* know in advance that the community will always choose more of all goods rather than less. We do in fact require to prove convexity before we can frame a consistency test. To show this we proceed to set up an example in which two goods only are involved. By this means the two problems, integrability and convexity, may be conveniently separated, for we know before we begin that, on reasonable assumptions,‡️ the integrability condition cannot fail in a two good world. A community-behaviour function must always exist.

Consider Fig. 6 due to Professor J. R. Hicks.§️ Goods x and z are measured along the axes.

---

†️ Technically this would mean an axiom as follows: if the cost of x^0 at prices p^0 is equal to the cost of x^1 at prices p^0 and x^0 is chosen, and if x^1 is chosen at prices p^1, then x^0 at prices p^1 is *cheaper* than x^1 at prices p^1 *and not dearer as in the usual axiom*.

‡️ Concerning continuity, cf. S. Karlin, *Mathematical Methods and Theory in Games, Programming and Economics*, p. 269, D. 4.

§️ *A Revision of Demand Theory*, chap. vi.

Assume the simplest kind of community, consisting of two individuals only. Suppose also that, whatever the community money income, individuals 1 and 2 share it equally. We have two situations A and B. In situation A each individual has income Oa (measured in terms of good x) and in situation B each

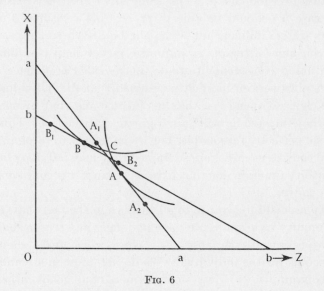

Fig. 6

has Ob. The lines aa and bb are the budget possibility lines of both individuals in each of the situations A and B. As incomes are always equal, the same budget line serves for both individuals. Suppose that in situation A individual 1 chooses the combination of goods x and z represented by the point A_1 and individual 2 chooses A_2. In situation B the choices are B_1 and B_2.

Now there is clearly nothing inconsistent about these choices on the part of individuals; for it is perfectly possible to draw a pattern of indifference curves for consumer 1 so that one curve is tangential to aa at A_1 and another is tangential to bb at B_1. Such curves can be drawn convex to the origin and need not cut one another. The same applies to individual 2. In short there is nothing in the theory of individual consumers' demand which will rule out the choices postulated.

But consider the community choice. If we imagine that the scale of the whole diagram has been halved, the point A, midway between A_1 and A_2, will represent the community choice when community income is $20a$ and prices are as in situation A. Similarly the point B midway between B_1 and B_2 will represent the community choice when income is $20b$ and prices are as in situation B. This illustrates the construction of the behaviour function; for, given individual shares of money income, community choice is determined by prices and community income in precisely the same way as for individuals. And if we go on to consider all possible sets of prices and income we could cover the diagram with points like A and B each with its appropriate price ratio. Regarding the price ratios (slopes aa and bb) in the region of the points A and B as tiny pieces of market preference curves, we have to ask the two questions:

(a) Do all these fragments join up into continuous curves (integrability)? and

(b) Are such curves convex to the origin (maximization)?

In the case of two goods only, we have already asserted that, except in very extraordinary cases which have no economic meaning, the fragments of curve *will* join up into continuous behaviour curves. What is clear from our diagram, however, is that in the case under review behaviour curves when drawn *cannot possibly be convex to the origin*. It is obviously impossible to draw continuously convex curves tangential to bb at B and tangential to aa at A which do not cut. And if they cut (say at C) we contradict what we take to be an economic fact of the real world; namely that, given money incomes, there is only one price ratio which will just and only just clear the market of the 'basket' of goods C. What Professor Hicks's example proves is not that behaviour curves might not exist but rather that they might not be convex to the origin.

To put this in the language of revealed preference, community behaviour does not, in Professor Hicks's case, meet the consistency test as framed for the individual. It is not consistent with the hypothesis that the community is attempting to maximize a behaviour function; for if it were, it would prefer a higher behaviour curve to a lower. Thus with budget line bb, B must be on a higher behaviour curve than A since it is chosen when A in fact costs less. But when the budget line is aa, we infer for the same reasons that A is on a higher behaviour curve than B, which is inconsistent.

On the other hand, it will be seen that, in our special case, community behaviour is *not* inconsistent with the hypothesis that a behaviour function is being *minimized* subject to the condition that income must be spent. For if all income must be spent, A is unattainable in situation B and B is unattainable in situation A. To put the matter the other way, we can easily draw curves, tangential to aa and bb at A and B, continuously *concave* to the origin. And such curves need not cut anywhere. We could frame a revealed preference axiom, which would be met, implying integrability but not convexity.

Clearly the possibility that the market preference function may be minimized in equilibrium is one which must be faced. We should note, at the same time, that this is not entirely destructive of a theory of aggregate demand; for the marginal conditions for minimizing a behaviour function are precisely the same as those for maximizing it. If it were known that the community behaves as if it were minimizing a behaviour function, the theory of aggregate demand would still look very much like the theory of individual demand. The symmetric properties of substitution effects would remain. The difference would be that direct substitution effects would be positive instead of negative. We should still be able to say that the change in demand for x due to an income compensated rise in the price of good z is equal to the change in demand for z due to an income compensated rise in the price of good x. But the change in demand for good z due to an income compensated change in the price of good z will be positive instead of negative.

Looked at this way, however, most economists would in-tuitively reject concave market preference curves as an unlikely case; for in such a case, if substitution effect outweighed income effect, demand curves would slope upward to the right.

Fortunately we do not have to rely entirely upon intuition to show that Professor Hicks's case is not likely to be very important in practice and that, in any event, aggregate demand curves slope downwards. In the first place by definition we have

$$X = x_1 + x_2.$$

That is, total demand for X equals the sum of the demands of individuals 1 and 2. Accordingly, writing $\partial X/\partial Y$ for the aggregate income response, i.e. the change in aggregate demand for X due to unit increase in national income, and using similar symbols with small letters for income responses of individuals 1 and 2, we have

$$\frac{\partial X}{\partial Y} = \frac{\partial x_1}{\partial y_1}\,dy_1 + \frac{\partial x_2}{\partial y_2}\,dy_2. \qquad \text{3.2 (ii)}$$

This merely says that the change in aggregate demand for X is the sum of the changes in individual demands for X when unit increase in community income is shared in the proportions dy_1 and dy_2. Thus, as

$$dy_1 + dy_2 = 1,$$

equation 3.2 (ii) is only another way of saying that the community income effect is equal to a weighted average of individual income effects, weights being equal to the share of money income of each individual. More generally, as long as income is always shared in the existing proportion we have

$$\frac{\partial X}{\partial Y} = \frac{y_1(\partial x_1/\partial y_1) + y_2(\partial x_2/\partial y_2)}{Y}. \qquad \text{3.2 (iii)}$$

Again, by definition we have

$$\frac{\partial X}{\partial p} = \frac{\partial x_1}{\partial p} + \frac{\partial x_2}{\partial p} \qquad \text{3.2 (iv)}$$

which states that the change in aggregate demand, due to unit change in price, is the sum of the individual changes. In passing we note that we need go no farther than equation 3.2 (iv) to show that aggregate demand curves never slope upwards (i.e. the left-hand side of 3.2 (iv) is never positive), unless individual demand curves slope upward also. Even if the aggregate substitution effect were positive, as in Professor Hicks's example, it could never outweigh the income effect.

But we can say much more than this. Breaking up all the terms of 3.2 (iv) into their income and substitution effects we can write

$$\Gamma - X \frac{\partial X}{\partial Y} = -x_1 \frac{\partial x_1}{\partial y_1} - x_2 \frac{\partial x_2}{\partial y_2} + \sigma_1 + \sigma_2,$$

where Γ is the community substitution effect and σ_1 and σ_2 are the individual substitution effects.

Making use of 3.2 (iii) above, we rearrange this last equation as follows

$$\frac{\Gamma}{X} - \frac{x_1(\sigma_1/x_1) + x_2(\sigma_2/x_2)}{X}$$

$$= \frac{y_1(\partial x_1/\partial y_1) + y_2(\partial x_2/\partial y_2)}{Y} - \frac{x_1(\partial x_1/\partial y_1) + x_2(\partial x_2/\partial y_2)}{X}. \quad 3.2 \text{ (v)}$$

3.2 (v) is a fundamental relationship which clearly holds, however many goods and however many individuals are involved. It may be expressed in words as follows:

The difference between the aggregate percentage substitution effect and the arithmetic weighted average (quantity weights) of the individual percentage substitution effects is equal to the difference between the average individual income effects, weighted by incomes and by quantities.

This property may be used to identify, in a general way, the conditions which give rise to Professor Hicks's case. We have seen that the minimized behaviour function is equivalent to a positive Γ/X. For this to occur the right-hand side of 3.2 (v) must be positive and greater in magnitude than the average individual substitution effect, which must be negative. But the right-hand side of 3.2 (v) is likely to be small, since a considerable change of weights is needed to make an appreciable difference to an average, and (taking all prices to be unity) the quantities to be averaged are in any case all less than unity. What is more important is the fact that, on normal economic assumptions, we should expect a fairly close correlation between the weights x and y. Generally speaking, consumption of any good goes up when income goes up. If consumption of x increased proportionately to income, in every case the right-hand side of 3.2 (v) would be zero. It would be positive and have a significant value only if there were a positive correlation between y and $\partial x/\partial y$ and a lower or a negative correlation between x and $\partial x/\partial y$. Intuition suggests that this is only possible for a very odd configuration of tastes.

Moreover, even if the right-hand side were to have a significant positive value, it would be necessary for it to outweigh the average substitution effect which *must* be negative. It can do this only in cases where the substitution effect is very small indeed. But this is just the case where all goods are complementary to one another. And goods which are complementary are usually required in the same fixed proportions by rich and poor, which as we have seen means that the right-hand side of 3.2 (v) tends to zero.

In short it seems likely that the market-preference curves will behave in very much the same way as individual indifference curves. If individual indifference curves show high substitution possibilities, so will the market-preference curves. If goods are complementary so that indifference curves degenerate into a single point, so will the market-preference curves. Only in an extreme case is it possible (but unlikely) that the community curves will tend to a sharp corner pointing *away* from the origin instead of towards it. Such a possibility is best thought of as a perversity somewhat analogous to the celebrated Giffen paradox noted in individual demand theory.†

In the light of all this let us look again at Professor Hicks's diagram. To fulfil all required conditions we are bound to draw indifference curves for individual 1 in such a way that x is an inferior‡ good. For individual 2, z must be an inferior good. And this in spite of the fact that 1 consumes a larger quantity of his inferior good than 2, and vice versa. For good x, the fact that the negative income response for individual 1 is much more heavily weighted than the larger positive income response for

† The case where income effect is positive and greater than substitution effect, so that elasticity of demand is positive.

‡ i.e. $\partial x/\partial y$ is negative and income effect positive.

individual 2 makes it possible to bring down the quantity weighted average to something in the region of zero. On the other hand, the income weighted average is approximately $\frac{1}{2}$ (with relative prices near to unity). Thus community substitution elasticity could be positive and up to, say, $\frac{1}{2}$ in magnitude. Even so, to achieve the required result very small average *individual* substitution elasticities are needed. This would be more than extraordinary in view of the shapes of the individual 'Engel' curves.

Professor Hicks (loc. cit.) goes on to argue that, even if tastes are identical, it is possible to have an 'inconsistent' case, provided incomes are different. This is, of course, true; but the reader who attempts to construct one following the principles outlined above will see that it is not possible without unlikely contortions of Engel curves.† The contortions become greater the greater the substitution possibilities exhibited in the individual indifference patterns. On the other hand, the smaller the substitution possibilities the less justifiable on economic grounds become even the smallest contortions of the Engel curves.

It is important to note also that the task of producing a perverted case becomes all the more difficult once we introduce a large number of individuals whose incomes are distributed so that the vast majority have incomes which are very little different. A small proportion of rich persons will not appreciably affect the averages in the right-hand side of 3.2 (v).

So far, of course, we have not proved very much. The fact that community behaviour curves are bound to exist in a two-good world does not imply that they must also exist where there are any number of goods. Moreover, the heuristic argument above establishes no more than a likelihood that the sign of the direct compensated price response Γ_{ii} (that is, the response of the ith good to the ith price) will be negative. This is not sufficient to establish the convexity of the market preference function where there are n goods.

† With two individuals only the curve must be 's'-shaped despite high complementarity.

Nevertheless, the ground has been prepared, and both points will be taken up more generally in the next section.

3.3. The general case

We seek first to establish integrability, or what might be called 'approximate' integrability, when there are three or more commodities. It is convenient to begin by drawing attention to an example devised by Wold and Juréen,† which makes it clear that we cannot hope to prove that a market-preference function exists in the most general case. What we shall try to show, however, is that it does exist on not unreasonable economic assumptions and that, in any event, the maximum error which could be involved in assuming integrability is bound to be small.

The Wold–Juréen example assumes a community of two individuals A and B, whose utility functions are

$$U_A = (x_1+1)(x_2 x_3)$$
$$U_B = x_1 x_2 (x_3)^2,$$

x_1, x_2, and x_3 are the quantities consumed of three goods 1, 2, and 3. Money national income is assumed to be at all times equally shared by A and B.

The actual working out of the example is somewhat tedious; accordingly, only an outline is given here. Applying the marginal utility conditions for equilibrium to the above functions we obtain individual demand equations as functions of commodity prices p_1, p_2, and p_3, and individual money incomes y_A and y_B. Summing individual demand equations for each good and using the fact that

$$y_A = y_B = \tfrac{1}{2}Y \quad \text{(where } Y \text{ is community income)}$$

aggregate demands (X_1, X_2, X_3) may be expressed as functions of prices and community income Y. Now, using the fact that

$$\sum p_i X_i = Y,$$

aggregate demand equations may be solved for p_1, p_2, and p_3 in terms of X_1, X_2, and X_3 (Y being regarded as a parameter). This corresponds precisely to the procedure described verbally

† Loc. cit., example (27), p. 143.

in section 3.2. For every basket of commodities X_1, X_2, X_3, we have a corresponding set of prices. These prices define tiny fragments of a plane in three-dimensional space which may or may not join up to form market-preference surfaces. They will join up if and only if the differential equation

$$\sum p_i \, dX_i = 0$$

possesses a solution. For a solution to exist the integrability condition

$$p_1\left(\frac{\partial p_2}{\partial X_3} - \frac{\partial p_3}{\partial X_2}\right) + p_2\left(\frac{\partial p_3}{\partial X_1} - \frac{\partial p_1}{\partial X_3}\right) + p_3\left(\frac{\partial p_1}{\partial X_2} - \frac{\partial p_2}{\partial X_1}\right) = 0 \quad \text{3.3 (i)}$$

must be fulfilled. It will be noticed that the Wold–Juréen example fails this test and no market preference function exists.

Were it not for this example, it would be tempting to conjecture that, because the aggregate differential equation is simply the sum of the individual differential equations

$$\sum p_i \, dx_i = 0$$

it must have a solution; for the individual differential equations must have solutions, namely the utility functions from which we began. What Wold and Juréen have shown is that such a conjecture is unjustified in general. Integrability of individual equations does impose some restriction, but it is clearly not the restriction we want.

On the other hand it is interesting to examine further the peculiarities of the Wold–Juréen example. From the aggregate demand equations we can find the value in terms of prices and Y of the aggregate analogue Γ_{12} of the individual substitution effects σ_{12}. This is given by the expression

$$\frac{\partial X_1}{\partial p_2} + X_2 \frac{\partial X_1}{\partial Y}.$$

Similarly we may find Γ_{21}. It will be noticed that

$$\Gamma_{12} - \Gamma_{21} = -\frac{1}{12 p_2}$$

which is independent of Y. The fact that Γ_{12} is not equal to Γ_{21}

is a consequence of non-integrability and illustrates the break-down of the usual conclusions of demand theory in this case. But it will be seen also that the separate expressions for Γ_{12} and Γ_{21} do involve Y, and are in fact both dominated by a term approximately equal to $Y/6p_1p_2$. Clearly when Y is very large relative to p, as it will be in all economically significant cases, the error involved in assuming $\Gamma_{12} = \Gamma_{21}$ will be very small relative to the substitution effects themselves. What is more important, we notice that most of the difficulties arise because the equation for X_1 takes the form

$$X_1 = \frac{7Y - 16p_1}{24p_1}.$$

This implies that when $7Y$ is smaller than $16p_1$, X_1 is negative, which is economic nonsense. *In other words the effect of non-integrability becomes significant only in the region where the model does not make economic sense*, that is, where p is of the same order of magnitude as Y.

All of this encourages us to hope that we may find that reasonable economic assumptions are equivalent, or approximately equivalent, to the integrability condition; and this in fact proves to be the case. We now proceed to show this in more general terms.

The straightforward approach would be to attempt to interpret in an economic sense the integrability conditions 3.3 (i). But this turns out to be unhelpful, for it is not easy this way to make use of the crucial fact that all individual differential equations are known to be integrable. A back-door method is more convenient.

Consider the identity

$$\sum_r x_i \equiv X_i,$$

the summation being for all individuals. Differentiating both sides with respect to the price p_j of the jth good and breaking up into income and substitution effects we obtain

$$\sum_r \left(-x_j \frac{\partial x_i}{\partial y} + \sigma_{ij} \right) = -X_j \frac{\partial X_i}{\partial Y} + \Gamma_{ij}. \qquad \text{3.3 (ii)}$$

Similarly

$$\sum_r \left(-x_i \frac{\partial x_j}{\partial y} + \sigma_{ji} \right) = -X_i \frac{\partial X_j}{\partial Y} + \Gamma_{ji}. \qquad \text{3.3 (iii)}$$

And we know that $\sigma_{ij} \equiv \sigma_{ji}$ for all individuals from the assumption that individual preference functions exist. We know also that $\Gamma_{ij} \equiv \Gamma_{ji}$ is a necessary and sufficient condition for integrability in all ordinary cases. By subtracting 3.3 (ii) from 3.3 (iii), therefore, we have a necessary and sufficient condition for integrability

$$\sum_r \left(x_j \frac{\partial x_i}{\partial y} - x_i \frac{\partial x_j}{\partial y} \right) - \left(X_j \frac{\partial X_i}{\partial Y} - X_i \frac{\partial X_j}{\partial Y} \right) \equiv 0 \qquad \text{3.3 (iv)}$$

which must be true for all possible pairs of goods ij and for all corresponding pairs of quantities $X_i X_j$.

The conditions 3.3 (iv) can be thought of as restrictions on the shapes and distribution of individual Engel curves. And looking at the problem from the point of view of any single set of Engel curves, corresponding to a given set of prices, we can make our problem simpler by imagining that units are chosen so as to make all prices unity. This is no more than a device to enable us to avoid continually writing prices into our conditions, so that we can say

$$\sum_{i=1}^n \frac{\partial x_i}{\partial y} \equiv 1 \quad \text{and} \quad \sum_{i=1}^n x_i \equiv y, \qquad \text{3.3 (v)}$$

where n is the number of commodities.

At this point it may be worth while to confirm what was asserted in section 2 above (and what we know from the theory of differential equations), namely that the integrability condition in this new form 3.3 (iv) *must* be met if there are no more than two goods.

First we note that for n commodities there are $(n-1)^2$ integrability conditions 3.3 (iv). But not all of these are independent; for, writing C_{ij} for the left-hand side of 3.3 (iv), it is clear that by symmetry

$$C_{ij} \equiv -C_{ji}.$$

Moreover,

$$\sum_{\substack{j=1 \\ j \neq i}}^n C_{ij} \equiv \sum_{j=1}^n C_{ij} \equiv 0$$

since C_{ii} is obviously zero and since

$$\sum_{j=1}^{n} C_{ij}$$

written in full, using 3.3 (v), and the definition (section 3.2)

$$\frac{\partial X_i}{\partial Y} = \frac{\sum_r y(\partial x_i/\partial y)}{Y}$$

becomes
$$\sum_r y \frac{\partial x_i}{\partial y} - X_i - \sum_r y \frac{\partial x_i}{\partial y} + X_i$$

which is identically zero.

Thus of our $(n-1)^2$ conditions 3.3 (iv), only $\frac{1}{2}(n-1)(n-2)$ are independent. If $n = 2$, $\frac{1}{2}(n-1)(n-2) = 0$, and a market-preference function must exist.

We recognize also that $\frac{1}{2}(n-1)(n-2)$ is precisely the number of independent integrability conditions required in the case of a differential equation in n variables.† This confirms that our use of the fact that individual preference functions exist imposes no further constraints of the kind we need as yet. We have already anticipated this in view of the Wold–Juréen example. Further constraints must be imposed on economic grounds.

Using again the fact that

$$\frac{\partial X_i}{\partial Y} = \frac{\sum_r y(\partial x_i/\partial y)}{Y}$$

we may transform the integrability conditions 3.3 (iv) further into

$$\sum_r \left[\left(\frac{\bar{x}_i}{\bar{y}} y - x_i \right) \frac{\partial x_j}{\partial y} - \left(\frac{\bar{x}_j}{\bar{y}} y - x_j \right) \frac{\partial x_i}{\partial y} \right] \equiv 0$$

where $\bar{x}_i$ and $\bar{y}$ are the mean values of x_i and y so that X/Y may be written $\bar{x}/\bar{y}$.

Moreover,

$$\sum_r \left(\frac{\bar{x}_i}{\bar{y}} y - x_i \right) \equiv 0 \equiv \sum_r \left[\frac{\bar{x}_j}{\bar{y}} \left(\frac{\bar{x}_i}{\bar{y}} y - x_i \right) \right]$$

so that 3.3 (iv) is equivalent to

$$\sum_r \left[\left(\frac{\bar{x}_i}{\bar{y}} y - x_i \right) \left(\frac{\bar{x}_j}{\bar{y}} - \frac{\partial x_j}{\partial y} \right) - \left(\frac{\bar{x}_j}{\bar{y}} y - x_j \right) \left(\frac{\bar{x}_i}{\bar{y}} - \frac{\partial x_i}{\partial y} \right) \right] \equiv 0.$$

† Cf. E. L. Ince, *Ordinary Differential Equations*, p. 54.

Now writing $\qquad x_i = f_{is}(y)$

for the sth individual's Engel curve for the ith good, we may define functions

$$F_{is}(y) \equiv \left(\frac{\bar{x}_i}{\bar{y}} y - f_{is}(y) \right)$$

so that our integrability condition becomes

$$\sum_{s=1}^{r} (F_{is} F'_{js} - F_{js} F'_{is}) \equiv 0, \qquad \qquad 3.3 \text{ (vi)}$$

where F' is the derivative of F with respect to y.

An oversufficient condition for this to be true would be

$$F_{is} F'_{js} - F_{js} F'_{is} = 0$$

for all s. It is worth while to make use of this oversufficient condition to prove that expected bias, due to skew income distribution and the known tendency for luxury goods to be taken in a higher proportion as income rises, does not impart any bias towards non-integrability. To this end we assume for the moment that all individual Engel curves are identical (i.e. similar tastes). This is, of course, the basic assumption made by empirical workers attempting to establish the form of Engel curves from family budget data.[†] We now state that if the function defining the Engel curve for the ith good, common to all consumers, takes the form

$$x_i = \alpha_i y^2 + \beta_i y, \qquad \qquad 3.3 \text{ (vii)}$$

where α_i and β_i are arbitrary parameters, the integrability condition will be fulfilled. We note that this functional form is very closely allied to the log linear form

$$x_i = \alpha_i y^{\beta_i} \qquad \qquad 3.3 \text{ (viii)}$$

which Wold and Juréen claim to have found satisfactory in empirical studies (loc. cit., p. 2). Both have two parameters and both represent families of curves passing through the origin[‡] which may be concave to the y-axis (necessaries) or convex to the y-axis (luxuries), according to the value of the parameters

---

[†] Cf. Wold and Juréen, loc. cit., chap. 1.

[‡] In one sense the function 3.3 (vii) is *more* flexible than 3.3 (viii) since we may have $x_i = 0$ for $y > 0$, which means that the effective part of the function might not pass through the origin.

α, β. Either can be a straight line through the origin (i.e. unit elasticity), if $\alpha = 0$ in the case of the first, and if $\beta = 1$ in the second.

To prove the claim above we define a new parameter 'a' such that

$$\beta_i = \frac{\bar{x}_i}{\bar{y}} - \alpha_i(\bar{y}+a),$$

or

$$a = \frac{1}{\alpha_i}\left(\frac{\bar{x}_i}{\bar{y}} - \alpha_i\bar{y} - \beta_i\right);$$

but

$$\bar{x}_i = \sum_r \left(\frac{\beta_i y + \alpha_i y^2}{r}\right)$$

so that, measuring y about its mean $\bar{y}$, we have

$$\frac{\bar{x}_i}{\bar{y}} = \beta_i + \alpha_i\bar{y} + \alpha_i\frac{m^2}{\bar{y}},$$

where m^2 is the variance of the distribution of incomes. Thus

$$a = \frac{m^2}{\bar{y}}$$

and is independent of both parameters α_i and β_i. More important, since m^2 and $\bar{y}$ are the same for all goods, the parameter, a, must be the same for all goods. The function F_{is} defined above now takes the form

$$F_{is} = -[\alpha_i y^2 - \alpha_i(\bar{y}+a)y] \qquad \text{3.3 (ix)}$$

with a common parameter $(\bar{y}+a)$ for all goods. Functions of this form meet the oversufficient integrability condition

$$F_{is}F'_{js} - F_{js}F'_{is} = 0.$$

Thus the assumption, that Engel curves are the same for all individuals and take the function form 3.3 (vii), is a sufficient condition for the existence of a market preference function.

This assumption is not unreasonable as a first approximation, and the argument above is probably quite enough to justify the free use of market-preference functions wherever the classifications of goods i, j are broad. It is unlikely, however, that the functional form proposed for Engel curves will hold for very narrow classifications. For example, the Engel curve for golf-

clubs is unlikely to fall into the required regular shape, even
though the curve for 'expenditure on sporting activities' may.
It would be interesting to know something of the magnitude of
the error which would be introduced if the facts ceased to
correspond to our assumption.

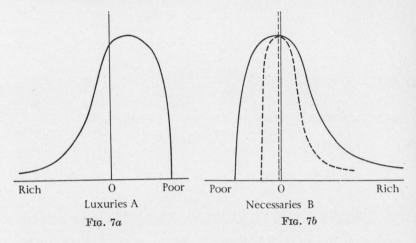

Rich   O   Poor   Poor   O   Rich

Luxuries A   Necessaries B

Fig. 7a   Fig. 7b

To this end we examine in a quite general way the probable
shape of the distribution of the values for the r individuals of
the function

$$F_{is} = \left(\frac{\bar{x}_i}{\bar{y}}y - x_i\right).$$

On the most reasonable economic assumptions, with a skew
distribution of income among the population, the distributions
of F_{is} will also be skew and will take forms similar to those
illustrated in Fig. 7 (unbroken lines). In words, F_{is} is the difference between (a) what the individual would spend on x_i if he
spent on it the same proportion of his income as the average
consumer, and (b) what he actually does spend. We have
already noted that the mean value of F_{is} is always zero. If $\partial x_i/\partial y$
is increasing with income (luxury good), F_{is} will be positive for
incomes less than average and negative for incomes greater than
average. The reverse applies for necessary goods. We explain
again that the skewness of the distributions is due partly to the
fact that the distribution of incomes is itself likely to be skew,

and partly to the fact that, when $\partial x_i/\partial y$ is increasing with income, F_{is} decreases at an increasing rate. Conversely, if $\partial x_i/\partial y$ is decreasing with income, F_{is} increases at an increasing rate.

Now the integrability condition is

$$\sum_s F_{is}\left[\frac{\partial x_j}{\partial y}\right]_s - \sum_s F_{js}\left[\frac{\partial x_i}{\partial y}\right]_s = 0$$

so that if there were no correlation between F_{is} and $\partial x_j/\partial y$ or F_{js} and $\partial x_i/\partial y$, it is bound to be met. For both $\sum F_{is}$ and $\sum F_{js}$ are zero. Unfortunately, however, in the normal case, we must expect correlation since all elements are probably correlated with individual incomes, y_s. Consider the effect of this correlation upon the means of the distributions of

$$F_{is}\frac{\partial x_j}{\partial y}.$$

If i and j are both necessaries $\partial x_j/\partial y$ will be negatively correlated with income and hence negatively correlated with F_{is}. The distribution of their product therefore is likely to take a form similar to the broken line in Fig. 7. Since

$$\frac{\partial x_j}{\partial y} < 1$$

it lies inside the old distribution with its skewness decreased. The mean will be negative. If i is a necessity and j is a luxury, the range of the product distribution will be decreased as before, but the skewness increased. The mean will be positive. If i is a luxury and j a necessity, on the other hand, skewness is decreased and the new mean is positive (since skewness is now oppositely orientated). If both i and j are luxuries, again the new mean is negative; skewness is increased. We conclude that the signs of mean $F_{is}\,(\partial x_j/\partial y)$ and mean $F_{js}\,(\partial x_i/\partial y)$ are always the same.

But the mean of the differences

$$F_{is}\frac{\partial x_j}{\partial y} - F_{js}\frac{\partial x_i}{\partial y}$$

in which we are interested is the same as the difference of the means

$$\overline{F_{is}\frac{\partial x_j}{\partial y}} - \overline{F_{js}\frac{\partial x_i}{\partial y}}.$$

And we have shown that these means will, on reasonable economic assumptions, be of the same sign.

Consider now the order of magnitudes of the $F_{is}(\partial x_j/\partial y)$. We note first that, even on the most extreme assumptions, the effective range of the distribution F_{is} is unlikely to exceed $\bar{x}_i$ and will normally be a great deal less. Hence the range of the distribution $F_{is}(\partial x_j/\partial y)$ will normally be of an order of size smaller than $x_i(\partial x_j/\partial y)$. Moreover, with highly leptokurtic income distributions such as we should expect in the usual case where the great majority of incomes lie in the region of the mean income, the value of the modulus

$$\left| \overline{F_{is}\frac{\partial x_j}{\partial y}} \right|$$

will be very much less than the range, which has already been shown to be not greater than the mean individual income effect $\overline{x_i(\partial x_j/\partial y)}$.

Moreover, we have shown that

$$\left| \overline{F_{is}\frac{\partial x_j}{\partial y}} \right| \geqq \left| \overline{F_{is}\frac{\partial x_j}{\partial y} - F_{js}\frac{\partial x_i}{\partial y}} \right|$$

and by definition

$$\Gamma_{ji} - \Gamma_{ij} = \sum_s \left(F_{is}\frac{\partial x_j}{\partial y} - F_{js}\frac{\partial x_i}{\partial y} \right) = r\left(\overline{F_{is}\frac{\partial x_j}{\partial y} - F_{js}\frac{\partial x_i}{\partial y}} \right).$$

Hence

$$\Gamma_{ji} - \Gamma_{ij} \leqq r\left| \overline{F_{is}\frac{\partial x_j}{\partial y}} \right|$$

which has been shown to be very small compared with

$$r\left(\bar{x}_i\frac{\partial \bar{x}_j}{\partial y} \right) = X_i\frac{\partial \bar{x}_j}{\partial y}.$$

In short, the difference between aggregate substitution effects will be negligible compared with aggregate income effect $X_i(\partial X_i/\partial Y)$.[†] There can be little doubt that for all practical

_____

† The following numerical example should serve to allay any doubts the reader may have at this point. The error $\Gamma_{ji} - \Gamma_{ij}$ expressed roughly as an

purposes the existence of a market-preference function can be
safely assumed. It is evident also that properly framed consistency tests could be applied to aggregate data with virtually
the same degree of confidence as in the case of the individual.

We are now in a position to reconsider quite generally all
other properties of substitution effects Γ_{ij}.

First we notice that, from the argument leading to equation
3.2 (v) of section 2, we can, in our new notation, write the
general substitution effect Γ_{ij} as under:

$$\Gamma_{ij} = \sum_{s=1}^{r} \sigma_{ij} + \sum_{s=1}^{r} F_{js}\frac{\partial x_i}{\partial y}. \qquad 3.3 \text{ (x)}$$

In order to establish strict identity between aggregate and
individual demand theory we should need to show

(i) that $\sum_j p_j \Gamma_{ij} = 0$ (where p_j is the price of the jth good),
and

(ii) that the determinant $|\Gamma_{ij}|$ is the discriminant of a negative
semi-definite quadratic form (i.e. that market preference
hypersurfaces are convex).

To prove (i) we note that for the sth individual $\sum_j p_j \sigma_{ij}$ is
zero by individual demand theory and that by definition

$$\sum_j p_j F_{js} = y_s - y_s = 0.$$

The required result follows at once.

elasticity (i.e. $(\Gamma_{ji} - \Gamma_{ij})/X_i$ prices being taken as unity) has been shown to be
less than, or at most equal to,

$$(r/X_i)\overline{\left|F_{is}\frac{\partial x_j}{\partial y}\right|} = (1/\bar{x}_i)\overline{\left|F_{is}\frac{\partial x_j}{\partial y}\right|}.$$

Making the most extreme assumption that the range of the distribution of
$F_{is}(\partial x_j/\partial y)$ is as large as $\bar{x}_i(\partial x_j/\partial y)$, and the further not unreasonable assumption
that the mean is distorted away from zero by, say, 1 per cent of the range,
we have a possible error in elasticity of demand of not more than 1 per cent
of $\partial x_j/\partial y$. Thus, if the marginal propensity to consume the commodity concerned is, say, 0·1, the error will be approximately 0·001 of the elasticity,
which must have an income effect of 0·1.

In other words, the percentage error in any forecast of consumption due to
non-integrability will be of the order of 0·001 per cent of the percentage price
change, i.e. 0·001 per cent for a 1 per cent price change, or, in absolute terms,
0·00001 times the quantity consumed.

That (ii) cannot be proved for the general case we have seen from section 3.2. It is possible, however, to get very close. First we note that $\left|\sum_r \sigma_{ij}\right|$ by itself is the discriminant of a negative semi-definite quadratic form, for it is the discriminant of the sum of the r quadratic forms with discriminants $|\sigma_{ij}|_s$, which are negative semi-definite by stability of individual choice. In other words we need only find the conditions under which

$$\left|\sum F_{js} \frac{\partial x_i}{\partial y}\right|$$

by itself is the discriminant of a negative semi-definite form.

It is now easy to show that the form of function 3.3 (ix), which we have already seen is oversufficient for integrability, is likewise oversufficient for convexity; for the determinant $\left|\sum F_{js}(\partial x_i/\partial y)\right|$ is identical with the determinant $\left|-\sum F_{js} F'_{is}\right|$ and from 3.3 (ix) we note that the general element $-\sum F_{js} F'_{is}$ can be written $\alpha_i \alpha_j [\phi(y)]$ where $\phi(y)$ is common to every element. Every principal minor of order greater than one must therefore be zero. And we have already noted that

$$-\sum F_{is} F'_{is} = \sum F_{is}(\partial x_i/\partial y)$$

is always negative, whether i is a luxury good or a necessity.

The same conclusion could have been derived by showing $\phi(y)$ to be negative for all reasonable values of y. Clearly also $|\alpha_i \alpha_j [\phi(y)]|$ is symmetric, so that $\left|\sum F_{js}(\partial x_i/\partial y)\right|$ is the discriminant of a negative semi-definite form and the market preference function must be convex.

More generally we recall that with no more than the weakest economic restrictions we have already shown the elements $\sum F_{js}(\partial x_i/\partial y)$ to be very small relative to income effects $X_j(\partial X_i/\partial Y)$. Unless, therefore, any of the principal minors, of any order, of the determinant $\left|\sum \sigma_{ij}\right|$ are also very small indeed, the character of the determinant $|\Gamma_{ij}|$ will be no different from $\left|\sum \sigma_{ij}\right|$, which, as we have seen, is the discriminant of a negative semi-definite form. Moreover, it will be shown in Chapter 4 that very small principal minors of $\left|\sum \sigma_{ij}\right|$ usually imply a high degree of complementarity between all of the commodities involved. It can be seen, therefore, that what has just been said is no more than a generalization of the two-dimensional arguments of section 3.2 above. If convexity seems likely to break down at all, this must be because of an extra-ordinarily high degree of complementarity between two or more goods. But if complementarity is present we must expect goods to be consumed in the *same* fixed proportions by all individuals, so that all appropriate F_{js} will be zero. And with zero F_{js} convexity remains despite the complementarity.

We conclude that, as a first approximation, economists need have no inhibitions in regard to the use of community market-preference curves analogous to individual indifference curves, provided only limited welfare significance is attributed to them. Welfare problems are considered in the section following. Aggregate elasticities are likely to possess precisely the same properties of sign and symmetry as individual elasticities. Tests of consistency may be applied with almost equal confidence, and for the same reasons, both to aggregate and individual consumption data. In the empirical work of later chapters we assume group demand equations to be subject to all the restrictions applicable in the case of the individual.

3.4. The community welfare approach

It is probably true that some part of the willingness of economists to apply the results of individual demand theory to aggregate data is based upon an approach quite different from that set out in the foregoing sections. Indeed, in at least one case, this has been explicitly claimed (see below). It would be wrong, therefore, to leave the working out above as it stands without further comment on what might be thought to be an alternative possibility.

Evidently, if we could define a social-welfare function analogous to individual utility and if, in addition, we could show that the community behaves *as if it were attempting to maximize the function so defined*, we should at once have an aggregate theory similar in all respects to individual theory. No further work

other this is so
it is doubtful to say
at least

would be necessary. Unfortunately, however, the proviso itali-cized is crucial. It is a simple matter to set up any one of an infinity of possible welfare functions (according to one's brand of ethics), but there is no reason to suppose that market behaviour is the outcome of an attempt to maximize any one of them.

Despite this there are at least two reasons why the welfare approach retains a certain appeal. First, it does not matter from the point of view of aggregate demand theory that there is no agreement about what might be meant by group welfare. If it can be shown that the community behaves as if it were maximizing any kind of function at all, this will do. The require-ments are only that the function should exist and that market equilibrium should be a maximum subject to a national money income constraint.

Secondly, there is a strong tradition in economics that equili-brium in a free market implies a greater satisfaction for all than any arbitrarily determined distribution of goods. This feeling is justified by simple observation of the fact that, given an arbitrary distribution of goods (say due to rationing), a black or grey market will form and exchange take place until a 'market' equilibrium is reached. In the market equilibrium some indivi-duals are better off whilst no one is worse off. Thus we can be sure that market equilibrium maximizes the function defined as the sum of satisfactions of all individuals, subject to the condition that all individuals should retain at all times the same propor-tionate share of real satisfaction which they have in the final market equilibrium.† To put it another way, in any market-equilibrium situation, provided the current distribution of money income, and hence real income, is 'just', group welfare is maximized subject to the national money-income constraint.

It is probably an awareness of this which gives rise to the widespread feeling that objections to 'community indifference curves' are no more than a technicality; that for all practical purposes such curves are all right and may be freely used in

† This measurable utility way of putting the proposition could easily be rephrased to satisfy those who object to this approach, but we shall not attempt this here.

analysis both for the derivation of qualitative conclusions and for the purpose of making certain welfare judgements.

Indeed an explanation by Professor W. J. Baumol of how such 'community indifference curves' might be constructed† has led Professor J. E. Meade to 'accept the assurance of Professor Baumol that [they] can be drawn'‡ and so to appeal to the familiar properties of elasticities even though these refer to aggregate demand.

This is not really satisfactory. If Professor Meade's work in fact rested on Professor Baumol's welfare function, either it would be implicitly assumed that every economic change discussed is always accompanied by a most complicated redistribution of money incomes, so that all gains and losses in real income are shared exactly according to some predetermined formula, or every equation in the theory of international trade as set out by Professor Meade has a term or terms missing. It is illuminating to expand upon this point.

Given some set of prices and some distribution of national income, let there be market equilibrium. This will determine the level of real satisfaction enjoyed by each individual. Now consider a small change in prices accompanied by an adjustment of money incomes leading to a new market equilibrium where every individual has exactly the same level of satisfaction as in the original position. Then, by definition, the two positions are points on a community indifference curve. The community is equally well off since all individuals in it are equally well off. Repeating the procedure for all possible combinations of commodity prices we may build up a complete community indifference curve. Other curves may be constructed similarly, once we have decided upon the way in which real satisfaction is to be shared for each level of community satisfaction.

These are Professor Baumol's community indifference curves and they define a social-welfare function. Obviously an infinite number of such welfare functions can be constructed, each one being determined by an arbitrary rule defining the division of

† W. J. Baumol, *Welfare Economics and the Theory of the State.*
‡ *The Balance of Payments,* Mathematical Supplement.

K

real satisfaction. More important, we know that market equilibrium is bound to maximize some one Baumol welfare function;
for, by construction, the slope of Baumol indifference curves is
always the same as the slope of individual indifference curves
which in turn is the same as relative prices in equilibrium.

Unfortunately, different positions of market equilibrium do
not maximize the *same* Baumol welfare function unless each set
of prices and community money income as it emerges is always
associated with the precise distribution which will divide real
satisfaction in the proportions subsumed in the construction of
the welfare function.

This will not happen in practice. If any community is in
market equilibrium and the current distribution of money, and
hence real, income is considered 'just', it is always possible to
define a Baumol welfare function based upon that value judgement. But if, in the course of any piece of economic analysis,
we suppose any commodity price to be changed, this may or
may not be accompanied by a money-income redistribution.
Whether it is or not, we can be certain that, in general, it will
not be accompanied by precisely that income redistribution
required to maintain the 'just' distribution of real income
assumed in the construction of the social-welfare function.
Hence our *new* position of equilibrium would *not* maximize the
social welfare function. We have a social-welfare function, but
it will be maximized only at one configuration of prices and
national income, namely that from which we commenced its
construction; and if we did not begin construction from a market
equilibrium, only by coincidence could it be maximized by any
market equilibrium. This is true for any possible Baumol
welfare function we may care to define based on any of the
infinity of possible distributions of real income. More generally
it is true for any social welfare function whatever.

On the other hand, our argument does suggest a procedure
which some economists might feel to be a useful one. We could
define arbitrarily some group-welfare function, say the Baumol
function, for existing equilibrium. We might then define 'net
income redistribution' as that redistribution of money income

needed, after any given price change, to ensure that market behaviour does maximize the chosen function. It is then open to us to show that observed aggregate elasticity of demand can be separated into three terms, income effect and substitution effect (derived from the welfare function), obeying the usual rules, and the 'net income redistribution effect'.

The extra term deducts net income redistribution effect because the income redistribution to which it refers does not in fact take place; for by definition net income redistribution is the difference between the redistribution which *does* take place and that which would be required to allow us to write elasticity as income and substitution effects alone.

It is now clear why Professor Meade's declared justification of his method is open to criticism. Either he is assuming zero net income redistribution or terms are missing from his formulae. Moreover, even if all the formulae of *The Theory of Economic Policy* were reworked so as to include net income redistribution terms, we should still be no farther forward; for the concept of net income redistribution is non-operational. It can never in principle be measured or observed unless real satisfaction is measurable for every individual. And, if this were the case, we should have no need for any of the present discussion. In short, no meaningful theory of demand which could conceivably be falsified by observation can be derived from the notion of a social welfare function.

Fortunately it is open to economists to use Professor Meade's results without modification by appealing to the work of sections 3.1, 3.2, and 3.3, which are independent of any measurement of welfare. Elasticity of demand, as explained in section 3.2, can be defined as excluding all income redistribution in the hope that, having at some time measured individual marginal propensities to consume, we may estimate separately the effect of any observed income redistributions which might actually take place. The absence of income-redistribution terms in Professor Meade's work can be justified by the assumption noted in section 3.2 that there is no correlation between tastes and actual redistribution so that all extra terms are zero. This is likely to be the common case.

We now note that, having thrown out social welfare, it comes in again by the back door, as we should expect from the intuitive argument with which this section begins. We have seen that *any* market equilibrium maximizes *some* Baumol welfare function. It follows that maximizing (or in the unlikely perverse case minimizing) a market preference function also maximizes some social-welfare function. But the maximized welfare function may not be one accepted by all as measuring community welfare. In other words the distribution of real wealth may not be 'just'. But we notice that if we are not in a market equilibrium we cannot be maximizing *any* Baumol function; for we know that further exchange and redistribution could make *everyone* better off. In other words, maximizing a market preference function is a *necessary* condition for an optimum but not a *sufficient* one.

We notice, moreover, that the necessary condition is a condition of economic efficiency whilst the additional condition for sufficiency (namely a 'just' money income distribution) involves a value judgement. This suggests that we may continue to use the market preference function without inhibitions and in the usual way in discussions of such topics as 'optimum tariffs', or 'ideal' tax systems, provided that we bear in mind the basic assumption that we are concerned with questions of economic efficiency and not with questions of justice and injustice. If we identify an optimum tariff, this means that at such a tariff level all *could* be better off not that all *would* be better off without any income redistribution. With limited propositions of this kind economists must rest content.

4

COMPLEMENTARITY, SUBSTITUTABILITY, AND INDEPENDENCE

4.1. Introduction

IN this chapter we shall develop the argument that economic theorists have not yet, even from the purely qualitative angle, fully exploited all that can be learned from the theory of demand. Indeed it may well be that the use in comparatively recent times of more powerful mathematical tools of analysis, and the consequent discovery of the less intuitively obvious theorems of Chapter 1, has created exciting opportunities for advance which we have so far hardly begun to explore.

Consider, for example, the full range of sign conditions on substitution responses shown in 1.4 to be implicit in the straightforward utility maximizing assumption. In fact we know that

$$\sigma_{ii} < 0, \quad \begin{vmatrix} \sigma_{ii} & \sigma_{ij} \\ \sigma_{ji} & \sigma_{jj} \end{vmatrix} > 0, \quad \begin{vmatrix} \sigma_{ii} & \sigma_{ij} & \sigma_{ik} \\ \sigma_{ji} & \sigma_{jj} & \sigma_{jk} \\ \sigma_{ki} & \sigma_{kj} & \sigma_{kk} \end{vmatrix} < 0,$$

and so on. Of these conditions none but the first could ever have been established without the possibility of appeal to purely mathematical theorems which are far from simple to understand. And perhaps because of this none but the first has yet played any great part in economic theory.

Common sense on the other hand suggests that, in any really general theory, we ought to find all sign conditions to be of parallel importance. If all are equally necessary to full consumer equilibrium, then each of itself imposes some meaningful restriction on demand functions, and, accordingly, on admissible changes in the variables. To fail to make use of every condition is to lose information.

It is instructive to consider why these obvious truths have, so it seems, scarcely made themselves felt as yet. First we recall how much economic theory is based either on the assumption,

(a) that two goods only exist, or

(b) that all σ_{ji} $(j \neq i)$ are negligible.

In both cases only the first sign condition is relevant; for in case (a), σ_{ij} is given when σ_{ii} and σ_{jj} are known, by the fact that

$$\sum_i p_i \sigma_{ij} = 0.$$

And in case (b) all determinants become products of direct substitution effects, σ_{ii}, so that higher-order sign conditions follow directly from the first.

We shall not attempt to dispute the usefulness of assumptions (a) and (b) as a first approximation. If they were never justified very little economic theory would be left. But we shall argue most emphatically that there are times when neither is justified, and we shall try to show how failure, in such circumstances, to recognize more than the first of the sign conditions on σ_{ij} has led either to incorrect inference or loss of information.

For example, in the theory of international trade it has been the custom to classify all goods into two composite commodities, importables and exportables, so as to simplify certain complex problems. If we could be sure that all goods do in fact fall into one or other of these classes, and that the individual prices of all elements of the composite good, exportables, move always in proportion, and if the same were true for importables, such a procedure would be justified.† Unfortunately, in the very nature of the international trade problem, this cannot be the case; for in every country there exists a class of goods and/or services which cannot enter into trade at all, and whose prices do not change proportionately either with importables or exportables, except in unusual circumstances. To suppose that they do is to invite results which have no applicability to the real world.

In international-trade theory we have no alternative but to work in terms of at least three composite goods. Nor is it

† Cf. Chapter 1, p. 38, n. ‡.

possible with a three good model to simplify by assuming (b); for the condition

$$\sum_i p_i \sigma_{ij} = 0$$

ensures, with such a small number of goods, that the order of magnitude of σ_{ij} ($j \neq i$) is, in general, not very different from the order of magnitude of the direct substitution responses σ_{ii}.

Despite all this, economists working in the field of international trade have followed both practices. Two good models have been used in argument in support of policy, and appeal has been made to assumption (b) under the dignified title 'partial equilibrium analysis'. We do not claim that the results thus obtained are necessarily false, for they are usually qualitative only, and variables are not free to move in any other direction than up or down. On the other hand, we have to face the fact that, until more general models have been worked out, our traditional conclusions rest rather more heavily upon intuition than is desirable in an exact science. And common sense suggests that when more general models are worked out it will be found necessary to appeal to higher than first-order sign conditions on σ_{ij} before even qualitative conclusions can be reached.

As an alternative to assumptions (a) and (b) other writers have made use of ambiguously defined concepts such as 'the elasticity of demand for exports', as if the quantity of exports could be written in functional form, independently of the problem under review, in the same way as consumer demand. Of course, it is well understood that it cannot be so written, and that exports depend on exchange rates, demand functions, supply functions, and incomes, both of the home country and the rest of the world, in a very complicated fashion. Nevertheless it has proved, in some quarters, hard to resist the temptation to attach a sign, and sometimes even an approximate magnitude, to the elasticity of demand for exports, as if it were an ordinary demand response.

Again it is not the intention to be critical, although the present writer is far from convinced that there is much value in concepts such as the elasticity of demand for exports. The intention is rather to make one point, namely, that, in anything more than a two-good world, to set a sign on elasticity of demand for exports must necessarily involve appeal to higher than first-order sign conditions on σ_{ij}. Examples to illustrate all that has been said above will be given later in this chapter.

We now come to an even more important point. Besides putting a sign on σ_{ii}, economists frequently attempt to set rough limits on its magnitude, based on introspectively derived ideas about the nature of the ith commodity. We occasionally say, for example, that two classes of goods i and j are highly complementary, so that there are few possibilities of substitution between them. Thus σ_{ii} will tend to be small. This can often help to determine the expected direction of change of certain variables.

As with sign conditions, however, the argument seldom goes beyond the case of the single substitution effect σ_{ii}. On the other hand, it is clear, from what has already been said that, if more general models are to be developed, it will be equally necessary to make parallel judgements about the probable magnitude of higher order determinants of substitution effects. And it is easy to show that qualitative ideas like substitutability and complementarity may be appealed to in this connexion just as in the simple case. In the next sections we reconsider the notion of complementarity and its reciprocal, substitutability, not only for its own sake, but with the broader end in view. We then apply the theory developed to particular cases by way of illustration.

4.2. Complementarity

In ordinary language complementarity means the property of 'belonging to' or 'going with'. Presumably, therefore, the expression 'complementary in consumption' should be reserved to describe goods which tend to be required in fixed proportions in all circumstances of price and income. Most economists would in fact agree with such a definition, and indeed it is usually in this sense that the idea is used in verbal argument. Cups and saucers or knives and forks are often quoted as examples. At the same time a mathematical definition has come to be generally accepted which does not seem to accord fully with this verbal definition.† As a first step we attempt to explain why the mathematical definition was chosen and what the difficulties connected with it are.

For reasons which will later become clear we introduce temporarily at this point another slight change in notation. So far we have put

$$\sigma_{ij} = \Delta_{ij}/\Delta,$$

where Δ is the bordered Hessian determinant

$$\begin{vmatrix} 0 & u_i \\ u_j & u_{ji} \end{vmatrix}$$

of the utility function u, and Δ_{ij} is the co-factor of the element u_{ij}. λ, the marginal utility of money is, as before, taken to be unity in the region of equilibrium, so that it does not appear. It will be seen in due course that all measures proposed are independent of the choice of utility index so that there is no loss of generality in putting $\lambda = 1$, so long as we remember that it does not stay constant.

The change made in this section is simply to write

$$\sigma_{ij}/\Delta = \Delta_{ij}/\Delta \quad \text{or} \quad \sigma_{ij} = \Delta_{ij}.$$

This is desirable since it becomes important to consider cases where Δ approaches zero. At the same time we wish to emphasize the connexion between Δ_{ij} and the substitution response which has been written throughout earlier chapters as σ_{ij}. We shall revert to the old notation with due warning as soon as it is convenient.

The generally accepted criterion for complementarity between goods i and j is simply that σ_{ji}/Δ should be negative. The common-sense justification of this is as follows. Beginning from the straightforward consideration of the sign of $\partial x_j/\partial p_i$ we see that if this is negative (i.e. if it is of the same sign as $\partial x_i/\partial p_i$ which must be negative), then a fall in the quantity consumed of good i has induced also a fall in the quantity taken of good j.

† The mathematical definition is usually attributed to Professors J. R. Hicks and R. G. D. Allen, 'A Reconsideration of the Theory of Value', *Economica*, 1934. It seems also to have been proposed by Professor Eugen Slutsky, 'Sulla Teoria del Bilancio del Consumatore', *Giornale degli Economisti*, 1915.

This occurs despite the fact that j is now relatively cheaper. The presumption, therefore, is that there is something about goods i and j which makes one of no use without the other; they go together, that is, they are complementary. The proportions in which the two are consumed changes less than would be the case if $\partial x_j/\partial p_i$ were positive. A positive $\partial x_j/\partial p_i$, on the other hand, would imply that j can take the place of i in consumption and hence is substitutable for it.

A difficulty arises, however, which is immediately obvious when we separate $\partial x_j/\partial p_i$ into income and substitution effects. The sign of the income effect $-x_i\,(\partial x_j/\partial y)$ is always negative, so that $\partial x_j/\partial p_i$ could be negative even if σ_{ji}/Δ were positive. This means that although j can take the place of i in consumption there will appear to be complementarity because the positive substitution effect is outweighed by the negative income effect. For this reason it has been judged better to accept the sign of the substitution effect alone as the criterion for complementarity, that is, the sign of σ_{ji}/Δ. The commonly accepted definition of complementarity therefore is a refinement of the simple idea that, if the cross elasticity of demand between two goods is negative, then there must be complementarity. It is made more acceptable by eliminating the income effect which must be negative whether there is complementarity or not.

So far as it goes all this is intuitively reasonable. Unfortunately, however, further serious difficulties arise. Some of these are now listed. Proofs will emerge in the course of the following discussion.

(i) On the definition above it is impossible to have complementarity unless there are more than two classes of goods. This flatly contradicts our intuition, for we can easily imagine a primitive society in which only two classes of goods exist, say food and clothing, and where these two items tend to be taken in fixed proportions. Most economists would wish to describe this as complementarity.

(ii) It is easy to show, as a kind of generalization of objection (i), that in any case there may be a very high degree of complementarity between i and j even though σ_{ji}/Δ is not negative, provided there is also complementarity between i and j and all other goods so that σ_{ji}/Δ is close to zero.

(iii) σ_{ji}/Δ is not a measure of the *degree* of complementarity. It will be evident from what follows that it is easy to choose cases where σ_{ji}/Δ is large and negative but where there is very little complementarity, if any at all.

Objection (iii) gives a clue to the fundamental difficulty which has beset all suggestions so far made for a criterion of complementarity.† All have been framed as if substitutability and complementarity were mutually exclusive. As if, in fact, the existence of any small degree of complementarity meant that there could be no substitutability at all and vice versa. But consideration of the two-good case shows at once that any measure of complementarity must be a kind of reciprocal of the measure of substitutability. Complete complementarity, i.e. fixed proportions, means, simply, no possibility of substitution. If there is only a small degree of substitutability there is high, but not complete, complementarity and so on.

It may be thought that the Slutsky/Hicks/Allen criterion does give effect to this idea by fixing an arbitrary line

$$\sigma_{ji}/\Delta = 0$$

on the one side of which we define i and j as substitutes, and on the other as complements. This might be satisfactory if σ_{ji}/Δ were a continuous measure of complementarity but unfortunately, as we shall see, it is not.

Objection (i) above is, of course, well known, and has been pointed out even by writers who introduced the traditional criterion.‡ It is helpful, however, to show geometrically why in the two-good case σ_{ji}/Δ is always positive since the geometry provides a useful starting-point from which to develop new proposals.

We know to begin with that σ_{ii}/Δ must always be negative. $\sigma_{ji}/\Delta < 0$ therefore implies $\sigma_{ji}/\sigma_{ii} > 0$. Now σ_{ii}/Δ is, by defini-

† See Henry Schultz, *The Theory and Measurement of Demand*, pp. 607–54, for a summary of the various proposals.

‡ See, for example, R. G. D. Allen, *Mathematics for Economists*, p. 509.

tion, the small change in i due to unit change in the price of i, when income compensation is given so as to keep the consumer on the same indifference surface. And σ_{ji}/Δ is the change in j due to the same income compensated price change. σ_{ji}/σ_{ii} therefore is, quite generally for n goods, the slope of the projection on to the i,j-axis plane of the small movement of the equilibrium-point on the indifference surface, generated by the change in the price of i. If there are two goods only, i and j, then the indifference surface is simply a curve lying in the i,j-axis plane; and its projection on to the i,j-plane is itself. The slope of the projection of a small movement on the indifference curve is in fact the slope of the indifference curve. This can easily be checked by writing down σ_{ji}/σ_{ii} in full from equation 1.4 (xiv). In this way we see that

$$-\frac{\begin{vmatrix} 0 & u_j \\ u_i & u_{ij} \end{vmatrix}}{\begin{vmatrix} 0 & u_i \\ u_i & u_{ii} \end{vmatrix}} = -\frac{u_j}{u_i} = \text{slope of indifference curve.}$$

Since the slope of an indifference curve must be negative in sign it follows that σ_{ji}/Δ must be positive and that there can be no complementarity as traditionally defined. It is evident also that if there are only two goods i and j, and if these are required in absolutely fixed proportions, the pattern of indifference curves must degenerate into a set of points lying on a line through the origin,† the slope of which defines the fixed proportion in which i and j are always taken. In such a case σ_{ji}/Δ must be zero, for clearly no compensated price change can affect the quantities of i and j consumed if the indifference curve is a single point. But

$$\sigma_{ji} \equiv u_i u_j$$

which can never be zero in any economically significant case, u_i being marginal utility. σ_{ji}/Δ can approach zero, therefore, only as Δ approaches ∞.

† In other words a single Engel curve which is a straight line through the origin. This implies, of course, complete complementarity everywhere as distinct from complementarity in the region of a point only. Throughout this chapter complementarity means complementarity everywhere.

It should be noted in passing that the rate of change of slope (i.e. the curvature) of any indifference surface in a direction parallel to the i, j-axis plane may be written†

$$\frac{1}{u_j^2} \begin{vmatrix} 0 & u_i & u_j \\ u_i & u_{ii} & u_{ij} \\ u_j & u_{ji} & u_{jj} \end{vmatrix}. \qquad\qquad 4.2 \text{ (i)}$$

In the two-good case the determinant in 4.2 (i) is Δ. Obviously as the indifference curve tends to degenerate into a point,‡ the rate of change of its slope approaches ∞, i.e. $\Delta \to \infty$. Since σ_{ji} cannot be zero $\sigma_{ji}/\Delta \to 0$ only when $\Delta \to \infty$, which is our conclusion above.

Complete complementarity therefore implies, in the two-good case, that Δ is very large. We now proceed to generalize this idea. Consider the three-good case. Any plane parallel to the i, j-axis plane will cut any indifference surface in a curve. This curve will tend to degenerate into a point as its rate of curvature gets very high just as in the two-good case. As before, the rate of curvature is given by the expression 4.2 (i) above. By analogy with the two-good case we define complete complementarity as existing between i and j when every such curve degenerates into a point. In other words, when no compensated price change can affect the proportion in which i and j are taken. This time it is the *projection* of degenerate indifference surfaces on to the i, j-axis plane which becomes a straight line through the origin. The slope of this projection again indicates the fixed proportions in which i and j are taken. To put it another way, complete complementarity exists in the three-good case when every indifference surface takes the form of a curve in space, the projection of which on to the i, j-axis plane is a straight line through the origin. Any movement on such an indifference curve in space, whether generated by a compensated price change in i or a compensated price change in j, must have the same slope when projected on to the i, j-axis plane. That is, the condition

† This is simply $\dfrac{\partial(u_i/u_j)}{\partial x_j} u_i - \dfrac{\partial(u_i/u_j)}{\partial x_i} u_j.$

‡ The point may be thought of as the corner of a right angle.

of complete complementarity is

$$\frac{\sigma_{ji}}{\sigma_{ii}} = \frac{\sigma_{jj}}{\sigma_{ij}} = r, \qquad\qquad 4.2\ (ii)$$

where r is the fixed ratio in which i and j are consumed.

Consider the common sense of this. 4.2 (ii) means that the changes in the consumption of goods i and j due to a compensated price change in good i will be in the same proportion as the changes in their consumption due to a compensated price change in j. Clearly goods i and j must possess the property of 'going together' in a high degree if a change in the price of i leads the individual to change his consumption of i and j in exactly the same proportion as he does when the price of j changes. This is all the more obvious when we identify the ratio of the changes with r, which is the proportion in which the goods are consumed; for then 4.2 (ii) means simply that the proportion in which the two goods are taken is unchanged by either price change. If i and j were substitutes we should expect a rise in the price of i to induce consumers to take more of j and less of i and vice versa for a rise in the price of j. With complete complementarity consumption of both i and j falls, and falls in the same proportion whether the price rise is in i or in j.

If there is a high *degree* of complementarity but some substitutability σ_{ji}/σ_{ii} will tend to be less than σ_{jj}/σ_{ij}. A rise in the price of i relatively will induce a fall in the quantity of j taken because there is some complementarity; but because j can also, in some degree, be taken *instead* of i the fall in j will not be so great numerically as if complementarity were complete. Similarly σ_{jj}/σ_{ij} will tend to be larger. It should be noted that σ_{ji}/σ_{ii} can never be numerically greater than σ_{jj}/σ_{ij} since this would imply

$$\begin{vmatrix} \sigma_{ii} & \sigma_{ij} \\ \sigma_{ji} & \sigma_{jj} \end{vmatrix} < 0$$

which is impossible if the indifference surface is to be convex to the origin. To measure the degree of complementarity we must measure the extent to which the proportions σ_{ji}/σ_{ii} and σ_{jj}/σ_{ij} differ.

The diagram below (Fig. 8) represents the projection on to the i,j-axis plane of movements of the equilibrium point on an n-dimensional indifference surface, generated by compensated price changes in goods i and j. O is the projection of the point from which the experiment begins. If the compensated price

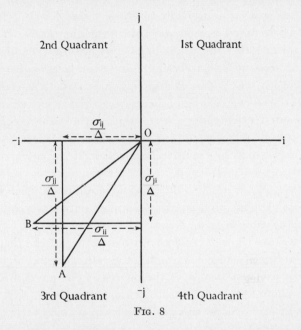

2nd Quadrant   1st Quadrant

3rd Quadrant   4th Quadrant

Fig. 8

change is in i the consumer moves to a point on his indifference surface of which B is the projection. If the price change is in j then the consumer moves to the point of which A is the projection. If A is in the third quadrant then B must also lie in the third quadrant since σ_{ii}/Δ and σ_{jj}/Δ are necessarily negative. A and B in the third quadrant correspond to $\sigma_{ij}/\Delta < 0$, i.e. to the traditional criterion for complementarity. If $\sigma_{ij}/\Delta = 0$ then A lies on the j-axis and B lies on the i-axis. If $\sigma_{ij}/\Delta > 0$ then A lies in the fourth quadrant and B lies in the second quadrant. The limiting cases are:

1. A and B coincident in the third quadrant. This, as we have seen, corresponds to complete complementarity.

2. A and B lying on a straight line through O in the second

and fourth quadrants. This, it will be shown, corresponds to complete substitutability. The convexity condition noted above

$$\left|\frac{\sigma_{ji}}{\sigma_{ii}}\right| \leqq \left|\frac{\sigma_{jj}}{\sigma_{ij}}\right|$$

implies that the angle BOA can never be greater than $180°$.

We are now in a position to show more clearly why σ_{ji}/Δ cannot be accepted as a *measure* of complementarity. If σ_{ji}/Δ is large and negative the angle BOA may still be very big if σ_{ii}/Δ and σ_{jj}/Δ are approximately equal and even larger, say ten times as big as σ_{ji}/Δ. The degree of complementarity between i and j will be quite small even though σ_{ji}/Δ is large and negative. In fact a compensated price change in i would induce the consumer to change purchases of j and i in the proportions $1:10$ whilst this proportion would be completely reversed if the price rise were in good j. Clearly there is no very strong property of 'going together'. Again σ_{ji}/Δ could be very small even when OB and OA are coincident, that is, when complementarity is complete, if at the same time both σ_{ii}/Δ and σ_{ij}/Δ were also small. The truth of these statements is evident on inspection of the diagram.

The argument above strongly suggests that the angle BOA is a most useful indicator of the degree of complementarity. It is a measure of the extent to which changes in the relative prices of i and j affect the proportions in which they are taken. It is most convenient to define complementarity as minus the cotangent of angle BOA since this will be $-\infty$ when complementarity is complete, zero when σ_{ij}/Δ is zero (i.e. when a compensated change in the price of j leaves the quantity of i consumed unchanged), and $+\infty$ when there is perfect substitutability.

Minus the cotangent of BOA may be expressed as follows.

$$-\cot(\widehat{iOA}-\widehat{iOB}) = -\frac{1+\tan\widehat{iOA}\tan\widehat{iOB}}{\tan\widehat{iOA}-\tan\widehat{iOB}}$$

$$= -\frac{1+\dfrac{\sigma_{jj}}{\sigma_{ij}}\dfrac{\sigma_{ji}}{\sigma_{ii}}}{\dfrac{\sigma_{jj}}{\sigma_{ij}}-\dfrac{\sigma_{ji}}{\sigma_{ii}}} = -\frac{\begin{vmatrix}\sigma_{ij} & \sigma_{jj}\\ -\sigma_{ji} & \sigma_{ii}\end{vmatrix}}{\begin{vmatrix}\sigma_{jj} & \sigma_{ji}\\ \sigma_{ij} & \sigma_{ii}\end{vmatrix}}. \qquad 4.2\ \text{(iii)}$$

This last expression 4.2 (iii) is a suitable measure of complementarity unless either:

(a) there are two goods only in which case the denominator is zero, or

(b) all substitution effects are zero, in which case there is complete complementarity between *all* goods whatever the value of 4.2 (iii).

These two exceptions merit some discussion. First of all we now recognize that in cases (a) and (b) the *measure* of complementarity does not break down because complementarity is not present. On the contrary, formula 4.2 (iii) was developed as a generalization of the two-good case where it does break down. Next we emphasize that cases (a) and (b) are really manifestations of the same difficulty. If there is high complementarity in the two-good case all substitution effects are small and indifference curves tend to degenerate into points. Similarly with n goods indifference surfaces may degenerate into points in space so that there are no possibilities of substitution anywhere in the system. The measure of complementarity breaks down not because the property of complementarity cannot be present but because complementarity is so complete and widespread that it cannot be revealed by the behaviour of the consumer. If it is not possible to compensate for a price change except by increasing the quantity of all goods in fixed proportions then net changes in consumption must tend to zero. Thus 4.2 (iii) becomes an indeterminate form.† Similarly if all goods are complementary to the same degree, then the measure 4.2 (iii) will be positive however great the tendency to take all goods in fixed proportions. The absolute values σ_{ij}/Δ will get smaller as the degree of overall complementarity increases.

In brief, 4.2 (iii) measures the degree of complementarity between any pair of goods i and j, whilst the size of the elements σ_{ij}/Δ gives a clue to the degree of complementarity between the pair i, j and all other goods generally. Whether individual

† It should be remembered that the σ_{ij}'s of 4.2 (iii) are really σ_{ij}/Δ which $\to 0$ as $\Delta \to \infty$.

elements are small or not, 4.2 (iii) always tells us whether i and j are more complementary than the pair, say, j and k. But if all pairs are complementary in the same degree or even if this is not so, 4.2 (iii) tells us nothing about the overall degree of substitutability in the system as a whole. This can be measured only by the average size of the elements σ_{ij}/Δ. Smallness of the elements is a necessary and sufficient condition for high complementarity between all goods. Either 4.2 (iii) large and negative, or the elements of 4.2 (iii) small, implies high complementarity between i and j. Small elements imply in addition high complementarity between j and k and i and k, etc.

Reconsidering the two-good case we now see that the second of the conditions above will be present when complementarity is high for, as we have already noted, $\sigma_{ij}/\Delta \to 0$ in the two-good case as substitutability becomes small. In practice, however, we are not likely to be bothered by low substitution effects, for the existence of one substitute anywhere in the system is sufficient to permit complementarity to reveal itself and to justify the measure 4.2 (iii). Clearly also in adopting 4.2 (iii) as a measure we have overcome all the difficulties of the traditional criterion mentioned above.

It is, of course, inelegant to choose a measure which breaks down in a world where all goods are complementary, but there are good reasons for doing this. It will be shown in the course of the discussion below that u_j^2/Δ, which, in the two-good case, ranges from zero to infinity as substitutability increases (see 4.2 (i) above) can be generalized quite simply. It could therefore be used instead of 4.2 (iii), particularly as it does not fail when all goods are complementary. On the other hand, there is no way in which the value of u_j^2/Δ can be measured, even in principle, other than by observation of the responses σ_{ij}/Δ, so that nothing can be gained by its use. Hence 4.2 (iii) has been chosen rather than u_j^2/Δ. The latter has been mentioned only as an aid to our understanding of the problem.

Consider now the properties of the full adjoint of the bordered Hessian determinant when complementarity is present. Inspection of 4.2 (iii) indicates that

$$\begin{vmatrix} \sigma_{ss} & \sigma_{st} \\ \sigma_{ts} & \sigma_{tt} \end{vmatrix} \to 0$$

is a necessary condition for high complementarity between goods s and t, provided none of the elements, σ_{ss}, σ_{st}, σ_{tt} are very large. In order to meet the possibility that some element might be very large, as in fact turns out to be the case for complementarity, we rewrite this condition as

$$\begin{vmatrix} \dfrac{\sigma_{ss}}{\Delta} & \dfrac{\sigma_{st}}{\Delta} \\[2mm] \dfrac{\sigma_{ts}}{\Delta} & \dfrac{\sigma_{tt}}{\Delta} \end{vmatrix} \to 0$$

and assume that the new elements σ_{st}/Δ, etc., are not large. This assumption is justified since substitution effects σ_{st}/Δ, etc., cannot approach infinity unless some other good, k, is a perfect substitute for either s or t. This would be exceptional. Similarly σ_{st}/Δ could not all be zero unless all other goods were completely complementary to both s and t. This again would be exceptional. We state now that it can be shown that the condition

$$\begin{vmatrix} \dfrac{\sigma_{ss}}{\Delta} & \dfrac{\sigma_{st}}{\Delta} \\[2mm] \dfrac{\sigma_{ts}}{\Delta} & \dfrac{\sigma_{tt}}{\Delta} \end{vmatrix} = 0$$

implies also that

$$\begin{vmatrix} \dfrac{\sigma_{ss}}{\Delta} & \dfrac{\sigma_{sk}}{\Delta} \\[2mm] \dfrac{\sigma_{ts}}{\Delta} & \dfrac{\sigma_{tk}}{\Delta} \end{vmatrix} = 0$$

where k is any other good. That is, it implies that rows s and t and columns s and t of the $n \times n$ determinant, made up of the elements of the unbordered adjoint divided by Δ, are proportional. Hence any minor of this determinant containing part of rows s and t or columns s and t is zero. Proof of this theorem is tedious and has accordingly been relegated to an appendix to this section.

We have noted above also that, if there is to be any curvature of the indifference surface in the general direction i, j, then the appropriate third-order principal minor of Δ,

$$\begin{vmatrix} 0 & u_i & u_j \\ u_i & u_{ii} & u_{ij} \\ u_j & u_{ji} & u_{jj} \end{vmatrix}$$

which we write as Δ_{iijj}, cannot be zero (see 4.2 (i) above). This is only another way of saying that we assume that there exists some pair of goods i and j which are not completely complementary when t and s are completely complementary. Moreover, by Jacobi's theorem on the minors of the adjugate, Δ_{iijj} must be equal to the complementary minor of the adjugate $(C_{iijj} \operatorname{adj} \Delta)$ divided by Δ^{n-3}. Dividing both sides by Δ we have

$$\frac{\Delta_{iijj}}{\Delta} \equiv \frac{(C_{iijj} \operatorname{adj} \Delta)}{\Delta^{n-2}}. \qquad 4.2 \text{ (iv)}$$

But by the theorem of the previous paragraph we know that the right-hand side term of 4.2 (iv) tends to zero as we tend to complete complementarity, for we may think of it as a determinant with the general element σ_{ij}/Δ containing two rows s and t proportionate. As Δ_{iijj} is not zero, it follows that the condition for high complementarity must be $\Delta \to \infty$ and all $\sigma_{ij} \to \infty$ including those involving s and t. All σ_{ij} must tend to infinity if substitution effects σ_{ij}/Δ are to have any value.

We now note that $\quad \dfrac{(C_{ss.tt} \operatorname{adj} \Delta)}{\Delta^{n-2}}$

is not small since it excludes the proportionate rows and columns. Hence $\Delta_{ss.tt}/\Delta$ is not small, again by Jacobi's theorem. But $\Delta \to \infty$ hence $\Delta_{ss.tt} \to \infty$. As previously claimed, therefore, we could accept $u_s^2/\Delta_{ss.tt}$ as a general measure of complementarity and note that it is a generalization of the two-good case, where $\Delta_{ss.tt}$ is the whole Hessian determinant. We now use the theorem of the appendix to this section to establish a relationship between the elasticities of demand for complementary goods.

It is reasonable to suppose that if complementarity manifests itself in substitution effects it will do so also in income effects.

That is, it does not follow necessarily, but we may assume, that as

$$\frac{\sigma_{ss}}{\sigma_{ts}} \to \frac{\sigma_{st}}{\sigma_{tt}}$$

then

$$\frac{\partial x_s / \partial y}{\partial x_t / \partial y} = \frac{\Delta_s}{\Delta_t} \to \frac{\sigma_{ss}}{\sigma_{ts}}.$$

Similarly we should expect the fixed proportion, σ_{ss}/σ_{ts}, in which the two goods are required, to be the same as the ratio of the quantities, x_s and x_t, actually consumed.

We now write down in full the elasticities of demand E_{ss} and E_{tt} for goods s and t

$$E_{ss} = \frac{\partial x_s}{\partial p_s} \frac{p_s}{x_s} = \left(\frac{p_s}{x_s} \frac{\sigma_{ss}}{\Delta} - \frac{p_s \Delta_s}{\Delta} \right)$$

$$E_{tt} = \left(\frac{p_t}{x_t} \frac{\sigma_{tt}}{\Delta} - \frac{p_t \Delta_t}{\Delta} \right).$$

Using the fact that

$$\frac{\sigma_{ss}}{\sigma_{st}} = \frac{x_s}{x_t} = \frac{\Delta_s}{\Delta_t} = \frac{\sigma_{st}}{\sigma_{tt}}$$

we obtain

$$\frac{E_{ss}}{E_{tt}} = \frac{p_s x_s}{p_t x_t}. \qquad 4.2 \text{ (v)}$$

That is, we have a theorem, by no means intuitively obvious, that two goods which are highly complementary will tend to have elasticities of demand proportional to the quantities of money spent on them.

Similarly, if we write down the cross elasticities E_{st} and E_{ts}, we find that these also are proportionate to total spending on goods t and s respectively. Indeed

$$E_{ss} = E_{ts} \quad \text{and} \quad E_{tt} = E_{st}.$$

Using now the appendix theorem

$$\frac{\sigma_{ss}}{\sigma_{st}} = \frac{\sigma_{sk}}{\sigma_{tk}}$$

we have, in addition, the general relation

$$E_{sk} = E_{tk}.$$

These last three relations are, in contrast to the first, trivially obvious since, if two goods are always taken in fixed proportions any change in any price must bring about the same proportionate change in the quantities consumed of these goods. Since they are derived from the appendix theorem, however, they may serve to set at rest any doubts the reader might have concerning earlier use of that theorem.

In passing it is worth noting also the implications of the result $E_{ss} = E_{ts}$ for theories of business behaviour. In developing theories of monopoly, oligopoly, or monopolistic competition we must be prepared to recognize that cross-elasticities of demand are often as important as the straightforward direct elasticities. How can we discuss, for example, the demand curve for motorcars, independently of the demand curve for petrol when a change in the price of petrol may have the same proportionate effect on the sales of cars as it will have on the sales of petrol itself and vice versa?

Turning now to the other end of the complementarity scale, it remains to show that, when the measure 4.2 (iii) takes the value $+\infty$, there is perfect substitutability between the two goods involved (say s and t). Perfect substitutability must mean that there is only one price ratio at which the consumer will take some of both goods. At all other price ratios the consumer will take all of one good and none of the other. In other words, the indifference surface must be coincident with the budget plane along any line parallel to the s, t-axis plane. The rate of change of slope of the indifference surface in the s, t direction must be zero. More generally, there will be perfect substitutability in the region of a point if the indifference surface is coincident with the budget plane over a finite distance.

Evidently the measure of substitutability 4.2 (iii) $\rightarrow +\infty$ once again as

$$\begin{vmatrix} \sigma_{ss} & \sigma_{st} \\ \sigma_{ts} & \sigma_{tt} \end{vmatrix} \rightarrow 0 \quad (\sigma_{rs} > 0).$$

By Jacobi's theorem

$$\begin{vmatrix} \sigma_{ss} & \sigma_{st} \\ \sigma_{ts} & \sigma_{tt} \end{vmatrix} = \Delta(C_{ss.tt}\Delta),$$

where $(C_{ss.tt}\Delta)$ is the appropriate complementary principal minor of the Hessian determinant, Δ. Now $(C_{ss.tt}\Delta)$ will normally not be zero and for the moment we assume this. The justification for such an assumption emerges when we come to consider the consequences. It follows that as 4.2 (iii) $\to \infty$, $\Delta \to 0$.

From this we see that the substitution effects σ_{ss}/Δ, σ_{st}/Δ, and σ_{tt}/Δ must be very large (that is, t and s must be very close substitutes), as long as σ_{tt}, σ_{st}, and σ_{ss} are not zero which is assumed (see below). Moreover, if the general substitution effect for other goods

$$\frac{\sigma_{ij}}{\Delta} \quad (i \neq s,\, i \neq t,\, j \neq s,\, j \neq t)$$

is to have a value which is not very large σ_{ij} must tend to zero.

Again, by Jacobi's theorem

$$(C_{ss.tt}\,\mathrm{adj}\,\Delta) \equiv \Delta^{n-3}\Delta_{ss.tt}$$

or

$$\frac{(C_{ss.tt}\,\mathrm{adj}\,\Delta)}{\Delta^{n-2}} \equiv \frac{\Delta_{ss.tt}}{\Delta}.$$

But the left-hand side of this last equation will normally have a value not zero or infinite since it may be thought of as a determinant whose elements are made up of the substitution effects σ_{ij}/Δ which have no special characteristics. As $\Delta \to 0$ therefore $\Delta_{ss.tt} \to 0$. Thus the indifference surface must be coincident with the budget plane in the s, t direction, since $\Delta_{ss.tt}/u_s^2$, the measure of its curvature in this direction, must be zero when $\Delta_{ss.tt}$ is zero. t and s therefore are perfect substitutes.

We may check these results by appeal to intuition. Perfect substitutability means that a pennyworth of s is indistinguishable from a pennyworth of t. That is, a pennyworth increase in consumption of s has the same effect on the marginal utility of t (or any other good i) as does a pennyworth increase in s. Hence

$$u_{ts} = u_{tt}\left(\frac{u_s}{u_t}\right)$$

and in general

$$u_{is} = u_{it}\left(\frac{u_s}{u_t}\right). \qquad 4.2\ (\text{vi})$$

This means that the tth and sth row and column of Δ must be proportionate. Any co-factor σ_{ij} containing both the tth and

sth rows or columns will be zero. That is, all co-factors except σ_{ss}, σ_{st}, and σ_{tt} will be zero. This confirms the conclusion noted above. Obviously the utility conditions 4.2 (vi) also imply

$$\Delta_{ss.tt} = 0.$$

APPENDIX TO SECTION 4.2

To show that

$$\begin{vmatrix} \dfrac{\sigma_{ii}}{\Delta} & \dfrac{\sigma_{ik}}{\Delta} \\[2ex] \dfrac{\sigma_{ji}}{\Delta} & \dfrac{\sigma_{jk}}{\Delta} \end{vmatrix} = 0$$

when
$$\begin{vmatrix} \dfrac{\sigma_{ii}}{\Delta} & \dfrac{\sigma_{ij}}{\Delta} \\[2ex] \dfrac{\sigma_{ji}}{\Delta} & \dfrac{\sigma_{jj}}{\Delta} \end{vmatrix} = 0 \quad \left(\dfrac{\sigma_{ij}}{\Delta} \neq 0 \right).$$

Extending the notation introduced in the text we write $\Delta_{ij.st}$ for the minor of the Hessian determinant of order two containing as its diagonal elements u_{ij} and u_{st}. $(C_{ij.st}\Delta)$ is its complement in Δ. $\mathrm{Adj}_{ij.st}$ is the second-order minor of adj Δ containing as its diagonal elements σ_{ij} and σ_{st}. $(C_{ij.st}\mathrm{adj}\,\Delta)$ is its complement. In this new notation we are required to prove that

$$\frac{\mathrm{adj}_{ii.jk}}{\Delta^2} = 0$$

when
$$\frac{\mathrm{adj}_{ii.jj}}{\Delta^2} = 0.$$

We begin by noting that $(C_{ii.jk}\,\Delta)$ is a co-factor of all co-factors of Δ which appear as elements of $\mathrm{adj}_{ii.jk}$. That is, it is a co-factor of σ_{ii}, σ_{ik}, σ_{ji}, and σ_{jk}. In particular it is a co-factor of σ_{ii}. Similarly $(C_{ii.jj}\,\Delta)$ and $(C_{ii.kk}\,\Delta)$ are co-factors of σ_{ii} and

$$\begin{vmatrix} (C_{ii.jj}\,\Delta) & (C_{ii.jk}\,\Delta) \\ (C_{ii.kj}\,\Delta) & (C_{ii.kk}\,\Delta) \end{vmatrix}$$

is a principal minor of adj σ_{ii}. Hence, by Jacobi's theorem,

$$\begin{vmatrix} (C_{ii.jj}\,\Delta) & (C_{ii.jk}\,\Delta) \\ (C_{ii.kj}\,\Delta) & (C_{ii.kk}\,\Delta) \end{vmatrix} = D\sigma_{ii},$$

where D is the appropriate complementary principal minor of σ_{ii}. Now if Δ is the discriminant of a negative definite form, $D\sigma_{ii}$ must be $\geqq 0$

since if σ_{ii} is of order m, D must be of order $m-2$. Dividing both sides by Δ^2, which is necessarily positive, gives

$$\begin{vmatrix} \dfrac{(C_{ii.jj}\Delta)}{\Delta} & \dfrac{(C_{ii.jk}\Delta)}{\Delta} \\[2ex] \dfrac{(C_{ii.kj}\Delta)}{\Delta} & \dfrac{(C_{ii.kk}\Delta)}{\Delta} \end{vmatrix} \geqq 0.$$

From this it follows that if

$$\frac{\text{adj}_{ii.jj}}{\Delta^2} \equiv \frac{(C_{ii.jj}\Delta)}{\Delta} = 0$$

then

$$\frac{(C_{ii.jk}\Delta)}{\Delta} = 0.$$

But

$$\frac{(C_{ii.jk}\Delta)}{\Delta} \equiv \frac{(\text{adj}_{ii.jk})}{\Delta^2}.$$

Therefore

$$\frac{\text{adj}_{ii.jk}}{\Delta^2} = 0$$

when

$$\frac{\text{adj}_{ii.jj}}{\Delta^2} = 0.$$

4.3. Applications in international trade theory

The practical value of the somewhat heterogeneous collection of results of section 4.2 is best demonstrated by reference to particular problems. We choose as the most convenient vehicle for such a demonstration, the theory of international trade, where, as previously explained, it is usual to aggregate all commodities into three groups, importables, exportables, and home goods. Home goods are those which by their nature are excluded from trade. We shall call these three classes, i goods, e goods, and h goods respectively.

We refer first to a well-known argument by which it is shown that currency depreciation will worsen rather than improve the balance of payments of a devaluing country if the elasticities of demand for imports at home and in the rest of the world sum (numerically) to less than unity. Many writers† have, of course, pointed out in this connexion that the elasticity of demand for imports, which may be, and usually is, a function of elasticities of supply and of the balance of payments itself, is not the same

† Including the author, cf. I. F. Pearce, 'The Problem of the Balance of Payments', *International Economic Review*, January 1961.

thing as the elasticity of demand for importables, which depends on consumer preferences alone. Some importables may be home produced. Even so, intuitively based claims that the price response for importables is likely to be low, have been used in practice to defend policies alternative to devaluation. It is worth while, therefore, to examine the low elasticity argument in this context.

Consider as an example the suggestion that, 'if official restrictions have already reduced imports to bare necessities, which cannot be produced locally, it would be optimistic to expect that devaluation would effect much further reduction'.† Now it is impossible to take exception to this remark if by 'official restrictions' we mean, as its author does in part, 'quotas, exchange control, price control and consumer rationing'; for in this case, by definition, price changes are not permitted to affect the quantities taken. But the whole passage seems to imply something more than this. The inclusion of 'tariffs' among the 'restrictions' and the use of the expression 'bare necessities' suggests that even if the price mechanism were allowed to operate there is something in the fact that trade has been reduced to a minimum which implies that elasticities will be low.

Evidently there are two issues here. It is perfectly true that, if trade is balanced only by means of import quotas, in both countries, then devaluation would mean that quotas would have to be reduced or a trade deficit would appear. The earnings of foreign currency would fall. But this says nothing about whether devaluation would or would not 'shorten the queue' for imports. That is, it says nothing about whether or not devaluation represents a step towards the freeing of controls. Paradoxically a worsening of the trade balance could represent a step towards the ultimate removal of quota arrangements. Whether this is the case or not depends simply on what the elasticity of demand for imports would be if there were no rationing. That is, on how far any rise in import prices can serve to check demand.

The passage which forms the subject of present comment

† Professor B. Tew, *International Monetary Co-operation 1945–52*, p. 51.

could therefore be taken to be a claim that the crucial import elasticity is likely to be low. We consider in the following paragraphs how the 'bare necessity' argument would have to be expressed in the light of the work of sections 1.4 and 4.2. At this point also we revert to our old notation, writing σ_{ii} for the σ_{ii}/Δ of section 4.2.

First we recall that elasticity of demand cannot be less numerically than the marginal propensity to consume the good in question for, from 1.4 (xi),

$$\frac{p_i}{x_i}\frac{\partial x_i}{\partial p_i} = -p_i\frac{\partial x_i}{\partial y} + \sigma_{ii}\frac{p_i}{x_i}$$

both terms on the right-hand side being negative in sign. Only when σ_{ii} tends to zero can elasticity tend to the marginal propensity to consume importables.

We now proceed to show that, in a three-commodity world such as international trade theorists postulate, σ_{ii} approaching zero usually implies both σ_{ee} and σ_{hh} approaching zero also. Consider the three equations like 1.4 (x), namely

$$\sum_{\substack{j \\ (j=i,e,h)}} p_i\sigma_{ij} = 0 \quad (i = i, e, h).$$

The problem is simplified if we choose units so that all p_i are unity. Adopting this convention we deduce from the three equations above that

$$\tfrac{1}{2}\sigma_{ii} - \sigma_{eh} = \tfrac{1}{2}(\sigma_{ee} + \sigma_{hh}).$$

And we know from 1.4 (xix) that

$$\begin{vmatrix} \sigma_{ee} & \sigma_{eh} \\ \sigma_{he} & \sigma_{hh} \end{vmatrix} \geqq 0$$

or $\quad\quad \operatorname{mod}\sigma_{eh} \leqq \operatorname{mod}\sqrt{(\sigma_{ee}\sigma_{hh})}.$

And, since the modulus of the arithmetic mean of two numbers is always greater than, or equal to, the geometric mean, we have

$$\operatorname{mod}\tfrac{1}{2}(\sigma_{ee} + \sigma_{hh}) = \operatorname{mod}(\tfrac{1}{2}\sigma_{ii} - \sigma_{eh})$$
$$\geqq \operatorname{mod}\sqrt{(\sigma_{ee}\sigma_{hh})} \geqq \operatorname{mod}\sigma_{eh}$$

or, as σ_{ii} tends to zero,

$$\operatorname{mod}\sigma_{eh} \to \operatorname{mod}\sqrt{(\sigma_{ee}\sigma_{hh})}$$

and accordingly $\qquad \begin{vmatrix} \sigma_{ee} & \sigma_{eh} \\ \sigma_{he} & \sigma_{hh} \end{vmatrix} \to 0.$

Again, by the conditions

$$\begin{vmatrix} \sigma_{ii} & \sigma_{ih} \\ \sigma_{hi} & \sigma_{hh} \end{vmatrix} \geqq 0$$

and $\qquad \begin{vmatrix} \sigma_{ii} & \sigma_{ie} \\ \sigma_{ei} & \sigma_{ee} \end{vmatrix} \geqq 0$

we have $\sigma_{ih} \to 0$ and $\sigma_{ie} \to 0$ when $\sigma_{ii} \to 0$. It follows that when $\sigma_{ii} \to 0$ all principal minors of order two of the determinant

$$| \sigma_{ij} | \qquad (i = i, e, h \text{ and } j = i, e, h)$$

approach zero. But we have seen in section 4.2 that this is a necessary condition for complete complementarity between every possible pair of goods, i and e, e and h, and h and i, in which case every substitution effect is small. The necessary condition for complementarity is not quite sufficient, however.

If the measure of complementarity 4.2 (iii) has a positive numerator with a zero denominator it becomes large and negative so that we can be sure of complete complementarity. But we have already proved that σ_{ih} and σ_{ie} approach zero as σ_{ii} approaches zero. From 1.4 (x) we know also that

$$\sigma_{ei} + \sigma_{ee} + \sigma_{eh} = 0$$

so that, when σ_{ii}, and hence σ_{ei}, approaches zero, σ_{ee} approaches $-\sigma_{eh}$. Similarly σ_{hh} approaches $-\sigma_{eh}$. It follows that the numerator $\qquad \begin{vmatrix} \sigma_{he} & \sigma_{ee} \\ -\sigma_{eh} & \sigma_{hh} \end{vmatrix}$

of the complementarity measure 4.2 (iii) is negative rather than positive when σ_{ii} approaches zero, as long as the elements σ_{eh}, σ_{ee}, and σ_{hh} are not small. We appear to have perfect substitutability between e and h. An exception which merits some discussion is clearly possible.

Geometrically it is possible that a zero σ_{ii} requires only that the indifference surface should degenerate into a single curve parallel to the e, h-axis plane rather than a point in space. This degenerate surface may show a low rate of curvature implying that e and h are highly substitutable, or a high rate of curvature implying that they are not. But whatever the rate of curvature it must always lie in a plane parallel to the e, h-axis plane, so that no compensated price change whatever, whether in i, e, or h, can change consumption of i.

It is important to note that this is not a case where i and e are complementary and where i and h are complementary, but where the pair i, e is a good substitute for the pair i, h. This would certainly require that the indifference surface should degenerate into a curve in space; but such a curve would not lie in a plane parallel to the e, h-axis plane. If it did the proportions in which i and h and i and e are chosen would vary with relative prices, contradicting the idea of complementarity. It is clear that even when we have complete complementarity between i and e and i and h, σ_{ii} is not zero if there is any substitutability at all in the system.

In fact the exception we have before us is a case where there is no true complementarity anywhere, but where, despite this, no compensated rise in any of the prices i, e, or h can ever induce the consumer to take more of i. This must imply that a rise in total expenditure would not lead to any greater consumption of imports either; nor presumably would a fall in total expenditure lead to a reduction. Our exception seems to point to a contradiction.

If we think of x_i as an absolute minimum requirement, as Professor Tew suggests, it is plausible to suppose that neither a fall in expenditure nor a rise in relative price will reduce consumption. It is not plausible, however, to suppose that neither a rise in expenditure nor a fall in relative price will increase consumption as would follow from zero income and substitution effects. Only a discontinuity in the Engel curve can satisfy all requirements.

On the other hand, if we think of x_i as completely satiating wants, then it is plausible to assume that no fall in relative price or increase in expenditure can raise consumption. This also means zero elasticity of demand. But again intuition is not satisfied without a discontinuity in the Engel curve when we ask what would be the result of a rise in relative price or a fall in total expenditure. Moreover, we have already noted in section 1.4 certain other logical difficulties connected with the idea of want satiation.

We reflect also that even if a discontinuity exists and i is a minimum requirement we have by our very argument developed a strong case for a high marginal propensity to consume i in an upward direction. This means that for values of x_i only very slightly above the point of discontinuity elasticity will be at least as large as the high marginal propensity to consume i.

In short, the analysis of 4.2 has helped us to discover that a low elasticity of demand for imports (low enough that is to sustain the anti-devaluation argument) of necessity implies very high complementarity between *all three* goods i, e, and h. Alternatively it implies a discontinuity in Engel curves with attendant logical difficulties.

Evidently Professor Tew's 'bare necessities' can be interpreted as either of these cases. Two saucers is a minimum requirement if we already possess two cups. Or, if Bogus Island produces only fish which it exports to a country whose inhabitants detest fish but are bound by religious rules to eat it on Fridays, then the elasticity of demand for its exports may be very low. The quantity x_i imported by the foreign country represents simultaneously a bare minimum and full want satiation. Such situations are possible but when all of the logical implications of low elasticities are laid bare they seem much less likely and much more easily recognizable in practice than is sometimes thought.

We do not claim to have reached any positive conclusion from the more formal analysis. We do claim, however, that an understanding of the work of 4.2 cannot fail to improve our chances of making truly informed judgements in particular cases. An argument, which is equivalent to a contention that the current equilibrium lies in the region of a discontinuity, is one calling for close examination, whilst the test for complementarity is simple and revealing. If two goods i and e are complementary then an increase in i goods, e constant, is worth almost nothing in terms of utility to the consumer. If i is 'cups' and e is 'saucers', for high complementarity, two cups must be of considerably less value (in use) than one cup and one saucer. Not many cases of suspected complementarity seem to survive this test particularly when we are thinking of three classes of goods which together form the whole of total consumption, and when the complementarity must be evident between every pair which can be selected from the three.

The above account of the consequences of assuming one elasticity of demand to be small has been given for what it is worth, and because this type of judgement has been used in defence of actual policy decisions. To the present writer, however, it seems clear that the real value of the analysis of section 4.2 lies much more in its power to enable us to say something constructive about probable magnitudes of *determinants* of substitution effects rather than substitution effects alone. We shall now give an example to illustrate this point, again taken from the theory of international trade.

Attention has already been drawn to the fact that the elasticity of demand for imports is not the same thing as the elasticity of demand for importables. The former is a total elasticity, that is, it is the total response to some primary price change *plus* the response to any secondary income or price changes in other goods necessary to re-establish general equilibrium. In the nature of the case no theory can exist to tell us anything about either the sign or the magnitude of a total elasticity, independently of the context in which it occurs. Clearly no problem can be said to be solved if the answer is expressed only in total elasticities.

The elasticity of demand for importables, on the other hand, is the ordinary partial demand response to a change in price, other prices and income constant. All of the sign and magnitude restrictions of section 1.4 immediately apply to it. In order to check the validity of conclusions drawn from solutions to problems set out in terms of total elasticities only, it is evidently necessary to express the total elasticities themselves as functions of the ordinary partial elasticities which go to make them up.

In many cases economists have attempted to do this intuitively. Consequent disagreements suggest that there is really no substitute for explicit mathematical formulation.

A notable beginning has been made by Professor J. E. Meade† and we now refer to one of his results. As soon, of course, as we come to define a total elasticity we face the need to specify precisely the number and nature of variables in the model in which it occurs. Professor Meade, working with a two good model which supposes that all goods are classifiable into importables and exportables, obtains a formula for the effect on the balance of payments of currency depreciation which, in the notation of this book, can be written

$$-[(\sigma_{ii}+\sigma'_{ii})/(1-C'_i-C_i)]+1, \qquad 4.3 \text{ (i)}$$

where the prime denotes 'belonging to the foreign country' and $C_i = p_i(\partial x_i/\partial y)$. For simplicity of exposition prices are taken to be unity in the region of equilibrium.‡ We continue to use i for importables, e for exportables, and h for home goods as before. It should be noted also that Professor Meade assumes no home production of importables in either country and full employment, which, in a two-good world, is equivalent to zero elasticities of supply.

The reader is now invited to compare the formula 4.3 (i) with an analogous result, 4.3 (ii), obtained by the present writer for a three-good world with importables, exportables, and non-traded goods:

$$-[(\psi_{ih}+\psi'_{ih})/(1-\phi_{ih}-\phi'_{ih})]+1. \qquad 4.3 \text{ (ii)}$$

Some importables are produced at home so that elasticities and

† *The Theory of International Economic Policy.*

‡ Cf. *The Balance of Payments—Mathematical Supplement*, table iv (*b*), p. 50. The formula 4.3 (i) can also be written

$$-x_i(E_{ii}+E'_{ii}+1)/(1-C'_i-C_i),$$

where x_i is the quantity of imports and E is the ordinary partial elasticity. This may be compared with the traditional sum of the elasticities formula referred to at the beginning of this section, namely

$$-x_i(\epsilon_{ii}+\epsilon'_{ii}+1),$$

where the ϵ's are total elasticities. Even in this very simple case it is far from easy to see intuitively why the $(1-C'_i-C_i)$ appears when we switch from total to partial elasticities. Do we really know anything about the sign of ϵ_{ii}?

cross elasticities of supply are also involved.[†] We shall purposely be mysterious about the meaning of ψ_{ih} and ϕ_{ih} until further formulae have been quoted.

In the simple two-good world of Professor Meade it is easy to show that the percentage change in the real terms of trade, due to the imposition of a 1 per cent tariff on imports, is given by the formula 4.3 (iii) below,[‡]

$$\frac{\sigma'_{ii}/x'_i}{1-C'_i-C_i+\sigma'_{ii}/x'_i+\sigma_{ii}/x_i}. \qquad \text{4.3 (iii)}$$

It is rather more difficult, but still possible, to show that in the three-good world with non-zero elasticities of supply the corresponding result is[§] 4.3 (iv)

$$\frac{\psi'_{ih}/x'_i}{1-\phi'_{ih}-\phi_{ih}+\psi'_{ih}/x'_i+\psi_{ih}/x_i}. \qquad \text{4.3 (iv)}$$

Again it is well known that, in a certain limited sense, it is possible to identify an optimum tariff. In Professor Meade's world the optimum tariff rate is given by the formula 4.3 (v)[||]

$$\sigma'_{ii}/x'_i - C'_i = -\left(1+\frac{1}{t}\right), \qquad \text{4.3 (v)}$$

where t is the tariff rate and as before foreign prices are taken to be unity.

This result generalizes to[††]

$$\psi'_{ih}/x'_i - \phi'_{ih} = -\left(1+\frac{1}{t}\right).$$

[†] Cf. 'The Problem of the Balance of Payments', *International Economic Review*, Jan. 1961, formula (15).
[‡] Cf. 'Optimum Tariffs Reconsidered', I. A. McDougall—forthcoming.
[§] Cf. 'Towards a More General Theory of Tariffs', S. F. Harris, I. A. McDougall, and I. F. Pearce—forthcoming.
[||] For a detailed discussion of the meaning of various formulae corresponding to 4.3 (v) but expressed in terms of total elasticities, cf. H. G. Johnson, *International Trade and Economic Growth*, pp. 56–61. 4.3 (v) can easily be seen to be precisely the same as equation (2) (p. 58) in Johnson, if we use his formula (4) (p. 58) to convert the elasticity of the offer curve into its equivalent partial elasticity. It is worth noting, however, that equation (4) in Johnson holds only in a two-good world with zero supply elasticities. With three goods the relation can be shown to involve ψ_{ih} and ϕ_{ih}.
[††] Cf. 'Towards a More General Theory of Tariffs', Harris, McDougall, and Pearce—forthcoming.

It must by now be clear that the parameters ψ_{ih} and ϕ_{ih} are valuable generalizations of the concept of substitution and income effects, and it is time to define them and discuss their properties. We have already hinted in the opening section of this chapter that the determinant of substitution effects is likely to be important in economic theory and this will prove to be a case in point. The value of section 4.2 will become apparent in the following discussion.

Before introducing precise definitions of ψ_{ih} and ϕ_{ih} general comments on the problem of aggregation may help to provide an intuitive understanding of the principles involved. In economics it is often useful to talk of a composite commodity, say, 'meat', knowing perhaps that it is made up of two distinct elements, mutton and beef. In the circumstances we may wish to form an impression of the magnitude of the elasticity of demand for meat as a whole, based upon previously measured, or intuitively guessed, elasticities of demand for the separate items mutton and beef.

If demand elasticities for mutton and beef were known to be large it might, at first sight, be tempting to argue that the elasticity of demand for meat would also be large, being some kind of weighted average of the two elements. Against this many economists would feel, on intuitive grounds, that the elasticity of demand for meat is not likely to be as high as that for either of its elements.

The explanation of the paradox is simple. Some part of the high elasticity of demand for mutton stems from the fact that it is a good substitute for beef and vice versa. This implies that the cross elasticity of demand for beef with respect to a change in the price of mutton is also high. And when we think of a rise in the price of meat as a whole, we usually think of a rise in the price of both mutton and beef. Thus any substitution out of mutton into beef, due to a rise in the price of mutton, is offset by a reverse substitution from beef into mutton.

And even if both prices rise other than proportionately, so that a relative price change between mutton and beef occurs, the high elasticities of the elements may merely bring about a change in the composition of meat consumption rather than a marked change in quantity.

All this is just one more reason for suspecting that, in a more than two-good world, determinants of the form

$$\begin{vmatrix} \sigma_{ii} & \sigma_{ij} \\ \sigma_{ji} & \sigma_{jj} \end{vmatrix}$$

will play an important part in measuring substitution possibilities, for high cross-substitution elements σ_{ij} can quite ordinarily have the effect of reducing the value of the determinant to something less than a weighted average of the direct elements σ_{ii} and σ_{jj}.

In the various international trade problems under review the crucial substitution possibilities appear to be those between importables and non-traded goods, thought of together as a composite commodity, and exportables. Some part of all other substitution possibilities has to be eliminated according to a complicated pattern involving the degree of complementarity between importables and home goods. The parameter ψ_{ih} achieves this result and therefore appears quite naturally in the formulae quoted. ψ_{ih} can in fact be shown to be

$$\psi_{ih} = \frac{\begin{vmatrix} (\sigma_{ii}-s_{ii}) & (\sigma_{ih}-s_{ih}) \\ (\sigma_{hi}-s_{hi}) & (\sigma_{hh}-s_{hh}) \end{vmatrix}}{(\sigma_{hh}-s_{hh})}, \qquad \text{4.3 (vi)}$$

where the s's measure elasticities and cross elasticities of supply.

The first thing we notice about ψ_{ih} is that the theory of demand enables us to determine unambiguously its sign. Although we shall not attempt a proof here, it can be shown, by methods analogous to those of section 1.4, that as long as the production transformation surface defining optimum production possibilities with a fixed factor endowment is concave to the origin,† then sign conditions can be imposed on s_{ih} corresponding to those on σ_{ih} (cf. 1.4 (xix)). In fact we have

$$s_{ii} > 0 \quad \text{or} \quad -s_{ii} < 0$$

† As we usually assume it to be—cf. P. A. Samuelson, *The Foundations of Economic Analysis*, p. 234.

and $\qquad \begin{vmatrix} s_{ii} & s_{ih} \\ s_{hi} & s_{hh} \end{vmatrix} > 0 \quad \text{or} \quad \begin{vmatrix} -s_{ii} & -s_{ih} \\ -s_{hi} & -s_{hh} \end{vmatrix} > 0.$ 4.3 (vii)

Clearly the determinant $| -s_{ih} |$ is the discriminant of a negative semi-definite quadratic form. And since the sum of two negative semi-definite quadratic forms is itself negative semi-definite it follows at once that the determinant

$$| \sigma_{ih} - s_{ih} |$$

is again the discriminant of a negative semi-definite form. The numerator of 4.3 (vi) therefore is positive. And by the conditions 1.4 (xix) and 4.3 (vii) both σ_{hh} and $-s_{hh}$ are negative so that ψ_{ih} is necessarily negative.

But this is not all. We can infer also something about the magnitude of 4.3 (vi) from the work of 4.2. Clearly the numerator of ψ_{ih} is formed by summing the separate demand and supply matrices, and the determinant of the demand matrix is the denominator of the measure of complementarity, 4.2 (iii), between goods i and h. It is worth while to consider how the value of the demand determinant will change as i and h pass from complete complementarity to complete substitutability.

We know from the work of 4.2 that

$$\begin{vmatrix} \sigma_{ii} & \sigma_{ih} \\ \sigma_{hi} & \sigma_{hh} \end{vmatrix} \to 0$$

as i and h tend to complete complementarity. This accords with common sense for, in the case where supply responses s_{ih} are zero, the consumption of home goods cannot change and therefore, i and h being required in fixed proportions, the consumption of i cannot change either whatever price changes occur. It is impossible to substitute exportables for either home goods or importables. On the other hand, it should be noted that, if home goods and importables are not produced under conditions of complete joint production (the supply analogue to complete complementarity) then high σ_{ii} and σ_{hh} continue to play a part in raising the value of the denominator of 4.3 (vi) even though complementarity is complete. This is because, as shown above, a high σ_{ii} can exist with complete complementarity if the joint i, h good can be freely substituted for exportables. This substitutability can be exploited as long as supply responses are not zero.

Turning now to the other end of the scale we have seen from section 4.2 that, for perfect substitutability, the demand determinant is again zero. This is something of an illusion, however, for, again from section 4.2, we learn that the closer we come to perfect substitutability the closer the elements σ_{ii}, etc., tend to infinity. The limit of the whole expression 4.3 (vi) (with zero supply effects) as we approach perfect substitutability seems not to be zero but some figure depending upon the substitutability of e goods with h and i goods together. It is easy to see that this is so from the fact that, whenever we assume a two-good world with zero supply responses, 4.3 (vi) is replaced by σ_{ii} in the various formulae 4.3 ((i)–(v)). And it is clear that if two goods are perfect substitutes they are to all intents and purposes the same good so that our three-good world becomes in fact a two-good world.

In short, the parameter ψ_{ih} behaves very much like a direct demand response σ_{ii}. It is negative in sign. It is zero when complementarity *and* joint production are complete, either between i and h goods or between all three together. It increases in size as substitutability in production and consumption between e goods and the rest of the system increases, reaching a limit dependent mainly on the degree of that substitutability. The supply conditions are exactly analogous to consumption, joint supply being equivalent to complementarity, and infinitely elastic supply to perfect substitutability.

For the sake of completeness we now define the other new parameter ϕ_{ih}, although the reader will already have guessed that it must be a weighted sum of the marginal propensities to consume imports, C_i, and home goods, C_h. It is in fact

$$\phi_{ih} = \left(C_i - \frac{\sigma_{ih} - s_{ih}}{\sigma_{hh} - s_{hh}} C_h \right).$$

Again section 4.2 tells us that, in the normal case where there

is no complementarity or joint supply in the system, the coefficient of C_h must be negative and less than unity, for we
recall that

$$\sum_j p_j \sigma_{ij} = 0$$

and both σ_{ih} and σ_{eh} are positive where there is no complementarity. A similar restriction applies also to supply responses.
It is clear therefore that the sign and order of size of ϕ_{ih} is the
same as for any marginal propensity to consume.

This discussion is far from complete. There are clearly gaps
in our knowledge and we shall need, in due course, to know
something of the order of magnitude of higher order determinants
than three. We leave the subject at this point, however, in the
hope that the reader has at least been led to the conviction that
the beginning has been worth while. In case he has not we loose
one parting shot. From formula 4.3 (iv) we see, once we know
the sign of ψ_{ih} and the fact that the order of magnitude of ϕ_{ih}
is the same as that of a marginal propensity to consume some
good, that it is unlikely to point of impossibility that the imposition of a tariff could do other than improve the real terms
of trade.

On the other hand, the latest (and so far uncontradicted)
opinion known to the present writer on this subject is that of
J. de V. Graaf† who concludes that nothing can be said. The
reason for this difference of view is that given at the beginning
of this chapter. Graaf loses information because he is unable to
make use of sign conditions on higher than first-order determinants of substitution effects.

4.4. Independence

In Chapter 5 we shall be concerned with a phenomenon to
which it is proposed to give the name 'neutral want association'.
This term has already been mentioned in earlier sections and
it has been claimed that the property of neutral want association
can be thought of as a means of identifying groups of commodities bounded by a marked gap in the chain of substitutes.

---

† 'On Optimum Tariff Structures', *Review of Economic Studies*, 1949–50, p. 51

Another way of thinking of a group, which might appeal to readers who have followed the work of 4.2, would be to imagine all those goods which have the same *degree* of complementarity or substitutability one with another, as included in it.

This last way of looking at the matter marks the point from which the present writer originally began. It has seemed worth while, therefore, to set down in what remains of this chapter the substance of some paragraphs written at a time when the whole problem was less clearly understood. In this way we are led naturally from ideas of complementarity and substitutability to independence, and thence to neutral want association.

The identification of neutral want association with the boundary of a group presents us also with an opportunity to distinguish at an early stage between independent utility, which is a familiar concept,† and neutral want association. This is a point upon which there could be some misunderstanding in this section. We make the distinction by stating, as yet without proof, that in the unlikely event of *all* commodities forming a single group, as we shall define it, then independence and neutral want association impose precisely the same restrictions on consumer behaviour. If there is more than one group, however, this ceases to be true. We now proceed with the discussion.

Appeal to intuition leaves the impression that pairs of goods in consumption fall into three classes. There are pairs such as knives and forks where the element of complementarity is clearly more important than the element of substitutability; and pairs such as two kinds of breakfast foods where the reverse is true. There is also a large class of goods where neither one property nor the other seems to predominate. Clothing does not seem to be specially substitutable with food nor does it seem particularly complementary.‡ It is interesting to note that the broader the

† Independent utility means simply that the utility function $u(x_1,..., x_n)$ can be written in the form

$$u = u_1(x_1) + u_2(x_2) + ... + u_n(x_n)$$

so that the marginal utility of any good is unaffected by changes in the quantity of any other. Independent utility is sometimes called additive utility.

‡ On the other hand, we do recognize that, since complementarity is merely the inverse of substitutability, it is sometimes proper to say that goods are

classifications of goods which we choose the less clearly can we identify intuitively either complementarity or substitutability.†
If we group consumption goods crudely under four headings, say, food, clothing, housing, and entertainment, it seems possible that some broad assumption might be made which would impose a suitable limitation on the form of the utility function when expressed simply in terms of the four goods. This in turn might imply a relationship between the elasticities of demand for each group the existence of which could considerably simplify the problem of measurement.

First consider what we might mean intuitively by independence in consumption. It is tempting at first sight to define independence between goods i and j as existing when $\sigma_{ij} = 0$, that is, when the two goods are on the borderline between substitutability and complementarity. When $\sigma_{ij} = 0$ the measure of complementarity/substitutability (4.2 (iii) above) is, of course, also zero. By definition σ_{ij} zero means that a compensated price change in j will have no effect on the consumption of i and vice versa.

This accords fairly well with one view of independence. Unfortunately, however, from the point of view of mathematical elegance, this definition does not in fact give full expression to our intuitive ideas. Serious difficulties arise.

In the first place we note that σ_{ij} may be zero for two reasons. It may be that a compensated price change in good j has no effect either direct or indirect on the consumption of i. On the other hand, such a price change may have a direct effect and any number of indirect effects which cancel each other out. Clearly a compensated rise in the price of j could leave the ratio of marginal utilities of i and w unchanged with the same consumption of i, not because i and w are unrelated to j, but because the direct relation between j and i is offset by an indirect relation

complementary simply because they are not obvious substitutes. The distinction should be made between a relationship in use which can be recognized intuitively and the measure of substitutability proposed in section 4.2. The meaning of the passage above is then clear.

† Cf. also H. S. Houthakker, 'Additive Preferences', *Econometrica*, April 1960, p. 246 and footnote 8.

through w. That is, a change in the consumption of j, other things being equal, might tend to make the consumer want more of i, but the change in consumption of w also involved might make him want less. The net effect could be zero. This second case of zero σ_{ij} is in a sense coincidental and does not accord with the intuitive idea of independence.

If i is to be truly independent of j it must also be independent of any other good which is not independent of j. Moreover, it must be impossible to trace any connexion between i and j through any chain of intermediate goods however long. In brief it must be possible to decompose the adjoint of the Hessian determinant as under

$$\Delta^{n+1} \begin{vmatrix} \sigma_{11} & \cdot\cdot & \sigma_{1r} & \Delta_1 & 0 & \cdot\cdot & 0 \\ \cdot & & & & \cdot & & \cdot \\ \cdot & & & & \cdot & & \cdot \\ \sigma_{r1} & \cdot\cdot & \sigma_{rr} & \Delta_r & 0 & \cdot\cdot & 0 \\ \Delta_1 & \cdot\cdot & \Delta_r & \Delta_0 & \Delta_{(r+1)} & \cdot\cdot & \Delta_n \\ 0 & & 0 & \Delta_{(r+1)} & \sigma_{(r+1)(r+1)} & \cdot\cdot & \sigma_{(r+1)n} \\ \cdot & & & & \cdot & & \cdot \\ \cdot & & & & \cdot & & \cdot \\ 0 & \cdot\cdot & 0 & \Delta_n & \sigma_{n(r+1)} & \cdot\cdot & \sigma_{nn} \end{vmatrix}.$$

Goods 1 to r make up a sector of consumption entirely independent of goods $(r+1)$ to n. Compensated price changes in one sector leave quantities unchanged in the independent sector and vice versa.

Evidently this approach simply leads us back to complete complementarity between the two sectors, for from

$$\sum_j p_j \sigma_{ij} = 0$$

and

$$\sigma_{ij} = 0 \quad \text{for all } j \geq r,\ i \leq r+1 \text{ and } j \leq r,\ i \geq r+1$$

we have

$$\sum_j p_j \sigma_{ij} = 0 \quad i \leq r,\ j \leq r, \text{ etc.}$$

This means that price changes proportional to p's in either sector have no effect whatever on consumption anywhere in the system. To put it another way, if we assume that all prices vary proportionately within each sector so that the system reduces to two goods only,† i and j, then $\sigma_{ij} = 0$ which, as we have already noted, is the condition for complete complementarity in a two-good world.

At this point the reader may be wondering why in these circumstances the measure of complementarity between any two goods taken one from each sector stands at zero rather than $-\infty$. The answer is simply that, as long as there is substitutability within sectors, two goods (one from each sector) are not complementary even though there is a sense in which the sectors as a whole are; for any two individual commodities need not always be taken in absolutely fixed proportions. If, on the other hand, there is no substitutability within sectors, then all σ_{ij} reduce to zero and every complementarity measure degenerates to an indeterminate form.

We take warning from this case that in any attempt to infer the magnitude of the measure 4.2 (iii) from a knowledge of the relation in use between two goods we must not forget the rest of the system. For example, the fact that travel is usually an essential ingredient of a holiday by the sea should not lead us to suppose that motoring and other holiday expenditure are highly complementary in the sense of the measure 4.2 (iii). For the substitutability of railway and motor transport could mean that holidays and motoring are not taken in fixed proportions despite the strong complementary relationship in use.

Turning again to the apparent paradox whereby a property which we hoped would give expression to intuitive ideas of independence turns out to imply complementarity we reflect that this should not really surprise us; for in fact $\sigma_{ij} = 0$ is simply an arbitrary line dividing a continuous measure of complementarity/substitutability and carries no real implication of independence. Attention has already been drawn to the fact that, in general, goods will possess simultaneously an element of complementarity and an element of substitutability. The two properties are no more mutually exclusive than are the properties of elasticity and inelasticity in demand curves. Just as we sometimes choose unit elasticity as an arbitrary dividing-

† Cf. Chapter 1, p. 38, n. ‡, and section 4.2.

line between goods which are elastic and inelastic in demand, so we have chosen $\sigma_{ij} = 0$ as an arbitrary dividing-line between complementarity and substitutability. Similarly independence and substitutability cannot be mutually exclusive properties since there must always be some degree of substitutability between any pair of goods even if the measure of such substitutability is low enough to justify the use of the term complementarity. Clearly our first attempt to define independence will not do.

The proposal above for an independence criterion has been introduced and rejected only in part, because it is an interesting illustration of the weakness of the traditional criterion for complementarity. Another important reason for its inclusion in this chapter lies in its close relationship to a suggestion recently made by Professor H. S. Houthakker.†

Professor Houthakker draws attention to the fact that the utility function u can be written indirectly, as a function of prices and expenditure, instead of quantities x_i. This is because all x_i are themselves functions of prices and expenditure.

If the indirect utility function, which we call u^*, is additive in form, that is, if it can be written

$$u^* = u_1^*(p_1, y) + u_2^*(p_2, y) + \ldots + u_n^*(p_n, y), \qquad 4.4 \text{ (i)}$$

then we have what Professor Houthakker has called indirect additivity (independence). On this assumption we have

$$u_{ij}^* = 0 \quad \text{for all } i \neq j$$

as a consequence of which it is possible to show that

$$\frac{\partial x_i/\partial p_k}{\partial x_j/\partial p_k} = \frac{x_i}{x_j}. \qquad 4.4 \text{ (ii)}$$

In fact we know that, in general,

$$u_i^* = -\lambda x_i,$$

for x_i is the sum of money required to compensate for the loss of u_i due to unit change in price, p_i, and λ, the marginal utility

† 'Additive Preferences', *Econometrica*, April 1960.

of money, is the factor required to convert money units into utility. Thus

$$\frac{u_i^*}{u_j^*} = \frac{x_i}{x_j}.$$
4.4 (iii)

Furthermore, it can be shown, and we shall later prove (cf. below, p. 177), that the condition

$$\frac{\partial(u_i^*/u_j^*)}{\partial p_k} = 0 \quad \text{for all } i \neq j \neq k$$
4.4 (iv)

is equivalent to the additivity assumption 4.4 (i) as long as we are free to choose any utility indicator we like, say $F(u^*)$, to replace u^*.

Differentiating 4.4 (iii) by p_k using the condition 4.4 (iv) immediately yields Houthakker's result 4.4 (ii).

We now notice that, in constructing the measure of complementarity 4.2 (iii), we might just as easily have applied the argument to the uncompensated price response $\partial x_i/\partial p_j$ rather than the substitution parts, σ_{ij} only. In fact a very good case can be made out for this as is easily seen from the work leading to equation 4.2 (v). Following on from the full price response definition of complementarity we obtain

$$\frac{\partial x_i}{\partial p_j} = 0 \quad (i \neq j)$$
4.4 (v)

as a definition of independence analogous to the $\sigma_{ij} = 0$ definition discussed above.

But 4.4 (v) implies

$$-x_j \frac{\partial x_i}{\partial y} = -\sigma_{ij} = -\sigma_{ji} = -x_i \frac{\partial x_j}{\partial y}$$

or
$$\frac{\partial x_i/\partial y}{\partial x_j/\partial y} = \frac{x_i}{x_j},$$
4.4 (vi)

which if it is identically true means homogeneity of the preference pattern. All Engel curves are straight lines through the origin.

Now quite generally

$$\frac{\partial x_i}{\partial p_k} \bigg/ \frac{\partial x_j}{\partial p_k} = \frac{x_i}{x_j} \left[\frac{-(\partial x_i/\partial y)/(x_i + \sigma_{ik}/x_k x_i)}{-(\partial x_j/\partial y)/(x_j + \sigma_{jk}/x_k x_j)} \right]$$
4.4 (vii)

and as $-\sigma_{ik}$ approaches $-x_k(\partial x_i/\partial y)$ and the condition 4.4 (vi) is met, the expression in square brackets approaches unity. Professor Houthakker's result 4.4 (ii) holds. Moreover, if we differentiate 4.4 (iii) with respect to p_k using the fact that $\partial x_i/\partial p_k = 0$ for all $i \neq k$, we notice that 4.4 (iv) is met and we have indirect additive utility as we should expect.

Evidently, the full partial response definition of independence is a sufficient condition for indirect additivity though, of course, not a necessary one. In passing it should be noted that unlike the criteria $\sigma_{ij} = 0$ and $\partial x_i/\partial p_j = 0$, indirect additivity does not imply some particular level of substitutability, but rather a relation between substitution effects. This is a characteristic it shares with neutral want association. On the other hand, it is easy to see from 4.4 (vii) (where additivity requires that the expression in the square brackets should be unity) that the ratio σ_{ik}/σ_{jk} is not simply expressible in terms of x's and/or $\partial x/\partial y$'s. This is the basic reason why indirect additivity is not very rich in consequences, as Professor Houthakker has noted. Indeed it appears that indirect additivity invites investigation only because of the simple form of function and not because it has any intuitive appeal as an attractive hypothesis likely to fit the facts. This is an unsatisfactory motive. We need to begin from the facts as revealed by introspection rather than from a particular mathematical form of function.

Further reflection suggests that what we really mean by independence is that there is no *special* relation between two goods i and j which will lead us to expect that a change in the quantity of i consumed would have any particular effect upon our preference for j. If i and j are complements an increase in the quantity of i possessed makes us much more willing to exchange other goods, w, for j. If i and j are substitutes an increase in the quantity of i will affect willingness to exchange w goods for j goods in much the same way as would an increase in j goods themselves. If i goods are independent of j goods and w goods, willingness to exchange j for w is unaffected by an increase in i.

We could give mathematical expression to this idea by saying that there is independence when a small increase in i goods will not affect the *marginal* utility of j goods or w goods. This will, of course, leave unchanged the willingness to exchange j and w (i.e. the *ratio* of their marginal utilities). That is:

$$u_{ji} = 0 \quad \text{and} \quad u_{wi} = 0$$

so that
$$\frac{\partial(u_j/u_w)}{\partial x_i} = \frac{1}{u_w^2}\begin{vmatrix} u_w & u_{wi} \\ u_j & u_{ji} \end{vmatrix} = 0.$$

This is the usual mathematical definition of direct independent (additive) utility, $u(x_w, x_i, x_j)$ being regarded as the sum of separate functions $u_1(x_w)+u_2(x_i)+u_3(x_j)$.

There are, however, reasons why even this expression of independence is unacceptable. Our intuition tells us that the more goods we have the less we want more of them. The marginal utility of income diminishes. Thus, although there is no *special* reason why a small increase in i goods should affect the marginal utility of j goods it will do so generally because the consumer is made better off. It is dangerous therefore to put $u_{ji} = 0$. On the other hand, it does seem reasonable to suppose that the marginal utility of w will be affected in much the same way as the marginal utility of j by the increase in i, if i is independent of both. One pennyworth of j and one pennyworth of w both give less utility but both give the *same amount* less utility. The ratio u_j/u_w is unchanged but both u_j and u_w are changed by the small increase in i. In other words, we reject $u_{ji} = 0$ and $u_{wi} = 0$ but retain

$$\frac{\partial(u_j/u_w)}{\partial x_i} = 0$$

or
$$\begin{vmatrix} u_w & u_{wi} \\ u_j & u_{ji} \end{vmatrix} = 0$$

as the criterion for independence.

We may confirm the good sense of this by reminding ourselves that u is not really a measurable utility function uniquely determinable, since a consumer whose utility is measured by any function $F(u)$ would behave in an exactly similar way. Hence when we say that independence means

$$F_{ij} = 0$$

we imply something which approaches measurable utility. Or, to put it another way, we impose a limitation on the form of utility index F. For if the marginal utility of j is $F'u_j$, the change in marginal utility due to unit increase in the consumption of i will be

$$F'u_{ji} + F''u_j u_i.$$

For this to be zero we require

$$-\frac{F''}{F'} = \frac{u_{ji}}{u_j u_i}, \qquad\qquad 4.4 \text{ (viii)}$$

which is a restriction on the choice of utility index; for given that u is a function defining behaviour, and given that j and i are independent, the ratio F''/F' is determined.

It may be a fact that an individual *could* say with certainty that an increase in i would leave his marginal utility for j unchanged. But if he could, and if we could accept the correctness of this subjective estimate, then we are at least half-way towards the ideal of a measurable utility.

Since the term 'measurable utility' can mean a great many things† and since the matter has been much debated, it may be as well to expand a little upon the point above. First we explain that in the present context 'measurability' has been used in a narrow sense to imply that some objective phenomenon can be observed which it is agreed varies with the utility to be measured.

The word 'agreed' is important, for it is not often recognized how much measurability depends upon mutual agreement. For example, we are prepared to accept, for very good reasons, that variations in a column of mercury measure something which we call temperature. And this concept has many applications. We should be much less willing to agree, however, that Nebuchadnezzar would be right in supposing that he could inflict seven times more than normal pain on Shadrach, Meshach, and

---

† For a survey of the subject of measurement the reader is referred to Thrall, Coombs, and Davis, *Decision Processes*, pp. 26 ff.

Abednego by casting them into a fiery furnace heated 'seven times more than it was wont to be heated'. Similarly it has so far proved impossible to find any observable phenomenon which we can agree measures utility. If we could so agree then many of our economic troubles, if not all, would be over.

We can, of course, always measure the utility of a given quantity of one good by finding out how much of another the individual is willing to exchange it for. But two insurmountable difficulties limit the usefulness of this. The first is that the utility of every good, and for that matter the disutility of labour, is intimately bound up with the quantity of every other good possessed. Moreover, the precise nature of this connexion is not reflected by any observable phenomenon. The second difficulty is that, even if the first could be overcome, all practical applications would be confined to the individual, unless it could be *agreed* that some good, or perhaps labour, has the same utility or disutility for everyone.

The relevance of this to independence is that, if we could be sure that $F_{ij} \equiv 0$, then our first difficulty would be overcome. We know that the utility of i does not depend on the quantity of j possessed. We could measure the utility of i in terms of j. It is this approach in one form or another which various writers have sought to exploit. Future goods, labour, and the opportunity to gamble have variously been suggested as want satisfying commodities, j, likely to be independent of current consumption i. If we could be sure that this were the case then there would be immediate application in the field of individual decision theory. Unfortunately there is no experiment by which it is possible to decide whether F_{ij} is zero or not for, as we have seen, observable behaviour is independent of the utility index F. This is always true and no amount of wishful thinking can make it otherwise. And even if it were otherwise interpersonal comparisons would still be impossible.

It is for this reason that we have taken care to define independence more generally as

$$\frac{\partial(F'u_j / F'u_w)}{\partial x_i} = 0 \quad \text{rather than} \quad \frac{\partial(F'u_j)}{\partial x_i} = 0,$$

for this is equivalent to

$$\begin{vmatrix} F'u_w & F'u_{wi}+F''u_i u_w \\ F'u_j & F'u_{ji}+F''u_i u_j \end{vmatrix} = 0,$$

that is

$$(F')^2 \begin{vmatrix} u_w & u_{wi} \\ u_j & u_{ji} \end{vmatrix} = 0$$

which condition will be fulfilled when

$$\begin{vmatrix} u_w & u_{wi} \\ u_j & u_{ji} \end{vmatrix} = 0 \qquad\qquad 4.4\ (ix)$$

whatever utility index is chosen.

At a later stage, moreover, we shall distinguish 4.4 (ix) from direct additivity (independence in the old sense) by calling it neutral want association. It will be shown that neutral want association generalizes in a way that additivity does not.

Having made this clear we now proceed to retrace our steps. We begin by noting a remarkable fact.† Clearly if 4.4 (ix) holds for every pair of goods in the system, so that every good is neutrally want associated with every other, then

$$\frac{u_{ji}}{u_j u_i} = \frac{u_{wi}}{u_w u_i} \quad \text{for all } i \neq w \neq j. \qquad 4.4\ (x)$$

On this condition it is easy to show that the expression $u_{ji}/(u_j u_i)$ is a function of u alone. It would be tedious to set out a full proof of this, and unnecessary, since it may easily be worked by the interested reader in a straightforward way. The most convenient approach is to define

$$\rho = \frac{u_{ij}}{u_i u_j} = \frac{u_{ik}}{u_i u_k} = \frac{u_{jk}}{u_j u_k}, \text{ etc.}$$

If ρ_i is $\partial\rho/\partial x_i$ it can be seen at once that

$$\frac{\rho_i}{\rho_j} = \frac{u_{ik}}{u_{jk}} = \frac{u_i}{u_j}$$

provided ρ_i is obtained by differentiating that form of ρ, as

† The author is grateful to Professor P. A. Samuelson and to Mr. W. M. Gorman for pointing this out. It had seemed so obvious intuitively that the contrary was true that I was never tempted to test the proposition.

defined, which does not contain any subscript i, and so on. Clearly, therefore,

$$\sum_i \rho_i \, dx_i = 0$$

for any set of dx_i such that

$$\sum_i u_i \, dx_i = 0,$$

i.e. such that u is a constant. In other words ρ is constant whenever u is constant, i.e. ρ is a function of u alone.

If the right-hand side of 4.4 (viii) is a function of u alone and if 4.4 (x) holds it follows that we can write

$$-\frac{F''}{F'} = \psi(u)$$

in place of 4.4 (viii). In other words, given neutral want association everywhere, we can always choose a utility index F such that $F_{ij} = 0$. And since behaviour is independent of the choice of index we lose no generality in putting $u_{ij} = 0$ *provided we do not use this result to claim that utility is measurable in the sense above.*

The reader is especially asked to note that, although neutral want association is a restriction on behaviour, and although we can and shall indicate how experiment can detect it, we have not contradicted our claim that it is impossible to test for actual independent utility. This is because behaviour consistent with neutral want association is only a necessary and not a sufficient condition for independent utility. For behaviour is invariant under a transformation of the utility index. For the same reason, however, we are free to analyse behaviour on the assumption of independence *provided all goods are in neutral want association with all others.* This last proviso is crucial. It will become clear later that it is necessary to revert to the criterion 4.4 (ix) when we come to generalize in Chapter 5.

In the meantime intuition suggests that there probably exist in practice a wide range of classes of goods where, as a first approximation, it is safe to analyse market behaviour on the assumption that $u_{ij} = 0$. We might in fact be able to hive off

consumption goods into broad groups and make useful statements about elasticities of demand for such groups.

Suppose, for example, there are two such groups in the
economy. All commodities 1 to r are independent of all commodities $r+1$ to n and vice versa. Consider the properties of
the Hessian determinant, Δ, in such a case. Evidently every
minor of the adjugate of order two which contains two of the
bordering elements in the same commodity group 1 to r or $r+1$
to n, together with two elements of the same row, but in a column
belonging to the independent commodity group, will be zero.
That is,

$$\begin{vmatrix} \sigma_i & \sigma_{ik} \\ \sigma_j & \sigma_{jk} \end{vmatrix} = 0 \quad \begin{aligned} & (i \neq r+1,...,n) \\ & (j \neq r+1,...,n) \\ & (k \neq 1,...,r) \end{aligned} \qquad \text{4.4 (xi)}$$

or vice versa,† where $\bar{\sigma}_i$ is the expenditure response $\partial x_i/\partial y$ (cf.
section 1.4, p. 54). This result follows (by Jacobi's theorem)
from the fact that the complementary minor of the Hessian
determinant itself must be zero. For if we divide such a complementary minor according to the independent commodity groups
and expand by a Laplacian expansion, at least one of the
determinants in each term of the expansion will contain at least
two rows or columns zero (by our definition of independence).
This property enables us to express the cross demand elasticities
between all independent goods in terms of the marginal propensity to consume them and an undetermined multiplier *which is
the same for all independent goods*.

Consider a simple case. Suppose all consumption goods are
classified into three independent groups, say, clothing, housing,
and food, in such a way that we agree, as a first approximation,
that a rise in the quantity of food possessed will not affect the
willingness to exchange housing for clothes, etc. Call these
goods x_1, x_2, x_3, with prices p_1, p_2, and p_3 respectively.

† The simplicity of this result, which clearly implies that

$$\frac{\partial x_i/\partial p_k}{\partial x_j/\partial p_k} = \frac{\partial x_i/\partial y}{\partial x_j/\partial y} = \frac{\sigma_{ik}}{\sigma_{jk}},$$

is in contrast to the complicated indirect independence condition which
requires that the expression in the square bracket (4.4 (vii)) should be unity.

First we note that there is no loss of generality in writing

$$\sigma_{13} = \lambda_{13}\frac{\partial x_1}{\partial y}\frac{\partial x_3}{\partial y},$$

for whatever the values of $\partial x_3/\partial y$ and $\partial x_1/\partial y$ we can always choose some λ_{13} appropriately. We also see that from

$$\sigma_{13} = \sigma_{31}$$

we have

$$\lambda_{13} = \lambda_{31}.$$

Now applying 4.4 (xi) we obtain

$$\begin{vmatrix} \sigma_2 & \left(\lambda_{21}\dfrac{\partial x_2}{\partial y}\dfrac{\partial x_1}{\partial y}\right) \\[2ex] \sigma_3 & \left(\lambda_{31}\dfrac{\partial x_3}{\partial y}\dfrac{\partial x_1}{\partial y}\right) \end{vmatrix} = 0,$$

which since

$$\sigma_2/\sigma_3 = \frac{\partial x_2}{\partial y}\bigg/\frac{\partial x_3}{\partial y}$$

implies

$$\lambda_{21} = \lambda_{31}.$$

Similarly

$$\lambda_{23} = \lambda_{13} = \lambda_{21}.$$

Hence all λ are equal and subscripts may be dropped.

Accordingly we may write

$$\frac{\partial x_i}{\partial p_j} = -x_j\frac{\partial x_i}{\partial y} + \lambda\frac{\partial x_i}{\partial y}\frac{\partial x_j}{\partial y} \quad (i = 1, 2, 3; j = 1, 2, 3; j \neq i).$$

$$4.4 \text{ (xii)}$$

Using now the general result 1.4 (x)

$$\sum_j p_j\sigma_{ij} = 0$$

we have

$$\sum_{\substack{j \\ j \neq i}} p_j\sigma_{ij} = -p_i\sigma_{ii}$$

or

$$\lambda\left(1 - p_i\frac{\partial x_i}{\partial y}\right)\frac{\partial x_i}{\partial y} = -p_i\sigma_{ii},$$

from which we deduce

$$\frac{\partial x_i}{\partial p_i} = -x_i\frac{\partial x_i}{\partial y} + \lambda\left(\frac{1}{p_i} - \frac{\partial x_i}{\partial y}\right)\frac{\partial x_i}{\partial y} \quad (i = 1, 2, 3).$$

$$4.4 \text{ (xiii)}$$

4.4 (xii) and (xiii) make it clear that all demand responses can be expressed in terms of income responses and a single λ.

The reader should recall, however, that so far we have only one group of composite commodities comprising all goods. The single λ means crudely that all composite commodities have the same degree of substitutability one with another. In the next chapter we shall show how this idea may be generalized to many groups with many different degrees of substitutability or complementarity. It is a remarkable fact that even in very complex cases the same obvious computational advantages persist.

5

NEUTRAL WANT ASSOCIATION

5.1. Introduction and definition

IT is convenient to begin a systematic discussion of neutral want association from a point of view rather different from that of section 4.3. In 4.3 we postulated certain restrictions on the utility function and examined the consequences for behaviour. Where the specialization is very complicated, however, as in the present chapter, it is much more illuminating to state the hypothesis directly, as a condition on behaviour, leaving the utility implications for later consideration. For the time being also the emphasis is shifted away from pure theory towards econometrics in a narrower sense.

We have, so far, a well-developed theory which implies certain uniformities of consumer behaviour in the market. The next logical step is to show how past data might be analysed with a view to discovering these uniformities, i.e. to finding the actual numerical value of the $\partial x_i/\partial p_j$, or, what amounts to the same thing, the $\partial x_i/\partial y$ and σ_{ij}, which figure in the theory. We then have a basis for quantitative, as against qualitative, prediction.

The straightforward approach would be to set down $n+1$ equations of the type

$$\sum_j \frac{\partial x_i}{\partial p_j} dp_j + \frac{\partial x_i}{\partial y} dy = dx_i \qquad 5.1\ (\mathrm{i})$$

and to solve for $\partial x_i/\partial p_j$ and $\partial x_i/\partial y$. The dp_j, dy, and dx_i are, of course, observed changes in prices, spending, and consumption x_i, over each of $n+1$ suitable periods of time. Unfortunately, in their attempts to measure the various parameters by this method, and by ingenious developments of it, econometricians have been consistently frustrated by the simple fact that there are too many of them.

It is an inescapable truth that, in a general way, the consumption of every good depends to a significant degree on the price of every other good. This is not to deny, of course, that the change in the consumption of, say, petrol, due to a rise in the price of salt, can, in some contexts, be assumed to be negligible. But in the normal case where *all* prices change the total effect upon petrol purchases will be far from negligible. We have to recognize that, although many individual price effects are likely to be small, their number is usually sufficiently great to make it unrealistic to ignore their cumulative effect. Indeed, this proposition follows at once from homogeneity of the demand function, which implies that a 1 per cent rise in all prices, except that of petrol, is precisely equivalent to a 1 per cent fall in the price of petrol, combined with a 1 per cent fall in money income.†
In short, if *we wish to be able to predict changes in the pattern of consumption, given expected price changes, we must know all cross elasticities however small these may turn out to be on the average.*

All of this means that none of the $n+1$ parameters of 5.1 (i) can be taken to be zero. Accordingly, if there exist 1000 commodities we need 1000 equations, and hence 1000 observations of price, expenditure, and quantity changes before we can solve.

There would, of course, be no difficulty about this if it were possible to take an observation every minute. Unfortunately, as we have already noted in section 1.1, the average flow of consumption we are trying to measure is so uneven, because of seasonal and other factors not incorporated into the theory, that there is little possibility of taking meaningful observations at smaller intervals than one year. One thousand years would be needed to estimate parameters which, on the most optimistic view, are hardly likely to remain constant for more than a few years at a time.

†
$$\sum_j p_j \frac{\partial x_i}{\partial p_j} + y \frac{\partial x_i}{\partial y} = 0 \quad \text{(cf. 1.4 (v)) implies}$$

$$\sum_{\substack{j \\ j \neq i}} \frac{\partial x_i}{\partial p_j} dp_j + \frac{\partial x_i}{\partial y} dy = -\frac{\partial x_i}{\partial p_i} dp_i$$

if all dp's and dy are proportional to p's and y.

A great deal of thought has been given to ways and means of overcoming this fundamental difficulty but so far, at bottom, all approaches have been based upon the same principle. The greater number of the terms of 5.1 (i) are replaced by an error term ϵ which is assumed to be distributed randomly over the set of observations taken. Thus we have a stochastic equation in two variables,

$$\frac{\partial x_i}{\partial p_i}dp_i + \frac{\partial x_i}{\partial y}\,dy + \epsilon = dx_i. \qquad 5.1 \text{ (ii)}$$

By maximizing a likelihood function appropriately formed from a series of observations, notionally of type 5.1 (ii), it is possible to find the 'most likely' values of $\partial x_i/\partial p_i$ and $\partial x_i/\partial y$, from a much reduced set of data. The degree of probability that the results obtained are correct within preassigned limits can also be stated, on certain assumptions.

The usefulness of this technique is limited, however, by the fact that it rests upon the supposition that there is no correlation between the observed dp_i and the magnitude of the error term for the time period. Moreover, as the major influence on ϵ is probably other prices, and since the movements of different prices over time are usually highly correlated, this basic assumption is almost certainly not met. Again, where the error-term technique has been used to compute cross responses ($\partial x_i/\partial p_j$ ($j \neq i$)) which tend to be small, the estimates obtained are not often found to be statistically significant. There is indeed dispute among statisticians as to whether it is ever possible, even with the widest margins of probable error, to obtain estimates of more parameters than there are observations of the data.

Against all this we have already discovered good reasons for suspecting that, after all, there are not as many parameters to compute as we commonly suppose. And it is upon this belief that the work below is based. Indeed the reader will recognize that the approach described above appeals only to the crudest hypothesis it is possible to make, for it supposes no more than that the quantity consumed of each good is related in some completely unknown way to all prices and money income. The

n^2 responses of each of the n goods, to n price changes, are to be computed, together with the n responses to income changes. But we already have a theory which tells us a great deal more than this.

We have in fact shown, in Chapter 3, that $\sigma_{ij} = \sigma_{ji}$ (approx.) even where the data under examination refer to the community as a whole. Knowing this, we have, at one stroke, discovered $\frac{1}{2}(n^2-n)$ of the unknowns we wish to estimate; for we can easily build up price responses from their constituent income and substitution effects. Given marginal propensities to consume each good we can compute the elasticity of demand for petrol with respect to a change in the price of salt direct from a knowledge of the elasticity of demand for salt with respect to a change in the price of petrol, and so on. In what follows we shall make use of this result.

But the symmetry of substitution effects is not yet enough. $\frac{1}{2}n^2$ parameters are scarcely less unmanageable than n^2. We shall introduce, therefore, want neutrality assumptions which, at best, can reduce the number of parameters to something of the order of $2n$. Before turning to this, however, it is worth while to re-emphasize two points.

First, although we have brought the discussion to the present stage by drawing attention to the need to reduce the number of parameters, the reader will recall that the implications of gaps in the chain of substitutes were not originally studied by the writer for this purpose. On the contrary, we have already seen how we can be led towards the same idea by problems in international trade and by investigation into possible consequences of varying degrees of substitutability and complementarity, quite independent of any attempt at statistical analysis. The possibility of commodity grouping as explained below appears in no way less plausible than the utility maximizing assumption upon which the theory of demand is based. *In short, new assumptions are not introduced solely to simplify computations. Rather it is claimed as a matter of fact that groups as later defined do exist.*

Secondly, the reader is especially asked to note that it is not just one new hypothesis which we are about to propose but a scheme for testing a very large variety of hypotheses any one of which may or may not more closely approximate to the facts than any other. The assumptions actually tested in Chapters 6 and 7 are selected from a large class possible and are not particularly sophisticated examples at that.

To illustrate the procedure, consider a world in which there exist only six goods, white bread, brown bread, butter, cheese, cinema, and television. Some of these goods are highly substitutable, e.g. white and brown bread, some are highly complementary, e.g. bread and butter, whilst some have an in-between status as, for example, butter and cheese. The chosen example therefore covers a wide variety of relationships.

Quite naturally we might classify these commodities into two groups: 'food' and 'amusements'. Such a partitioning appears natural simply because the kind of want met by each group is in some sense distinct. A 'marked gap' separates them. But we need a more objective principle upon which a partition might be identified.

Consider the reasons why changes in expenditure on 'food' occur. These are either:

(a) because total expenditure on all goods has changed, prices remaining constant,

(b) because some prices in the group 'amusements' have changed, or

(c) because some prices in the group 'food' have changed.

Any change in expenditure on 'food' must be allocated to the various elements in the group. Obviously the principles of such allocation will depend very heavily on the prices of goods in the food group. But they may be unaffected by prices in the amusement group. To put it another way, we might find that whenever changes of the kind (a) or (b) above occur, in such a way as to leave the overall 'food' expenditure unchanged, then the allocation of expenditure within the food group remains unchanged also. In this case we say that goods in the group food are in *neutral want association* with goods in the group amusements.

What this means in effect is, that any change in prices outside the group food causes changes in consumption of the various goods inside the group which are in every case proportionate to income responses, i.e. proportionate to changes which occur if income rises with all prices constant. [The reader will imme- diately recognize that we have here *defined* neutral want associa- tion in terms of the behavioural consequences of the alternative definition of 4.4 (p. 177). But notice that we now propose a relation between a group of goods and all those goods outside the group and not a symmetric relation between *all* goods.]

If, in addition to the fact that goods in the food group are neutrally want associated with all goods in the amusement group, the converse also applies, i.e. amusement goods are neutrally want associated with food goods, then a natural partition may be made between the two. This is the objective principle by which we discover a marked gap.

The possibility of partitioning arises because wants them- selves fall into more or less loosely related groups. Any means of satisfying any kind of want is always in some degree substi- tutable for, or complementary to, any means of satisfying any other want. But there is no obvious reason why the *degree* of substitutability (or complementarity) between two goods which satisfy two distinctly *different* classes of wants should be any different from the degree of substitutability between any other two goods satisfying the same two classes of wants. To put it another way, 'food' and 'amusements' may be complementary commodities in such a way that the marginal pound's worth of 'food' is complementary in the same degree with the marginal pound's worth of 'amusements' however the pound is spent within each group.

At this point it may be as well to warn that our six-good example is an example only. No claim is made at this stage that as a matter of fact 'food' and 'amusements' can be parti- tioned. On the contrary, if we were to extend our commodities to include, say, peanuts and toffee; and if it were usual to eat only peanuts at the cinema, and to enjoy toffee only whilst watching television, then it would be necessary to include peanuts and toffee under 'amusements' rather than 'food' and the titles might then be inappropriate. All that is claimed is that it would be surprising if, among all commodities consumed, some partitioning were not possible *somewhere*. Part of the object of the exercise is to discover just where. We proceed by choosing an hypothesis which appears reasonable and by testing the chosen hypothesis at the bar of the facts.

Returning to our six-good example we now notice a further remarkable possibility. Consider the group 'food' consisting of brown bread, white bread, butter, and cheese. Suppose that no other goods exist but these. At once it appears plausible to make a partitioning of the 'food' goods into 'bread' and, shall we say, the 'appetizers', butter and cheese. Exactly the same rules for partitioning apply. Small changes in the prices of butter and cheese affect only the absolute amount spent on 'bread' and not the allocation between white and brown. Similarly, small changes in the prices of white and brown bread affect only the absolute amount spent on appetizers and not the principle of allocation between butter and cheese.

Notice especially that the plausibility of a partitioning between 'bread' and 'appetizers' depends absolutely upon the fact that we are not now thinking of 'amusements'. We should not, at stage one, have considered the possibility of partitioning 'bread' and all other goods for the obvious reason that changes in the price of bread will almost certainly affect the principles of allocation between butter and cinema. We now have a 'tree', Fig. 9,† with three levels of composite commodities. It will be noted that marked gaps reach down to different levels in what, in a more realistic case, could be a most complicated pattern. Some boundaries are stronger than others.

Again it is emphasized that the possibility of grouping commodities into a tree, as in Fig. 9, stems from the nature of wants themselves. Indeed the very words we use as headings for the different groups are sometimes descriptive of the wants rather

† Readers who know the work of Professor R. H. Strotz will notice the similarity between Fig. 9 and the 'Utility Tree'. Cf. 'The Empirical Implications of a Utility Tree', *Econometrica*, vol. 25, no. 2, 1957.

than the particular means of satisfying them, e.g. appetizers and amusements. Such classifications are used intuitively by the compilers of statistics, a fact which confirms that there probably exists a basis in fact for the neutral want association hypothesis.

The ultimate aim of partitioning is to divide all goods into basic groups consisting of not more than two goods in each group.

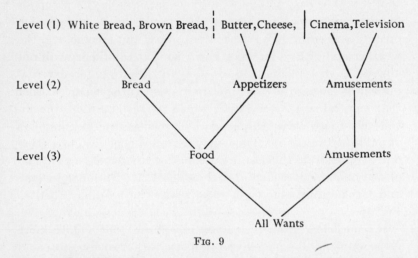

FIG. 9

Two goods taken from any basic group will be neutrally want associated with *all* other goods but two goods taken one each from two basic groups are not *necessarily* in neutral want association with *any* other good. They usually will be in neutral want association with some good, however. For example, on our assumptions, white and brown bread are neutrally want associated with every good, but white bread and butter are not neutrally want associated with either cheese or brown bread.

The reader who doubts the possibility of partitioning to the point where not more than two goods are left in each basic group is invited to try examples on his own account. It will be observed that each partition seems always to open up further possibilities of partitioning. Moreover, even if it does not, it is always possible to mend broken links in the chain at the cost of an index-number problem, by treating any offending group of goods as one single good. It is also emphasized that the partitioning procedure described here is not the only, or even the most general, way to make use of properties of neutral want association between goods. Each time such a property is noted at least one more parameter can be dropped. A fully general account of the possibilities will be given in section 5.4.

On the other hand, there is no wish to create the impression that it will be easy to find a 'correct' partitioning for all goods in any community. In the first place there are influences which operate on consumption other than prices and income, e.g. the weather and/or hire-purchase rules, so that the theory will not always apply precisely. Some way of allowing for external influences must be devised. Secondly, there are principles other than neutral want association which go to determine the intuitively based classifications actually chosen by the compilers of published statistics. These may require a good deal of sorting out. To illustrate this last point consider a possible partitioning of the nine goods which appear in the U.K. National Income and Expenditure blue book 1958, under the heading 'Food'— Fig. 10.

It seems clear, from even a first inspection, that a much more satisfactory preliminary hypothesis than that of Fig. 10 could be devised if the principles of classification employed by the compilers of the blue book were more consistent. For example, fruit and vegetables are separated, presumably on the ground that they meet separate wants. On the other hand, eggs are included with butter under dairy products, perhaps because of a common producer background. Similarly bread and cereals appear as one good although there is clearly a distinction between the kind of want satisfied by bread and say rice.

Evidently, in our attempts to use the concept of neutral want association to define more precisely what we mean by gaps in the chain of substitutes, we have, remarkably, and as a by-product, also defined composite commodities at various levels. In sections 5.2, 5.3, and 5.4 it will be shown that very simple empirical tests are available to discover exactly where marked gaps occur. We have, in fact, a ready means of confirming the

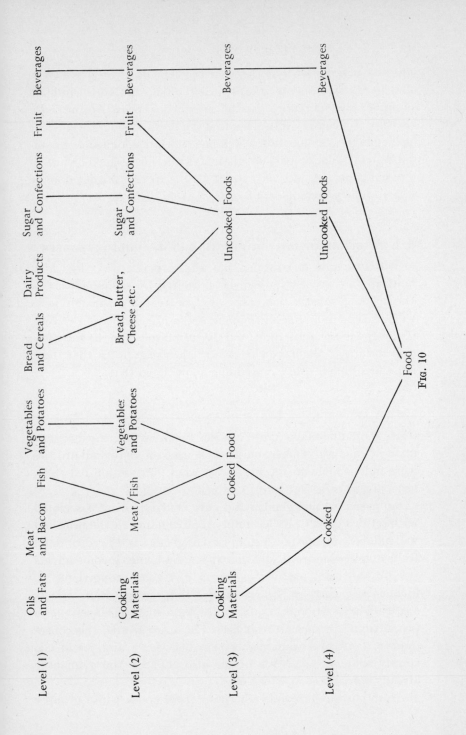

Level (1)   Oils and Fats   Meat and Bacon   Fish   Vegetables and Potatoes   Bread and Cereals   Dairy Products   Sugar and Confections   Fruit   Beverages

Level (2)   Cooking Materials   Meat/Fish   Vegetables and Potatoes   Bread, Butter, Cheese etc.   Sugar and Confections   Fruit   Beverages

Level (3)   Cooking Materials   Cooked Food   Uncooked Foods   Beverages

Level (4)   Cooked   Uncooked Foods   Beverages

Food

Fig. 10

validity of complex hypotheses of the type illustrated in Figs. 9 and 10. Even more remarkably it will be shown that the implied composite commodities can be assigned a price *free of index number difficulties*. For the first time we recognize a clear principle for classification which has enormous logical and computational advantages, as distinct from mere convenience in presentation. *A plea is entered that serious consideration be given to the general adoption of this principle by the compilers of consumption data.*

5.2. A technique for computation of demand responses

We turn now to consider one of the many ways in which neutral want association can be exploited by econometricians. Income and substitution responses are treated separately so as to gain the advantage of the symmetry of substitution effects.

For the moment we direct our attention solely to the substitution term, σ_{ij}. We have already noted in section 4.4 that there is no loss of generality in defining some λ_{ij} so that

$$\sigma_{ij} = \lambda_{ij} \frac{\partial x_i}{\partial y} \frac{\partial x_j}{\partial y}.$$

(Care should be taken not to confuse the λ_{ij} with λ, the marginal utility of money. There would be a connexion only if all utilities were independent in the narrowest sense; cf. section 5.3.) We have also shown that as $\sigma_{ij} = \sigma_{ji}$ then $\lambda_{ij} = \lambda_{ji}$.

Suppose now that goods i and j are neutrally want associated with a third good t. By assumption any change in the price of t will induce a change in consumption of goods i and j *proportional* to income responses $\partial x_i/\partial y$ and $\partial x_j/\partial y$. And since income effects $-x_t(\partial x_i/\partial y)$ and $-x_t(\partial x_j/\partial y)$ are in any case proportional to income responses it follows again that substitution effects $\lambda_{it}(\partial x_i/\partial y)(\partial x_t/\partial y)$ and $\lambda_{jt}(\partial x_j/\partial y)(\partial x_t/\partial y)$ must themselves be proportional to income responses. In other words, the consequence of neutral want association between i and j and t is simply that $\lambda_{it} = \lambda_{jt}$. We notice also that by the symmetry already referred to $\lambda_{it} = \lambda_{ti}$, etc.

An important principle emerges. If all goods i in a group r

are in neutral want association with some good t then every cross substitution response involving t can be written

$$\lambda_{rt} (\partial x_i/\partial y)(\partial x_t/\partial y),$$

where λ_{rt} is a single unknown common to the whole group r. In particular if the good t is taken to be any good in a group s all members of which are neutrally want associated with every member of r then all cross substitution responses σ_{it} can be written $\lambda_{rs} (\partial x_i/\partial y)(\partial x_t/\partial y)$, where λ_{rs} is a single unknown common to both groups.

To fix our ideas consider how this works out in the simple six-good case introduced in section 5.1 (Fig. 9). A table of the thirty-six income compensated responses is set up below. In successive cells of row 1 we write the responses of good one to a rise in the prices of goods one, two, three, etc., to six. In row 2 we have the responses of good two to changes in the prices of goods one to six, and so on. So far we know nothing about the values of the responses on the main diagonal (i.e. own price responses), so that these are identified simply by the name of the good. But we do know that off-diagonal elements can be written as some λ multiplied by the product of the income responses corresponding to the row and column number of the cell. To avoid complicating the table unnecessarily the income response products have been left out, leaving us free to concentrate upon the effect of commodity groupings on the various values of λ.

Our first partitioning in 5.1 (Fig. 9) separates cinema and television from all other goods. The assumption that cinema and television are in neutral want association with white bread implies that $\lambda_{51} = \lambda_{61}$ where the subscripts refer to row and column number respectively. Similarly the neutral want association between cinema and television and the remaining three goods implies $\lambda_{52} = \lambda_{62}$, $\lambda_{53} = \lambda_{63}$, and $\lambda_{54} = \lambda_{64}$.

Again neutral want association between the group of four goods, white bread, brown bread, butter, and cheese, and the single good cinema implies $\lambda_{15} = \lambda_{25} = \lambda_{35} = \lambda_{45}$. But $\lambda_{52} = \lambda_{25}$, etc., by the symmetry of substitution responses already noted.

It follows that if we divide Table 5.2.1 into four quadrants by lines between columns 4 and 5 and rows 4 and 5 all λ's in the top right quadrant and the bottom left quadrant are equal. For reasons which will become apparent later this common λ has been written λ (all) in the table.

Proceeding now to the second partitioning we notice that exactly the same principles apply. The top left-hand quadrant is divided by lines between columns 2 and 3 and rows 2 and 3.

TABLE 5.2.1

WHITE BREAD	λ (bread)	λ (food)	λ (food)	λ (all)	λ (all)
λ (bread)	BROWN BREAD	λ (food)	λ (food)	λ (all)	λ (all)
λ (food)	λ (food)	BUTTER	λ (appetizers)	λ (all)	λ (all)
λ (food)	λ (food)	λ (appetizers)	CHEESE	λ (all)	λ (all)
λ (all)	λ (all)	λ (all)	λ (all)	CINEMA	λ (amusements)
λ (all)	λ (all)	λ (all)	λ (all)	λ (amusements)	TELEVISION

The top right-hand and bottom left-hand quadrants of the smaller table are now seen to have common λ's labelled λ (food). λ_{12} and λ_{21} are equal by the symmetry of substitution responses and are accordingly shown as λ (bread). Similarly we have λ (appetizers) and λ (amusements). This system of successive division of tables and subtables is no more than another aspect of the tree-like diagrams of 5.1.

Clearly our assumptions have in this case reduced the number of parameters we are trying to find from thirty-six, plus six income responses, to five λ's, plus six income responses, plus six substitution responses on the diagonal. This is a notable gain. But we can now go further.

From the work of Chapter 1 we know that the sum of any row of substitution responses multiplied by the appropriate price must be zero $\left(\text{i.e. } \sum_j p_j \sigma_{ij} = 0\right)$. It follows that the substitution responses on the diagonal can be deduced at once from a knowledge of those in the off-diagonal cells. Our unknowns are now down to eleven and may be computed as follows.

Consider two goods i and j being in neutral want association with *every* other good. This will be a characteristic of every pair of goods in the smallest basic group, e.g. white bread and brown bread. In any period we observe changes in consumption dx_i and dx_j from consumption in the previous period. We observe also price changes dp_i and dp_j. Let us now introduce two parameters k_i and k_j which are proportional to the $\partial x_i/\partial y$ and $\partial x_j/\partial y$ we are trying to find and write

$$\frac{dx_i}{k_i} - \frac{dx_j}{k_j} = \frac{dp_j}{p_j} - \frac{dp_i}{p_i}. \qquad 5.2\ (i)$$

Clearly we can always choose some k_i and k_j such that equation 5.2 (i) holds for the observed price and quantity changes; for we may vary the factor of proportionality to make it true. But it is a remarkable fact that on our neutral want association assumptions k_i and k_j will be constant whatever the observations.† The common sense of this is clear; for any part of the change dx_i which is due to income or price changes other than dp_i or dp_j must by assumption be proportional to the income response and accordingly to k_i. Similarly with dx_j. Anything, therefore, which is not substitution around an indifference surface, due to changes dp_i and dp_j, cancels itself out on the left-hand side. The equation would hold if dx_i and dx_j were replaced simply by substitution response parameters (which are constants), multiplied by the percentage relative price change

$$\frac{dp_j}{p_j} - \frac{dp_i}{p_i}.$$

This relative price change cancels with the right-hand side leaving only k's and fixed parameters. If k's are by definition proportional to income responses and if equation 5.2 (i) must hold even when dx's and dp's are replaced by fixed parameters, then k's also must be fixed parameters and will remain constant whatever observations are taken. They are in fact dependent

† Cf. Theorem 3, section 5.4.

upon the shape of indifference curves and are closely associated with the values λ_{ij}.

It follows that from two sets of observations yielding equations of type 5.2 (i) we can at once compute k's; for we have two linear equations in two variables $1/k_i$ and $1/k_j$. Alternatively we might increase the number of observations and introduce error terms finding the 'most likely' values of k by the usual methods. In such a case it might be felt that account should be taken of possible changes in k due, say, to changes in consumer preferences. If so we could write

$$dx_i \frac{1}{k_i e^{it}} - dx_j \frac{1}{k_j e^{jt}} = \frac{dp_j}{p_j} - \frac{dp_i}{p_i}, \qquad 5.2 \text{ (ii)}$$

where i and j are the rates of change of k_i and k_j over time and e is the exponential number. Four observations are now sufficient to determine the four unknowns k_i, k_j, i, and j and hence the *ratio* of income responses between goods in the same basic group.† It is emphasized, however, that the discovery of the values of $k_i e^{it}$ does not at once give us the absolute values of income responses. To find absolute values requires much more work as will be shown.

In the meantime we note in passing that observations of type 5.2 (i) and 5.2 (ii) provide us with a convenient and easy empirical test of the validity of the particular neutral want association hypothesis chosen. In short, if the estimates of k obtained show a high level of significance then the neutral want association assumption is not contradicted.‡ Simple partial tests of this kind will help in the formulation of the more complex 'trees' of Fig. 9 and Fig. 10 above.

† The form of function 5.2 (ii) implies, of course, a constant rate of growth (positive or negative) of k. We are not restricted to this, however. An endless variety of approaches are possible on whatever assumptions appear attractive. The introduction of new commodities and the development of a market for them may easily be treated this way.

‡ A particularly simple test, actually used by the writer, can be applied if graphs of the linear equations 5.2 (i) in $1/k_i$ and $1/k_j$ are sketched for, say, five or six time periods. If all lines plotted cut in a single point the hypothesis is justified. If they do not it is contradicted. This type of graph also tests for the presence of multicollinearity. Estimates of k are much less reliable if the plotted lines tend to be parallel. The dating of graphs helps to show whether it is worth testing for a time trend.

The computation of absolute income responses depends upon the possibility of forming and defining composite commodities as in level (2) of Figs. 9 and 10 and repeating the process already described. This can best be understood in terms of the formal example of Fig. 9. Suppose that we have computed values k_w and k_b for white and brown bread respectively. We have to show that, without any index number approximation of any kind, and solely because of the 'marked gap' between these two commodities and all others, we can combine the two into a single composite commodity bread.

First we define a unit of the composite commodity 'bread' as one pound's worth at base year prices. We should now like to be able to say what we mean by a small change in the price of bread, so as to be sure that the response in the consumption of bread to a 1 per cent price change is always the same whatever price changes in white bread and brown bread separately go to make it up. In other words, a 1 per cent price change in bread made up, say, by a 2 per cent price change in white bread and no change in the price of brown should, if the index is satisfactory, have precisely the same effect on the total expenditure on bread as a 1 per cent price change, made up by a 2 per cent price change in brown bread and no change in white.

If no index can be found with this invariance property then there is no point in attempting to compute the elasticity of demand for bread as a whole, for no such elasticity exists. In point of fact it is not difficult to show that, on our assumptions, the only price index which can fulfil our requirement is a weighted arithmetic average of individual prices, the weights being proportional to the partial derivatives of the demand functions, i.e. to the responses of the individual commodities to unit change in individual prices. Clearly if we knew these weights we should know all elasticities and there would be no point in further computing. Moreover, even this index serves only for the direct partial derivatives and not for the cross partials.

On the other hand, in the present context, there does remain a way in which a precise meaning can be given to price changes for a composite commodity. This arises once again out of the fact that price responses can be divided into income and substitution effects. Clearly there is no difficulty about the income response $\partial X/\partial y$ of a composite commodity X; for, as long as quantity is defined as pound's worth at base year prices, $\partial X/\partial y$ is no more than the sum of the individual marginal propensities to consume the goods which form the composite commodity. Moreover, in any given instance, the money compensation part is always the sum of all $x_j \, dp_j$ where x_j is the quantity consumed of the jth (individual) good and dp_j is the amount by which its price has changed. This is simply the sum of money which, if awarded to the consumer in compensation, will always permit him to buy the same as before the price changes occurred. In any given instance, therefore, it is always possible to write down the income effect on any composite commodity of any other composite commodity price change, even though this income effect might not always be the same for the same percentage composite price change, as reflected by the chosen index. In short it would be sufficient if an index could be defined so that the substitution response only has the property of invariance necessary to give meaning to the parameter.

In fact it can be shown that if a price change in a composite commodity is defined to be a weighted arithmetic average of the price changes in the individual commodities which make it up, *weights being proportional to individual commodity income responses*, and if all goods forming the composite commodity are in neutral want association with all others, then a substitution response for the composite commodity does exist and possesses the necessary properties of invariance. Even more important, it can be shown that composite substitution responses have precisely analogous properties to those already noted for the individual commodities, and they can be written in terms of the λ's of Table 5.2.1 without modification.

We postpone a rigorous proof of this last proposition until we come to section 5.4 (p. 219) but there is nothing about it which will appear intuitively implausible to the reader. In fact we are saying no more than that, with composite commodity prices defined as weighted arithmetic averages of the prices of their components (weights proportional to marginal propensities to consume), the response in consumption of a composite commodity, say r, due to a compensated price change in the composite commodity, s, may be written as

$$\lambda_{rs} \frac{\partial X_r}{\partial y} \frac{\partial X_s}{\partial y},$$

where $\partial X_r / \partial y$, etc., is the income response and where λ_{rs} is the *same* λ_{rs} which appears in the responses of the individual components of the groups r and s.

Again to fix our ideas consider the following Table 5.2.2.

TABLE 5.2.2

BREAD	λ (food)	λ (all)
λ (food)	APPETIZERS	λ (all)
λ (all)	λ (all)	AMUSEMENTS

By forming the composite commodities, food, appetizers, and amusements the 6×6 Table 5.2.1 has been collapsed into a 3×3 Table 5.2.2. Table 5.2.2 has all the properties of Table 5.2.1; λ (bread), λ (appetizers), and λ (amusements) have disappeared but the remaining λ's take the same values as those of Table 5.2.1. Moreover, we notice that the λ (all) of row 1 column 3 is the same as the λ (all) of row 2 column 3. This tells us that the composite commodities bread and appetizers are in neutral want association with amusements so that equation 5.2 (i) is immediately applicable. Given a suitable price index we can compute a k (bread) and a k (appetizers) by the methods already discussed at level (1). As before, the new k's will be proportional to the income responses for the composite goods.

We now understand the crucial importance of first knowing the values of the k's for white and brown bread computed at level (1); for these are proportional to income responses and accordingly serve as the theoretically correct weights required to form the price index for bread at level (2). All that we need to know to form composite commodities is given, once all k's at level (1) have been found.

Similarly a knowledge of k (bread) and k (appetizers) computed at level (2) provides us with the weights necessary to form a composite commodity food. Accordingly we have a still further reduced Table 5.2.3 below, with two goods and only one λ, namely λ (all).

TABLE 5.2.3

FOOD	λ (all)
λ (all)	AMUSEMENTS

As before, we may now apply the basic equation 5.2 (i) which clearly always holds in a two-good economy. A k (food) and a k (amusements) can be found which are by definition proportional to the marginal propensity to consume food and the marginal propensity to consume amusements.

We are now in a position to determine absolute income responses for the final two composite goods; for we know their ratio and we know that they must sum to unity. (The reader is reminded that our responses are by definition responses to changes in consumption and not to changes in income, and that prices are unity.) This is the key to further work.

Although it will not be proved rigorously until we come to section 5.4 (Theorem 3) it will appear intuitively obvious by the argument of p. 195 above, that k (food) and k (amusements) are closely related to the λ (all) which measures the curvature of the indifference surface between them. In fact it will be shown that

$$k\,(\text{food})\bigg/\frac{\partial X}{\partial y}\,(\text{food}) = \lambda\,(\text{all})$$

$$= k\,(\text{amusements})\bigg/\frac{\partial X}{\partial y}\,(\text{amusements}). \quad 5.2\ (\text{iii})$$

When $\partial X/\partial y$ is known λ (all) is determined.

We now work back down through the various levels as follows. k (bread) and k (appetizers) are known and these are in the ratio of the marginal propensities to consume bread and appetizers. But we now know the absolute value of the marginal propensity to consume food as a whole, which is in turn the sum of the marginal propensities to consume bread and appetizers. The three absolute marginal propensities at level (2) can therefore be found. These results make it possible to compute λ (food) as follows.

Analogous to equation 5.2 (iii) we have the following:

$$k\,(\text{bread})\Big/\frac{\partial X}{\partial y}(\text{bread}) = C\,(\text{food})\,\lambda\,(\text{food}) + C\,(\text{amusements})\,\lambda\,(\text{all})$$

$$= k\,(\text{appetizers})\Big/\frac{\partial X}{\partial y}(\text{appetizers}) \quad 5.2\ (\text{iv})$$

where C is the marginal propensity to consume the good whose name follows in parentheses.†

The rule for forming these equations is a simple one. Replacing the λ (all) of equation 5.2 (iii) above we have (in the case of the more extended Table 5.2.2) a weighted average of all λ's appearing in the column of the table in which the good appears whose k is under consideration. Comparison of the equation above with Table 5.2.2 will make the rule clear. The weights are the marginal propensities to consume the composite good made up of elements with a common λ.

Alternatively our rule may be stated in terms of the tree diagram (Fig. 9, section 5.1). In this case we say

$$k_i\Big/\frac{\partial X_i}{\partial y} = \sum_s C_s \lambda_{rs},$$

where s is summed over all composite goods added at each junction when passing along the direct route on the tree (Fig. 9) from good i to the root (all wants) beginning with the first junction after the ith good. C_s is the marginal propensity to consume the composite good added at each junction. r identifies the group of the ith good.

All elements of the equation 5.2 (iv) are known except λ (food) which can therefore be determined.

We are now free to proceed to the next level. Again the known k (white bread) and k (brown bread), together with the new found marginal propensity to consume all bread, yield the absolute marginal propensities to consume white and brown bread.

† Cf. section 5.4, Theorem 3—compare with 5.2 (i).

λ (bread) can at once be computed from

$$k \text{ (white bread)} \bigg/ \frac{\partial X}{\partial y} \text{ (white bread)}$$

$$= C \text{ (bread)} \lambda \text{ (bread)} + C \text{ (appetizers)} \lambda \text{ (food)} +$$
$$+ C \text{ (amusements)} \lambda \text{ (all)}.$$

Similarly all elements of the original Table 5.2.1 can be found. In fact we have all income and substitution responses so that if desired a table of elasticities and cross elasticities of demand can be constructed.

5.3. The utility approach to neutral want association

The two previous sections represent an attempt to set out in the simplest way, without breaking into the intuitive argument with rigorous proofs, an explanation of the consequences of a powerful and plausible conjecture regarding the form of the utility function. It is now time to look again at the utility function to discover precisely what the restriction is. In order to do this we restate the want neutrality conditions as a condition on the utility function, and, at the cost of some slight repetition, show that this leads again to the results of sections 5.1 and 5.2. Or rather, we shall show that the hypotheses of Figs. 9 and 10 are special cases of an even more general set of possibilities.

Consider again the six goods of Fig. 9, butter and cheese, two kinds of bread, A and B, and two kinds of entertainment, cinema and television. We have already remarked in section 5.1 that these six goods exhibit, in all probability, a wide range of degrees of substitutability. We now look more closely at this, recalling that, in Chapter 4, it was suggested that a group of commodities might be formed by including within it all those goods with the same degree of substitutability, both with all goods outside the group *taken as a whole* and with each of its companion goods within the group.

Intuitively we should expect bread A and bread B to be very close substitutes, and butter and cheese to be substitutable, but less so than the two kinds of bread. The groups food and entertainment would be much less substitutable again. On the other hand, it might well be that an increase in the amount of either kind of entertainment enjoyed by any individual would not affect the marginal rate of substitution, i.e. the equilibrium price ratio, u_i/u_j, between butter and cheese. Similarly an increase in entertainment might not affect the marginal rate of substitution between bread A and bread B. Again a small increase in the quantity of either butter or cheese might not affect the marginal rate of substitution between the two kinds of bread or the two kinds of entertainment. But notice that it would not leave unchanged the willingness to substitute bread for entertainment. Nor would an increase in the quantity of, say, bread A, leave unchanged the willingness to exchange bread B for cheese or butter.

In other words, the six goods might be divided into three groups as under:

(i) Butter and cheese.
(ii) Bread A and bread B.
(iii) Cinema and television.

The relative marginal utilities of goods in group (i) are not affected by small changes in the quantities enjoyed of any good in groups (ii) or (iii). Similarly the relative marginal utilities of goods in group (ii) are not affected by small changes in the quantities enjoyed of goods in groups (i) and (iii), and so on. In other words, the first condition for the existence of a basic group such as (i), (ii), or (iii) is that any pair of goods taken from it must be in neutral want association† (cf. section 4.4) with all goods outside the group. Or, intuitively, every good in the group must have the same degree of substitutability with goods outside the group, taken as a whole. Notice that pairs of goods taken from different groups are *not* necessarily in neutral want association with any other good.

Groups may contain any number of goods or even a single good. But if the number exceeds two then we require as a second

---

† We have reverted here, as is clear from the verbal explanation, to the utility definition of neutral want association. The term 'neutral want association' was finally decided upon after reading a paper by Professor R. Frisch— 'A Complete Scheme for Computing Elasticities', *Econometrica*, April 1959— where the expression 'want independence' is used to signify true independence, i.e. $u_{ij} = 0$. We shall refer at length to this paper later.

condition that all goods within the group should be in neutral want association with all other goods within the same group. If, for example, group (i) consisted of three different kinds of butter with different trade names, it might be that the ratio of marginal utilities of any two kinds would be unaffected by changes in the quantity consumed of the third. In this case the three kinds of butter are neutrally want associated and may be included within the same group. This may also be interpreted as meaning that all goods within a group have the same degree of substitutability one with another.

It should be noticed that the necessity of neutral want association *within* the group is in no way a restriction; for if this property does not hold the group may be further subdivided until two goods only are left. In this case the required condition must be met. Conceivably, of course, it could prove impossible to find a companion for *any* good so that we end up with as many groups as there are commodities. But both intuition and the writer's experiments so far suggest that this is unlikely.

We note also that for companion goods to exist it is necessary that they should be distinguishable one from the other in the mind of the consumer. It should not be thought that we can always find a companion good for, say, cheese, simply by defining as separate goods two otherwise identical cheeses produced by different producers. In other words, goods with infinite substitution elasticities the prices of which cannot vary independently are necessarily the same good.

It is now easy to show that the existence of basic groups, say, r, s, t, implies that the utility function, u, can be written, not only as a function of quantities consumed, x_i, but alternatively as a function of functions ϕ_r, ϕ_s, and ϕ_t of the quantities consumed in groups r, s, and t respectively; i.e. u can be written

$$u = u(\phi_r, \phi_s, \phi_t).\qquad\qquad 5.3\text{ (i)}$$

In fact, if goods i, j, k, etc., form a group, r, then, by the definition of want neutrality

$$\partial(u_i/u_j)/\partial x_p = 0 \quad (i, j \text{ in } r; p \text{ not in } r)$$

or $\qquad u_i/u_j = h(x_i, x_j, x_k, \text{etc.}) \quad (i, j, k \text{ in } r).$

It follows that u_i and u_j may be written as the product of two functions
$$u_i = g[\phi_{ri}(x_i, x_j, x_k, \text{etc.})]$$
and
$$u_j = g[\phi_{rj}(x_i, x_j, x_k, \text{etc.})], \qquad \text{5.3 (ii)}$$
where g is a function of all commodities, the same for all u_i, u_j, u_k, etc., i, j, k, in r.

If the functions u_i meet the integrability conditions,† as they must by assumption, so that

$$\sum_i u_i \, dx_i = du \quad \text{(when only } x_i \text{ in } r \text{ have changed)}$$

then it follows from 5.3 (ii), by straightforward test, that the functions ϕ_{ri} also meet the integrability conditions and

$$g \sum_i \phi_{ri} \, dx_i = g \, d\phi_r = du$$

so that $g = du/d\phi_r$ where ϕ_r is the function implied by the functions ϕ_{ri}, ϕ_{rj}, etc.

Clearly u can be written

$$u = u(\phi_r, x_p, x_q) \quad (p, q, \text{etc., not in } r).$$

Considering now the groups s and t in turn, we easily obtain by similar methods the result 5.3 (i).

This property of the utility function has been given the name 'separability'.‡

Consider now the reduced utility functions 5.3 (i). By analogy we might hope to find a property which takes the same mathematical form as want neutrality, between the ϕ_r. In other words, we might hope to find in some cases that

$$\frac{\partial(u_r/u_s)}{\partial \phi_t} = 0, \qquad \text{5.3 (iii)}$$

where u_r is $\partial u/\partial \phi_r$. It is not hard to show that 5.3 (iii) does in fact hold whenever there is want neutrality between any pair of goods taken one each from groups r and s, and any good from group t. That is, whenever

$$\frac{\partial(u_i/u_p)}{\partial x_q} = 0 \quad (i \text{ in } r, p \text{ in } s, q \text{ in } t). \qquad \text{5.3 (iv)}$$

† Cf. Chapter 3 and R. G. D. Allen, *Mathematical Analysis for Economists*, p. 421.
‡ Cf. R. H. Strotz, loc. cit. See above p. 188, n.†.

This is proved very simply by writing u_i/u_p in the form

$$u_r \phi_i / u_s \phi_p,$$

where u_r is $\partial u/\partial \phi_r$, etc. Differentiating with respect to x_q and equating with zero as in 5.3 (iv) yields

$$\frac{u_{rt}}{u_r u_t} = \frac{u_{st}}{u_s u_t}, \qquad \text{5.3 (v)}$$

where u_{rt} is $\partial^2 u/\partial \phi_r \, \partial \phi_t$. 5.3 (v) is clearly equivalent to the want neutrality condition 5.3 (iii).

If 5.3 (v) holds, it is evident, not only that we can write the utility function as in 5.3 (i), but also that there is a higher level of separability so that

$$u = u(\phi_r, \phi_s, \phi_t)$$

takes the form $\qquad u = u(\psi_m, \psi_n),$

where $\qquad \qquad \psi_m = \psi_m(\phi_r, \phi_s)$

and $\qquad \qquad \psi_n = \phi_t.$

We notice that on the assumptions upon which we set up the six-good example in section 5.1 this higher level of want neutrality holds. For we supposed, in effect, that bread and cheese are neutrally want associated with cinema. We can in fact construct a utility function as demonstrated, Fig. 11.

A full expression for the utility function for the six goods of Fig. 11 on the assumptions of section 5.1 would be

$$u = u[\psi_1(\phi_1[x_1, x_2], \phi_2[x_3, x_4]), \psi_2(x_5, x_6)]. \qquad \text{5.3 (vi)}$$

We are now in a position to clear up finally any doubts the reader might still have regarding the need to distinguish carefully between independence proper and want neutrality. First we note that there is no trace of additivity whatever left in the function 5.3 (vi), despite the fact that all the computational advantages remain. It is also true that the function 5.3 (vi) is a great deal more general than it would be if the form of ϕ_r were

$$\phi_r = \phi_r[f_i(x_i) + f_j(x_j)]$$

and if u were simply $\psi_1 + \psi_2$.

Secondly, we may put the matter more directly. It is easy to see why, even when there are no more than two basic groups, there is a crucial sense in which actual behaviour is not the same under the two assumptions.

Consider the case where we have two basic groups A and B

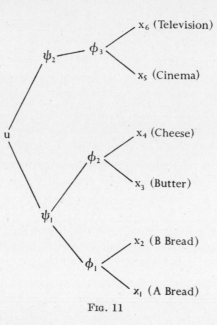

FIG. 11

defined as above. Want neutrality implies (cf. section 4.4) that

$$\frac{u_{ik}}{u_i u_k} = \frac{u_{jk}}{u_j u_k} \quad \text{(for all } i, j \text{ in group } A, k \neq i, j)$$

and $\quad \dfrac{u_{rk}}{u_r u_k} = \dfrac{u_{sk}}{u_s u_k} \quad$ (for all r, s in group $B, k \neq r, s$).

Suppose now that we have chosen the utility indicator, u, so that u_{ik} is zero. Then it follows that u_{rk} cannot possibly be zero. For if it were so we should have neutral want association also between goods i and r and good k where i and r are by definition in different groups. This contradicts the assumption that two distinct groups exist.

To put the matter the other way round, if we give expression to the assumption that two basic groups exist by putting $u_{ik} = 0$ and $u_{rk} = 0$, then we are surely imposing a further restriction upon the behaviour over and above that originally intended. The two groups become one.

Having said all this it must now be explained that, when there are three or more goods in a group, the condition that there should be want neutrality (the same degree of substitutability) within the group does impose additivity on the 'sub' function, ϕ_i. There is no need to prove this in full here, since it follows from the work of section 4.4. But the reader will see at once that, if

$$\frac{\phi_{ij}}{\phi_i \phi_j} = \frac{\phi_{ik}}{\phi_i \phi_k} = \frac{\phi_{jk}}{\phi_j \phi_k} = \rho,$$

which is the condition for want neutrality within a group i, j, k, then we know from section 4.4 that ρ is a function of ϕ alone.

As before we can choose some $F(\phi)$ such that

$$F''\phi_i \phi_j + F'\phi_{ij} = F_{ij} = 0 \quad \text{(for all } i, j, k \text{ in the group)},$$

where $F' = \partial F/\partial \phi$ and $F'' = \partial^2 F/\partial \phi^2$. Hence

$$F = f_i(x_i) + f_j(x_j) + f_k(x_k), \text{ etc.,}$$

which means, since $\phi = \phi(F)$, that ϕ can be written

$$\phi = \phi\{f_i(x_i) + f_j(x_j) + f_k(x_k), \text{ etc.}\}.$$

To understand fully the significance of this let us suppose that there are three kinds of bread instead of two in the example, Fig. 9, and three kinds of food. Appropriate want neutrality assumptions might then require that the new utility function corresponding to 5.3 (vi) should, by the argument above, be written

$$u = u[\psi_1\{\phi_1[f_1(x_1) + f_2(x_2) + f_3(x_3)] +$$
$$+ \phi_2[x_4, x_5] + \phi_3[x_6, x_7]\}, \psi_2(x_8, x_9)].$$

By an appropriate choice of utility index we could select u so that u_{ij} is zero for all i between 1 and 7 and $j = 8$ or 9. But we cannot make $u_{12} = 0$ by any choice of index, despite the want neutrality between goods 1, 2, and 3, and so on.

We have made much of the distinction between want neutrality and want independence largely because econometricians who have tried to make use of this kind of property have ordinarily done so in the 'independence' form. They have accordingly attracted a good deal of criticism which may very well be misplaced.

It is true, as critics have argued, that independence is a property which is not invariant under a general monotonic transformation of the utility function. On the other hand, want neutrality is invariant and is a condition equally useful from an econometric point of view. Again it is true that the independence assumption imposes a serious restriction on actual behaviour. In the extreme case where all utilities are independent the preference field has to be a so-called 'Gossen' map.† The answer to such criticism is, of course, that a restriction on behaviour which fits the facts is precisely what we are looking for. On the other hand, it has to be conceded that, except for very wide classes of goods, it would be rather surprising if a Gossen map did fit the facts. The virtue of the want neutrality approach, as must be evident from the work above, is that it offers all the computational advantages of the Gossen map whilst admitting a much wider range of possibilities, not Gossen maps, to investigate. The Gossen map is one restriction which has been tested, at least intuitively, and been found wanting. The work of this chapter shows how we might construct a vast number of other preference patterns to test in the hope that we shall eventually find one which is a close approximation to actual behaviour.

At this point, for completeness, it seems desirable to refer to the work of Professor R. Frisch.‡ Professor Frisch recognizes that cardinal utility is implied by want independence§ but argues, rightly, that it remains an hypothesis worth testing. Indeed he goes further and uses the independence property to determine a parameter which he calls 'money flexibility' and

† Cf. H. Wold and L. Juréen, *Demand Analysis*, pp. 60–62, and example 17, p. 142.

‡ 'A Complete Scheme for Computing Elasticities', *Econometrica*, vol. 27, no. 2, April 1959.

§ Professor Frisch's definition is expressed in terms of the inverse functions $x_i(u_1,..., u_n)$ but amounts to the ordinary definition in view of his relationship (28), loc. cit., footnote 11.

which in our notation would be written

$$\mu = \frac{\partial \lambda}{\partial y}\bigg/ \lambda,$$

where λ is the marginal utility of money.

In a general way μ is, of course, dependent on the choice of utility index. If we put all u_{ij} zero, however, for $i \neq j$, and solve for $\partial\lambda/\partial y$ from the equations like 1.4 (xiii), obtained by differentiating equilibrium equations by y instead of p_j, then it is not hard to show that μ is the reciprocal of the λ_{ij} of section 4.4 (p. 180). And we have already shown that this is observable and is the same for all goods where independent utilities are universal.

The relationship between μ, which is a measure of utility, and λ_{ij} which is not, disappears, however, as soon as we have more than one group; and in fact it disappears even in the case of one group if we substitute want neutrality for independence. As we have already suggested, our λ_{ij} is very little more than a measure of the general degree of substitutability, i.e. the curvature of indifference hypersurfaces. Professor Frisch, on the other hand, claims to be measuring something related to intensity of satisfaction. He has suggested that μ or, more strictly, $y\mu$, might be regarded as a parameter likely to remain fairly constant over time for given levels of real income. He proposes in fact that 'maps' of values should be prepared. Unfortunately it is harder to find a priori arguments to support the belief that our y/λ_{ij} will remain constant for very different sets of relative prices than is the case with $y\mu$, even when there is no more than one group. 'Maps' of values can only be of temporary significance.

This discussion leads us at once to an important point of principle. The assumption that any one of our parameters remains constant over a wide range of observations constitutes a restriction on the form of demand equations. On the other hand, as long as we can complete all of our calculations from as few as three or four observations of the data, involving only relatively small changes in prices and income, very little error is introduced, whatever the form of demand functions, by the assumption that every parameter remains constant over the range of observations. Parameters once computed must not be supposed to remain constant over time. They must be recomputed with the latest data so that their trend can be observed. The advantage of our present theory is that this procedure is now brought within the bounds of possibility.

To conclude our discussion of the utility view of want neutrality we appeal once more to intuition and point out what we really mean by neutral want association between goods i and j and good k is that there is no utility relation between two goods i and k different in any special way from the utility relation between goods j and k. But we must not say there is no relation. Intuition suggests that normally an increase in the consumption of any good increases welfare and hence diminishes the marginal utility of all goods in general. On the other hand, good j is affected in much the same proportion as the marginal utility of good i by any change in k. One pennyworth of i and one pennyworth of j both give less utility following a change in k but the utility of both pennyworths remains equal.

Similarly, if i, j, and k were highly complementary goods, it might be that the marginal utilities of i and j would be increased by an increased consumption of k despite the increase in general welfare. Even so neutral want association is still present if the increase in marginal utility is proportional.

We now revert to the simple notion of basic groups as defined above in utility terms. In the next section we consider the empirical implication of the existence of such groups at a slightly more general level than in sections 5.1 and 5.2.

5.4. The most general want neutrality theorems

As a first step we invite the reader to write out in full the now familiar Hessian determinant Δ of the utility function u for the six goods of section 5.1, bordered in the usual way by marginal utilities u_i. For convenience number the goods (butter, cheese), (bread A, bread B), (cinema and television) 1 to 6 in the order given. The goods bracketed form three basic groups number 1,

2, and 3. Assuming now that neutral want association properties hold between goods as conjectured in section 5.3, we can evidently write the off-diagonal elements u_{ik} as $\alpha_{rs} u_i u_k$, where r is the number of the group containing good i, and s is the number of the group containing good k. Also, from the fact that $u_{ik} = u_{ki}$ we have $\alpha_{rs} = \alpha_{sr}$.

The next step is to show that the bordered adjugate determinant can be written in precisely the same form. This follows at once from Jacobi's theorem on the minors of the adjugate which states that any minor of order n in the bordered adj Δ is equal to Δ^{n-1} multiplied by the complementary minor in Δ (if Δ is symmetric);† for the complementary minor in Δ to every minor of order two, containing two of the column bordering elements in the same commodity group, together with appropriate elements in any column belonging to a *different* commodity group, must be zero. To prove this it is convenient to divide such a complementary minor according to basic commodity groups and expand by a Laplacian expansion.‡ It will then be observed that, because of neutral want association, at least one of the determinants in every term of the expansion will contain at least two proportionate rows or columns.

Hence, temporarily writing σ_{ij} for the general element of the bordered adjoint multiplied by the marginal utility of money, and σ_i for the bordering elements, we have the general conclusion that

$$\begin{vmatrix} \sigma_i & \sigma_{ik} \\ \sigma_j & \sigma_{jk} \end{vmatrix} = 0 \quad \text{(for all } ij \text{ belonging to a different group from } k).$$

Thus, corresponding to the utility condition, we are free to write

$$\sigma_{ik} = \lambda_{rs} \sigma_i \sigma_k \quad \text{(where } r, s \text{ are the group numbers of } i \text{ and } k\text{).}$$
$$\scriptstyle i \neq k$$

We notice also in passing that, if the number of commodities within the group exceeds two, and if such commodities i, j, m are in neutral want association with one another, then by the

† Cf. A. C. Aitken, *Determinants and Matrices*, p. 98.
‡ Cf. A. C. Aitken, loc. cit., footnote 5 (13), p. 78. Compare chap. 4, section 4.4, p. 179.

argument above

$$\sigma_{ij} = \lambda_{tt} \sigma_i \sigma_j \quad \text{(for all } i, j, m \text{ in group } t\text{)}.$$
$$\tiny{i \neq j}$$

If we have only two commodities in each group parameters can always be introduced so that

$$\sigma_{12} = \lambda_{11} \sigma_1 \sigma_2, \quad \sigma_{34} = \lambda_{22} \sigma_3 \sigma_4, \quad \text{and} \quad \sigma_{56} = \lambda_{33} \sigma_5 \sigma_6.$$

But we know from section 1.4 that the elements σ_{ij} of the adjoint determinant divided by the bordered Hessian determinant, Δ, and multiplied by the marginal utility of money are in fact income-compensated partial derivatives with respect to price of the demand functions

$$x_i = x_i(p_1, ..., p_n y) \quad (i = 1, ..., n).$$

Moreover the bordering elements, σ_i, divided by Δ, are the partial derivatives of these functions with respect to y. And clearly the conditions on σ_{ij} hold whether or not we divide throughout by Δ. For convenience, therefore, we revert to our familiar notation, reading σ_{ij} as the σ_{ij} above divided by Δ multiplied by the marginal utility of money.

We have now proved:

THEOREM 1. *If commodities are divided into basic groups such that every possible pair of commodities which can be made up from within any group have the property of neutral want association with every other good, then all income-compensated cross partial derivatives of demand functions are proportional to income partial derivatives, the factor of proportionality being the same for all goods within the group.*

That is
$$\sigma_{ik} = \lambda_{rs} \frac{\partial x_i}{\partial y} \frac{\partial x_k}{\partial y}$$
5.4 (i)

(where r and s are the groups of i and k). Moreover, since

$$\sigma_{ik} = \sigma_{ki}$$

we have
$$\lambda_{rs} = \lambda_{sr}.$$

Using now
$$\sum_k p_k \sigma_{ik} = 0,$$

which is 1.4 (x), we obtain a similar expression for the direct substitution effects

$$\sigma_{ii} = -\frac{1}{p_i}\Big(\sum_s \lambda_{rs} \sum_{\left[\substack{k \text{ in } s \\ k \neq i}\right]} p_k \frac{\partial x_k}{\partial y} \Big)\frac{\partial x_i}{\partial y}. \qquad 5.4 \text{ (ii)}$$

From 5.4 (i) and 5.4 (ii) we may now write down

THEOREM 2. *On the assumptions of Theorem 1 all demand functions can be written in terms of n partial derivatives with respect to income and $\frac{1}{2}g(g+1)$ parameters λ_{rs} where n is the number of commodities and g is the number of groups.*

That is, we have

$$\frac{\partial x_i}{\partial p_i} = -x_i\frac{\partial x_i}{\partial y} - \frac{1}{p_i}\Big\{ \sum_s \lambda_{rs}\Big(\sum_{\left[\substack{k \text{ in } s \\ k \neq i}\right]} p_k \frac{\partial x_k}{\partial y} \Big)\Big\}\frac{\partial x_i}{\partial y} \qquad 5.4 \text{ (iii)}$$

and

$$\frac{\partial x_i}{\partial p_k} = -x_k\frac{\partial x_i}{\partial y} + \lambda_{rs}\frac{\partial x_i}{\partial y}\frac{\partial x_k}{\partial y}. \qquad 5.4 \text{ (iv)}$$

In the special case where there is one basic group only, that is, when all goods are in neutral want association with all others, 5.4 (iii) and 5.4 (iv) reduce to

$$\frac{\partial x_i}{\partial p_i} = -x_i\frac{\partial x_i}{\partial y} - \frac{\lambda}{p_i}\frac{\partial x_i}{\partial y}\Big(1 - p_i\frac{\partial x_i}{\partial y}\Big) \qquad 5.4 \text{ (v)}$$

and

$$\frac{\partial x_i}{\partial p_k} = -x_k\frac{\partial x_i}{\partial y} + \lambda\frac{\partial x_i}{\partial y}\frac{\partial x_k}{\partial y} \qquad 5.4 \text{ (vi)}$$

as in section 4.4.

So far we have not achieved very much. By grouping we have simply reduced the number of parameters to be determined from an unmanageable $\frac{1}{2}(n^2+3n)$ to a lesser but still probably unmanageable $\frac{1}{2}g(g+1)+n$, where g is the number of groups. Were it not for further remarkable possibilities foreshadowed in section 5.2 we should be very little further forward. We proceed therefore to state and prove:

THEOREM 3. *Under the conditions of Theorem 1, for any pair of goods i, j, within any basic group r we have*

$$\frac{dx_i}{\Big(\sum_s C_s\lambda_{rs}\Big)(\partial x_i/\partial y)} - \frac{dx_j}{\Big(\sum_s C_s\lambda_{rs}\Big)(\partial x_j/\partial y)} = dp_j/p_j - dp_i/p_i,$$

$$5.4 \text{ (vii)}$$

where dp, dx are observed price and quantity changes and C_s is $\sum p_k (\partial x_k/\partial y)$ for all k within the group s.

This result is obtained as follows:

$$dx_i = \sum_k \frac{\partial x_i}{\partial p_k} dp_k + \frac{\partial x_i}{\partial y} dy$$

or, using 5.4 (iii) and 5.4 (iv),

$$dx_i = -\frac{\partial x_i}{\partial y} \sum_k x_k\, dp_k + \left(\sum_s \lambda_{rs} \sum_{\left[\substack{k\ \text{in}\ s \\ k\neq i\ \text{in}\ s=r}\right]} \frac{\partial x_k}{\partial y} dp_k \right)\frac{\partial x_i}{\partial y} -$$

$$-\frac{1}{p_i}\left(\sum_s \lambda_{rs} \sum_{\left[\substack{k\ \text{in}\ s \\ k\neq i\ \text{in}\ s=r}\right]} p_k \frac{\partial x_k}{\partial y}\right)\frac{\partial x_i}{\partial y} dp_i + \frac{\partial x_i}{\partial y} dy$$

or, adding $\lambda_{rr} (\partial x_i/\partial y)^2 dp_i$ to term two and subtracting

$$\lambda_{rr} (\partial x_i/\partial y)^2 dp_i$$

from term three,

$$\frac{dx_i}{\partial x_i/\partial y} = -\sum_k x_k\, dp_k + \sum_s \lambda_{rs}\frac{\partial x_k}{\partial y} dp_k - \frac{dp_i}{p_i}\sum_s \lambda_{rs} C_s + dy.$$

$$5.4 \text{ (viii)}$$

Evidently a similar expression for $dx_j/(\partial x_j/\partial y)$ would have terms one, two, and four in common with 5.4 (viii) as long as j is in group r. Theorem 3 follows immediately.

The relationship 5.4 (vii) is a powerful one. In the first place it provides us with a simple test which can be applied, as explained in section 5.2, to determine whether in fact any two commodities are in neutral want association with all others; for thinking of 5.4 (vii) as a linear equation in two variables†

$$1\Big/\left[\left(\sum_s \lambda_{rs} C_s \right)(\partial x_i/\partial y)\right]$$

and

$$1\Big/\left[\left(\sum_s \lambda_{rs} C_s \right)(\partial x_j/\partial y)\right]$$

we may plot observations on a graph. Four successive observations of price/quantity data yield three equations which must be consistent with some unique value of the variables. If they are consistent the hypothesis of neutral want association is

† The reader will recognize these as the $1/k$ of section 5.2.

not contradicted. A group may be formed by testing for neutrality any pair. Once a pair is found any further good neutral with both members of the original pair can be added to the group and so on.

We now define $\qquad y_r = \sum_{i \text{ in } r} p_i x_i$

(y_r is total expenditure on group r goods), so that we have

$$\sum_{i \text{ in } r} p_i \frac{\partial x_i}{\partial y_r} = 1 \qquad\qquad 5.4 \text{ (ix)}$$

and $\qquad \dfrac{\partial x_i}{\partial y} = \dfrac{\partial x_i}{\partial y_r}\dfrac{\partial y_r}{\partial y} = \dfrac{\partial x_i}{\partial y_r} C_r$ (all prices constant).

Thus $\qquad \dfrac{\partial x_i}{\partial y} \bigg/ \dfrac{\partial x_j}{\partial y} = \dfrac{\partial x_i}{\partial y_r}\bigg/\dfrac{\partial x_j}{\partial y_r}$ (i, j in r).

Clearly also, if r is the number of goods in group r we can obtain, from at most three observations of the data, $r-1$ independent equations of the form

$$\frac{\partial x_i}{\partial y_r}\bigg/\frac{\partial x_j}{\partial y_r} = A_{ij} \quad (j \text{ in } r,\ j \neq i), \qquad 5.4 \text{ (x)}$$

where A_{ij} is the ratio of the solutions to equations 5.4 (vii). Solving the $r-1$ equations 5.4 (x) together with 5.4 (ix) yields values for $\partial x_i/\partial y_r$ and hence all $\sum_s \lambda_{rs} C_s C_r$ $(r = 1, 2, ..., g)$. A new theorem enables us to carry the work further.

THEOREM 4. *When a group of goods are in neutral want association with reference to all goods outside the group the partial derivatives of the demand equation for any good within the group may be written as under*

$$\frac{\partial x_i}{\partial p_i} = -x_i \frac{\partial x_i}{\partial y_r} + \sigma_{ii}^r + \frac{\partial x_i}{\partial y_r}\frac{dy_r}{dp_i} \qquad 5.4 \text{ (xi)}$$

and $\qquad \dfrac{\partial x_i}{\partial p_j} = -x_j \dfrac{\partial x_i}{\partial y_r} + \sigma_{ij}^r + \dfrac{\partial x_i}{\partial y_r}\dfrac{dy_r}{dp_j},$ 5.4 (xii)

where σ^r measures substitution into goods within group r only.

Theorem 4 does not require formal proof,† for the essence of

† 5.4 (xii) should be compared with 2.2 (xiv) recalling that

$$\left(\frac{1}{1-h}\right)\frac{\partial x_i}{\partial y} = \frac{\partial x_i}{\partial C} \quad \text{and} \quad \frac{\partial s}{\partial p_i} = -\frac{\partial C}{\partial p_i}.$$

the neutral want association assumption is that the *shape* of indifference hypersurfaces between goods within a group is not affected by changes in the quantities consumed of goods outside the group. In the simple three-good case, say goods i, j, k, for example, a section through the individual's indifference surfaces representing a given quantity of good k yields a two-dimensional set of indifference curves between goods j and i. Neutral want association means that wherever the section is taken (i.e. whatever the given value of k) the ji indifference curves will look the same even though the utility attached to each curve may change.

Thus, given y_r, all the usual demand theorems apply as if goods outside the group did not exist. These yield the first two terms of 5.4 (xi) and 5.4 (xii). The third term arises because we must now take into account the income effect due to the change in total consumption on goods within the group as a whole.

Moreover, as our group is chosen so that all goods within the group are in neutral want association with one another we may also apply Theorem 2 and write

$$\frac{\partial x_i}{\partial p_i} = -x_i\frac{\partial x_i}{\partial y_r} - \frac{\lambda}{p_i}\frac{\partial x_i}{\partial y_r}\left(1 - p_i\frac{\partial x_i}{\partial y_r}\right) + \frac{\partial x_i}{\partial y_r}\frac{dy_r}{dp_i} \quad \text{5.4 (xiii)}$$

and $$\frac{\partial x_i}{\partial p_j} = -x_j\frac{\partial x_i}{\partial y_r} + \lambda\frac{\partial x_i}{\partial y_r}\frac{\partial x_j}{\partial y_r} + \frac{\partial x_i}{\partial y_r}\frac{dy_r}{dp_j} \quad (j \text{ in } r,\ i \neq j).$$

$$\text{5.4 (xiv)}$$

By following the procedure of Theorem 3 we obtain from 5.4 (xiii) and (xiv) an alternative version of 5.4 (viii), namely

$$dx_i = \frac{\partial x_i}{\partial y_r}\left(dy_r - \sum_{(j \text{ in } r)} x_j\, dp_j + \lambda \sum_{(j \text{ in } r)} \frac{\partial x_j}{\partial y_r}\, dp_j - \frac{\lambda}{p_i}\, dp_i\right).$$

$$\text{5.4 (xv)}$$

Moreover, a comparison of 5.4 (vii) with its analogue derived from 5.4 (xv) makes it clear that the λ of 5.4 (xv) must be the $C_r \sum_s \lambda_{rs} C_s$ which has already been computed.

Evidently the observation of three sets of data for any one group has enabled us to estimate all of the parameters of 5.4 (xv). Given price changes and the change in money spending on the group as a whole we can now predict the allocation among the various goods. Already we have valuable information.

The reader interested in problems of oligopoly will also have noticed that the definition of a basic group might well turn out to be the most convenient definition of an oligopolistic group. Clearly we now have before us both a theory and a method of computing shares of the market which could be of immense significance.

We recognize, however, that we have not yet enough knowledge to evaluate the full partials 5.4 (xiii) and 5.4 (xiv), for we have not yet found dy_r/dp_i, etc. The straightforward method of procedure would be to look again at equations 5.4 (viii). What is needed is some estimate of the unknowns $\lambda_{rs} C_r C_s$ of which there are at least g. Thus in the most general case g observations of the data will be needed. As, for any group, only one equation of type 5.4 (viii) is independent after income effects have been computed, g observations can be made only from a time series of g years, which is too long.

Fortunately the most general case is highly unlikely to be met with in practice. It will almost always be reasonable to conjecture that some λ_{rs} is equal to some λ_{ts}, which simply means that pairs taken, one from group r and one from group t, are in neutral want association with goods from group s; $\lambda_{rr} = \lambda_{tt}$ is not, of course, implied. This is likely to occur over a wide range of groups. Each time it does we have extra equations which with 5.4 (vii) give a system of linear equations in the variables $(\lambda_{rs} C_r C_s)$. In general these may be solved by taking as many observations as are required.

But much more important possibilities may be open, as must be clear from the work of 5.2. From consideration of a systematic procedure to be described we see that a great deal more information (perhaps all) may be obtained from the same two sets of observations already used.

The key to later procedure is the fact that, once $\partial x_i/\partial y_r$'s within group r have been found it is at once possible to combine all goods in the basic group r into a single good r *without an index number problem*. It will then be found that composite goods r

and s may themselves be allocated to second-order basic groups with all the properties of first-order basic groups. After further computation the grouping process may be repeated until the nth order basic group includes the whole matrix. Everything is then determined. Conditions under which this can be done will be examined later.

In the meantime we *define* a composite commodity in the differential form

$$dX_r = \sum_{i \text{ in } r} p_i \, dx_i.$$

In other words, the unit of quantity is £1 worth at current prices. As all measurements are made in the region of a point the prices of all composite commodities are always unity. We must, however, define small price changes in terms of an index to be discovered.

Remarkably enough the index-number problem is greatly simplified if we think of demand X_r as being a function not of price and *money* income but of prices and *real* spending, I. The partial derivative with respect to price of this function is, of course, substitution effect only which we will call S_{rs} corresponding to σ_{ij}. The partial with respect to I is equal to $\partial X_r / \partial y = C_r$. As the form of dI is simply dy less income compensation for all price changes, i.e.

$$dI = dy - \sum x_i \, dp_i,$$

we can always write the total change in X_r, as long as we know substitution effects and income effects. This is, of course, a fact we have already used; and we might have kept this way of looking at things from the beginning. There may indeed be a quite general case for such a point of view as long as we remain in the region of a point. We now have, from our definition of X,

$$\frac{\partial X_r}{\partial P_s} dP_s = S_{rs} dP_s = \sum_{(k \text{ in } s)} \sum_{(i \text{ in } r)} p_i \sigma_{ik} \, dp_k$$

$$\text{(I constant)}$$

$$= \lambda_{rs} C_r C_s \sum_{(k \text{ in } s)} p_k \frac{\partial x_k}{\partial y_s} \frac{dp_k}{p_k}.$$

But

$$\sum_{(k \text{ in } s)} p_k \left(\partial x_k / \partial y_s \right) \left(dp_k / p_k \right)$$

is no more than a weighted average of percentage price changes in p_k; for

$$\sum_{(k \text{ in } s)} p_k \, (\partial x_k / \partial y_s) = 1.$$

Moreover we have already computed the weights $\partial x_k / \partial y_s$. It is natural, therefore, to define dP_s as this weighted average. Thus $S_{rs} = \lambda_{rs} C_r C_s$, which is invariant whatever price changes actually occur. Evidently we have no local index-number problem. But notice that if we write

$$\frac{\partial X_r}{\partial P_s} = -\left(\sum_{(k \text{ in } s)} \frac{x_k \, dp_k}{dP_s} \right) \frac{\partial X_r}{\partial y} + \lambda_{rs} C_r C_s,$$

as we are entitled to do, we have defined a parameter $\partial X_r / \partial P_s$ which is *not* invariant and does depend on the way in which unit change in the price P_s is made up. It is this fact which justifies the remark above that the 'real spending' form of the demand equation simplifies index-number problems. Evidently it is no use computing $\partial X_r / \partial P_s$ in the hope of using this for prediction purposes, but there is a great deal of point in computing S_{rs}.

When we define $S_{rs} = \lambda_{rs} C_r C_s$ we have the exact analogue of our initial definition $\sigma_{ij} = \lambda_{rs} (\partial x_i / \partial y)(\partial x_j / \partial y)$ (remembering that all composite prices are unity). If we have reason to suspect that any $\lambda_{rs} = \lambda_{ts}$ this is precisely the same thing as suspecting that the composite goods r and t are in neutral want association with the composite good s. Again we emphasize that, in general,

$$\lambda_{rr} \neq \lambda_{tt}.$$

The reader may satisfy himself of the likelihood of further grouping by recalling the example with which we began and the whole of the work of section 5.2. The primary basic groups were three, butter and cheese, bread A and bread B, and cinema and television. The composite goods become food A, food B, and entertainment. The possibility of further grouping exists if we consider that an income compensated rise in the price of entertainment will cause consumers to increase consumption of food A and food B proportionately to their respective marginal propensities to consume.

Intuition supports the view that the more we aggregate the more likely it is that we shall discover further possibilities of aggregation. The rule is that if $\lambda_{rs} = \lambda_{RS}$ for all r in R and for all s in S, including $R = S$ $(r \neq s)$, then we may form second-order basic groups R and S such that

$$S_{rs} = \lambda_{RS} C_r C_s$$

and, using $\sum_s S_{rs} = 0$ analogous to $\sum_j p_i \sigma_{ij} = 0$,

$$S_{rr} = - \sum_S \lambda_{RS} \Big(\sum_{\substack{t \text{ in } S \\ t \neq r}} C_t \Big) C_r.$$

These two results (except for income effects which may be treated separately) correspond precisely with 5.4 (iii) and 5.4 (iv). They can be used to obtain a second-order analogue to 5.4 (viii), namely

$$dX_r = C_r \Big(dy - \sum x_i \, dp_i + \sum_S \lambda_{RS} C_S \sum_{(s \text{ in } S)} \frac{\partial X_s}{\partial y_S} dP_s - $$
$$- \frac{dP_r}{P_r} C_R \sum_S \lambda_{RS} C_S \Big) \qquad \text{5.4 (xvi)}$$

and an analogue to 5.4 (xv)

$$dX_r = \frac{\partial X_r}{\partial y_R} \Big(dy_R - \sum_{(j \text{ in } R)} x_j \, dp_j + C_R \sum_S \lambda_{RS} C_S \sum_{(r \text{ in } R)} \frac{\partial X_r}{\partial y_R} dP_r - $$
$$- C_R \sum_S \lambda_{RS} C_S \, dP_r \Big). \qquad \text{5.4 (xvii)}$$

The variables in this equation are observable, dP_r being defined and weights computed. From a new inspection of the data *already used* we may now by the analogue of equation 5.4 (vii) compute all parameters of 5.4 (xvii). Thus, given price changes and changes in expenditure on second-order groups R and S, etc., we can determine the allocation right down to first-order groups; for

$$dy_r = dX_r + \sum_{(i \text{ in } r)} x_i \, dp_i$$

so that when dX_r is known dy_r is known and may be used in the solution of 5.4 (xv).

Next, groups R and S are treated as commodities, using price weights $\partial X_r / \partial y_R$ obtained from 5.4 (xvii), and third-order basic

groups sought. In our example these would be food and entertainment. These two 'goods' form a third-order basic group
which exhausts the matrix. There is in fact only one group. In
the third-order analogue of 5.4 (xvii) we find that $\partial X_r / \partial y_R$ is in
fact $\partial X_R / \partial y$. Once the third-order parameters are found we may,
given price changes and total money spending changes, allocate
expenditure to all goods right down to first order.

It now remains to identify the circumstances in which it will
always be possible to build up groups of higher and higher order
until the whole matrix is collapsed into one group of composite
commodities.

We begin by defining the notion of 'partitioning'. A matrix
of first-order commodities can be partitioned if it can be divided
so that *all* commodities within any division are in neutral want
association with all commodities outside *and all commodities
outside are in neutral want association with those inside*. A partition differs from a group in virtue of the italicized proviso and
the fact that goods within a division need not be in neutral want
association with one another.

Suppose we can carry out an initial partition. It may now
be clear that either or both divisions separated by the partitioning can be further partitioned provided we look upon each
division as a separate matrix ignoring everything outside it.
We now state:

THEOREM 5. *If it is possible to combine k, n-th order basic
groups into t, (n+1)-th order basic groups then*

(a) *Any p, n-th order groups forming a single (n+1)-th order
group must be divisions of a partitioning of that group, and*

(b) *Any pair (pq) of the (n+1)-th order groups formed from n-th
order groups must be divisions of a partitioning of the n-th order
commodity sub-matrix containing all elements of p and q.*

Condition (a) ensures that nth order composite commodities
forming an $(n+1)$th order group are in neutral want association
with one another.

Condition (b) ensures that they are in neutral want association
with every nth order composite commodity outside the group.

It follows that, if it is possible to carry out higher and higher order partitionings until the final division leaves only basic groups, then higher and higher order basic groups may be formed until the whole matrix consists of a single basic group.

This may be made clearer if our example is set out in full, Table 5.4.1, the symbol i, j being used for σ_{ij}. λ's are inserted initially subscripted to indicate the possibility of forming the three first-order basic groups.

TABLE 5.4.1

11	12	13	14	15	16
	λ_{11}		λ_{12}		λ_{13}
21	22	23	24	25	26
31	32	33	34	35	36
	λ_{21}		λ_{22}		λ_{23}
41	42	43	44	45	46
51	52	53	54	55	56
	λ_{31} =		λ_{32}		λ_{33}
61	62	63	64	65	66

The continuous lines mark out a first-order partitioning. This is possible only if $\lambda_{31} = \lambda_{32}$ which we have assumed in our example, entertainment (5 and 6) being in neutral want association with butter and bread (2 and 3) as well as (1 and 2) and (3 and 4).

The dotted line indicates a second-order partitioning of 1, 2, 3, 4 possible because $\lambda_{21} = \lambda_{12}$ as it must. The two partitionings lead to the first-order basic groups $(1, 2)$, $(3, 4)$, and $(5, 6)$. Composite commodities $1'$, $2'$, and $3'$ can be combined into two second-order basic groups $(1', 2')$ and $(3')$. We recognize $(1', 2')$ as a basic group by two criteria. First it contains only two goods. If there were three we should need to appeal to condition (a) of Theorem 5. In the case of two goods condition (a) is automatically fulfilled since any matrix of two groups only can be partitioned. Second, $(1', 2')$ is a basic group because $\lambda_{31} = \lambda_{32}$. If this were not so $1'$ and $2'$ would not be in neutral want association with $3'$ which is a condition for a group. Clearly if $\lambda_{31} = \lambda_{32}$ the full matrix can be partitioned. This is condition (b) of Theorem 5. If condition (b) were not met $(1', 2')$ could not be combined into a third-order composite commodity without an index number ambiguity. Table 5.4.1 is, of course, no more than a reconstruction of Table 5.2.1 of section 5.2.

Partitioning and grouping are simply twin devices for forming conveniently complex hypotheses concerning the interdependence of commodities, in such a way that they can be tested at the bar of the facts. It may well be that experience will show that there are other and better ways. No claim is made here to have said the last word on the subject. Indeed there is another way of looking at our own proposals which may prove to be rewarding in the long run. In order to complete all calculations from the minimum three observations, we require

(a) that the matrix of substitution effects should be decomposable as under (λ's only being written in)

$$
\begin{bmatrix}
A_{11} & \lambda & . & . & \lambda \\
\lambda & A_{22} & . & . & \lambda \\
. & . & . & . & . \\
. & . & . & . & . \\
\lambda & . & . & . & A_{mm}
\end{bmatrix}
$$

where A_{ii} are sub-matrices of substitution effects and where some constant λ replaces the zeros which are the usual requirement for decomposability; and

(b) that the sub-matrices A_{ii} should be decomposable in their turn each with a new λ, $λ_i$, and that second-order sub-matrices should be similarly decomposable and so on. Finally we must be left with nth order A's each composed only of goods forming a first-order basic group.

If the conditions of decomposability are not met it will usually be possible to mend any broken links at the cost of an index-number ambiguity.

We conclude with a few general remarks. First the extreme flexibility of computational methods based on want neutrality is emphasized. If desired there is nothing to preclude the use of an error term at any stage. Additional variables of any kind, other than prices and expenditure, may be simply introduced.

The work may easily be combined with the results of budget studies† based on sample surveys so as to reduce still further the number of unknowns.

Again, at the price of an index-number problem, it is possible to break into the computation at any level of aggregation we choose; for the calculations at each stage are precisely analogous to those of the previous stage. Similarly we can break off the computation at any point, confining our interest simply to one sector of the economy.

Moreover, if at any point it is found that further grouping or partitioning is impossible we are by no means entirely defeated. We have already noted that any group of offending commodities can always be treated as one commodity at the price of an index-number ambiguity. Experience will show the extent to which this is a serious problem.

Finally we emphasize again that the whole system is by no means a simple one. In general we can solve for something of the order of n distinct λ's which is more than sufficient to allow for a wide variety of degrees of substitutability and complementarity. All of this information can be distilled from two sets of price and quantity changes. With more observations even more complex cases can be treated. Computations are simple and can be carried out on a desk machine, the validity of chosen hypotheses being automatically checked at each stage of the work.

5.5. Implications of want neutrality for economic theory

It is possible that, in the present chapter, too much emphasis has been placed upon the value of the concept of want neutrality as an aid to computation, and too little upon its relevance to

† The object of budget studies is mainly to determine the expenditure partials $\partial x/\partial y$. Families are asked to keep a record of their expenditure over a suitable period. It is then assumed that tastes are the same throughout the community in the sense that every family on a given income can be taken to spend in the way in which the community as a whole would spend if all individuals received that income. Since different total expenditures are represented a relation between consumption and expenditure can be found. It is easy to see how a prior knowledge of all, or even some, $\partial x/\partial y$ would simplify the task of computing price responses by the methods of this chapter.

economic theory in a wider context. In an attempt to redress the balance, therefore, we shall conclude with a brief reference to the problem of oligopoly, one of the more obvious fields where it seems that want neutrality might prove to be important. It is not the intention to try to develop a definitive theory. This would be clearly out of place in the present work. Our purpose is simply to illustrate the point with which this paragraph began. Two theorems will be proved which are sufficient to suggest strongly that further inquiry would be profitable.

We begin by reminding the reader that the notion of a marked gap in the chain of substitutes was originally developed in connexion with the theory of production under conditions of imperfect competition,† the idea being that, when the number of firms manufacturing distinct but related competitive products is small, they could no longer take the market price of their output as given. One firm's activities could affect another firm's price in a way too obvious to be ignored. This is likely to occur when the separate commodities satisfy a single want, e.g. different brands of detergents.

We have already commented on the plausibility of the assumption that a group of goods of this kind forms a basic group as defined above. Attention has been drawn to the fact that, if it is a basic group, then we have a means of computing the share of the market each firm might hope to hold at various prices (cf. section 5.4, Theorem 4). But we can go further than this. Normative theorems might be deduced, particularly if the commodity group can be identified as a division of a partitioning, so that all goods outside the group are neutrally want associated with those inside (Theorem 5, section 5.4). Incidentally we find also a new use for the planning demand theory of section 1.5.

It will be sufficient to consider a group of three commodities only, i, j, k. Suppose first that i, j, and k form a basic group, but not a division of a partitioning. It is of great interest to know in what circumstances we can change prices and quantities produced of i, j, and k without setting up forces which will alter the pattern of production and consumption in the rest of

† Cf. J. Robinson, *The Economics of Imperfect Competition*.

the economy. Clearly this will be achieved if there is no change in any commodity price other than i, j, and k. We assume that relative input prices do not change throughout, although this is a matter which would have to be investigated in anything but an illustrative treatment of the subject. The assumption of identical homogeneous production functions for the three branded products is a sufficient condition for this.

First we recall that in section 1.5, when dealing with planning demand theory, it was proved in general that homogeneity of order one of the utility function is a sufficient condition for the identity

$$\frac{\partial p_i}{\partial x_j} = \frac{\partial p_j}{\partial x_i} \qquad\qquad 5.5 \text{ (i)}$$

to hold. In fact this is true of homogeneity of any order, for inspection of 1.5 (ix) shows that all we need for 5.5 (i) is

$$u_i \sum_i u_{ij} x_i = u_j \sum_j u_{ji} x_j. \qquad\qquad 5.5 \text{ (ii)}$$

And if $\sum_i u_i x_i = ru$ as it does, by Euler's theorem, for any homogeneous function of order r, we obtain 5.5 (ii) at once by differentiating with respect to x_i and x_j. This result should not surprise us, for choosing an order of homogeneity is equivalent to choosing a utility indicator. Behaviour as reflected by 5.5 (i) is unaffected.

As there is a good deal of evidence that utility functions are not homogeneous† in general, the theorem leading to 5.5 (i) would not ordinarily be of much interest. But consider the consequences of neutral want association. If i, j, and k form a group then

$$\sum_r u_{rj} x_r \Big/ \sum_r u_{ri} x_i = u_j/u_i \qquad (r \neq i, j, k). \qquad 5.5 \text{ (iii)}$$

In this case the conditions 5.5 (ii) reduce to

$$\sum_r u_{rj} x_r \Big/ \sum_r u_{ri} x_r = u_j/u_i \qquad (r = i, j, k). \qquad 5.5 \text{ (iv)}$$

It is easy to see that 5.5 (iv) is both a necessary and sufficient

† The very notion of a distinction between luxury goods and necessaries contradicts homogeneity. For, almost by definition, a luxury is a good, consumption of which increases more than proportionately to total expenditure.

condition that the sub-function (cf. section 5.3)

$$\phi(x_i, x_j, x_k)$$

is homogeneous of some arbitrary order r, apart from a possible constant of integration which we can take to be zero.

In other words the utility function

$$u = u(x_i, x_j, x_k, x^0),$$

where x^0 represents any fixed value of all x's other than i, k, j, is homogeneous in i, j, and k.

This restriction on utility, contrary to full homogeneity, is highly likely;† for if i is a luxury good so will j and k be, and vice versa. The concept of a group implies that no one member should be either a necessary or a luxury relative to any other. There is, for example, no reason to suppose that a rise in total expenditure on three brands of detergent, prices constant, will change the proportions in which they are purchased.

Making this restricted homogeneity assumption we conclude that 5.5 (i) holds for all i, j, and k in the group. We remind ourselves again that this is true for any basic group whether or not it is a division of a partitioning.

We now prove a lemma which says that for all members of such a group

$$p_j \frac{\partial \lambda}{\partial x_i} = p_i \frac{\partial \lambda}{\partial x_j}, \qquad\qquad 5.5 \text{ (v)}$$

where λ is the marginal utility of money. This result is easily obtained by differentiating

$$\lambda = u_i/p_i$$

with respect to x_j, which yields

$$\frac{\partial \lambda}{\partial x_j} = \frac{u_{ij}}{p_i} - \frac{\lambda}{p_i} \frac{\partial p_i}{\partial x_j},$$

and $$\lambda = u_j/p_j$$

† In this connexion cf. also W. M. Gorman, 'Separable Utility and Aggregation', *Econometrica*, vol. 27, July 1959. In particular we refer to the note 'The Empirical Implications of a Utility Tree—A Further Comment' which follows the reply by Professor Strotz.

with respect to x_i, giving

$$\frac{\partial \lambda}{\partial x_i} = \frac{u_{ji}}{p_j} - \frac{\lambda}{p_j}\frac{\partial p_j}{\partial x_i}.$$

Using now $u_{ij} = u_{ji}$ and $\partial p_i/\partial x_j = \partial p_j/\partial x_i$ 5.5 (v) follows.

Consider now any price p_r of some commodity not in the group i, j, k. We wish to find the change dp_r in p_r due to some shift of resources and consequent change in prices between goods in the oligopolistic group i, j, k. Accordingly we write

$$dp_r = \sum_i \frac{\partial p_r}{\partial x_i} dx_i \quad (i = i, j, k \text{ all other supplies constant}).$$

$$5.5 \text{ (vi)}$$

Since

$$p_r = u_r/\lambda$$

then

$$\frac{\partial p_r}{\partial x_i} = \frac{u_{ri}}{\lambda} - \frac{p_r}{\lambda}\frac{\partial \lambda}{\partial x_i},$$

so that

$$dp_r = \frac{1}{\lambda}\sum_i \left(u_{ri} - p_r\frac{\partial \lambda}{\partial x_i}\right)dx_i.$$

But on the assumption of want neutrality $u_{ri} = \alpha p_i$ for all i, j, k and $\partial \lambda/\partial x_i$ is proportional to p_i by lemma 5.5 (v). It follows that

$$dp_r = C \sum_i p_i\, dx_i \quad (i = i, j, k), \qquad 5.5 \text{ (vii)}$$

where C is some constant.

We are now in a position to appeal to a theorem developed elsewhere† by the present writer which proves that if the demand curve facing a monopoly is defined to be that curve *which would, under ideal conditions be found by experiment*,‡ then it is impossible that all firms in a group should be simultaneously maximizing profits unless total expenditure on the group as a whole is constant.

The result 5.5 (vii) makes it clear that when prices are proportional to marginal costs and there is a small shift in resources from one product to another in the group i, j, k, the change dp_r

---

† 'Total Demand Curves and General Equilibrium', *The Review of Economic Studies*, no. 53, 1952–3.

‡ This would be a 'total' demand curve, i.e. it takes into account all the repercussions of price and output changes in other products. It is discovered by changing output arbitrarily and noting the final effect on selling price.

in the rth price is zero; for with full employment, so that any resources released from one product must be used to increase the
output of another, we have

$$\sum (mc)_i \, dx_i = 0,$$

where (mc) is marginal cost.†

Conversely, if marginal costs are not proportional to prices,
dp_r cannot be zero for every price p_r not in the group i, j, k.
It follows that, in general, total expenditure on goods outside
the group, and hence on goods inside the group, will be constant
only when marginal costs are everywhere proportional to prices,
i.e. when all dp_r are zero. Thus equilibrium of all firms within
the group can only be attained when marginal costs are proportional to prices which is the same, from the point of view of
resource allocation, as the fully competitive equilibrium. This
in fact is the result shown by the writer to hold for a world of
monopolies.‡

A fully dynamic story of how such an equilibrium might be
reached, if it ever could, is very complex and we shall not attempt
to set it out.§ It is worth noting, however, that want neutrality
enormously simplifies this. Want neutrality within a group
implies that any change in output of, say, good i, changes prices
p_j and p_k proportionately leaving the ratio p_j/p_k unaffected.
There would be no change in the relative profitability of goods
j and k and hence no economic pressure to change output. It is
possible for two firms to become involved in experimental
changes in output without affecting any other.

This brings us to our final point. If the group i, j, k is also
a division of a partitioning then any changes in price and output
whatever within the group do not affect the ratio of prices
outside the group. The group itself could be completely isolated,
except via the rate of profit from all other activity. This fact
could be of very great importance in any dynamic analysis.

With these remarks we conclude our theoretical discussion.
The remaining two chapters are devoted to the results of
empirical work.

† Cf. P. A. Samuelson, *The Foundations of Economic Analysis*, pp. 238–9.
‡ Loc. cit., p. 229, n. †.   § But cf. the paper cited, p. 229, n. †.

6

THE FIRST EXPERIMENT

6.1. Introduction

THE purpose of this chapter is to set out the results of an early experiment undertaken on the basis of the theory outlined in the previous sections. It is emphasized that the work is intended to be illustrative† only. No single individual could hope to undertake personally more than a fraction of the statistical analysis necessary before the value of the approach can be said to have been fully tested.

What has been attempted in this and the following chapter is only the first word on the subject. The writer will be disappointed if it should turn out also to be the last. These are the considerations which have prompted the publication of estimates of demand elasticities at a stage when it is also necessary to urge that they should not be looked upon as firm results to be quoted or used in any kind of argument in support of policy.

6.2. An illustrative experiment described

The data analysed were taken from the United Kingdom blue book, National Income and Expenditure (1958). As already suggested in Chapter 5 the blue book does not give sufficient information to permit the design of any very satisfactory experiment. For this and other reasons therefore the simplest possible hypothesis was chosen, the fifteen composite commodities of Table 6.2.1 (below, p. 239) being assumed to form a single group. In other words only one λ and all income responses have to be

---

† The word 'illustrative' is used advisedly. In the first place it has become clear *ex post* that the experiment undertaken is far from being the most rewarding which might have been attempted. Secondly in the field of statistical analysis the present writer is very conscious of his amateur status; nor was there any advantage to be derived from being located some 11,000 miles from the source of the data under examination.

found. Any pair of goods taken at random from the fifteen are
supposed to be in neutral want association with all others. Some
slight alterations were made to the blue book groupings in order
to add plausibility to this assumption.

Our experiment is best thought of as the final stage of a process
similar to that described in section 5.2. We are seeking to find
the analogue of the λ common to the 'food' and 'amusements' of
our example. In order to break in at this final stage it is necessary
to accept an index-number ambiguity. We assume in fact that
the use of *average* propensities to consume as weights to determine
the price changes of composite commodities, gives a satisfactory
approximation to the theoretically correct marginal propensity
weighted average. It is worth noting in passing that this
assumption is sufficient to ensure that the whole price response
is invariant in the sense of the discussion of section 5.2 (p. 198).

The quantity unit of each composite commodity is £1 worth
at 1954 prices, i.e. the same as that used in the blue book.
Percentage price changes are easily computed from the value at
current prices table. Thus we have all the information needed.

Preliminary attempts to determine elasticities and cross
elasticities for 1953 and to use the results to predict consumption
changes in 1955 and 1956 suggested three things. First, for the
years concerned, a great deal of uncertainty must necessarily be
attached to any value obtained for λ. This is because of the
presence of multicollinearity. There is a strong tendency for
trends in the data to be continuous so that the changes in prices
and consumption each year are sufficiently like those of the
previous year to make *absolute* values of k_i (see 6.2 (i)) very
sensitive to observational errors. Some negative values of k_i
appeared which contradicts the indifference curve convexity
condition in this very simple case. The relationship of k_i to k_j,
however, by the same token, remained fairly certain.

Secondly it became obvious that factors other than prices and
income must have some considerable influence on consumption.
Reconsideration of the raw data and some introspection suggested that the weather, particularly hours of sunshine, and
changes in hire-purchase regulations were almost certainly of

importance. The initial hypothesis, therefore, was modified as under to include these as variables.

Thirdly, it was noted that, because of the interdependence of all variables in the system, it is almost impossible to guess without a great deal of calculation what would be the effect of errors in the estimation of λ, or, for that matter, how great will be the effect of the introduction of any new variable. This adds very much to the burden of computation where trial and error methods are desirable.

Hours of sunshine can be brought in in a quite straightforward way, the annual mean for the whole of U.K. as given in *Whitaker's Almanack* being taken as an indicator, h. We have now to determine values for $\partial x_i/\partial h$ (the reaction in consumption due to unit change in hours of sunshine) along with other parameters. The basic equation 5.2 (i) becomes

$$\frac{dx_i-(\partial x_i/\partial h)dh}{k_i} - \frac{dx_j-(\partial x_j/\partial h)dh}{k_j} = \frac{dp_j}{p_j} - \frac{dp_i}{p_i}. \qquad 6.2 \text{ (i)}$$

This can be thought of as a linear equation in four variables $1/k_i$, $1/k_j$, $(\partial x_i/\partial h)/k_i$, and $(\partial x_j/\partial h)/k_j$. Four observations accordingly give a complete solution.

In practice it seemed reasonable to assume further that only 'housing and fuel' and 'motoring and travel' are affected *directly* by changes in hours of sunshine. All other goods are subject to an indirect effect proportional to marginal propensities to consume (prices unity). That is, a fall in the hours of sunshine will change expenditure on 'motoring' and on 'housing and fuel' for reasons which are obvious, but other goods are affected only because the net change in expenditure must be spread elsewhere. The effect of this, where neither i nor j is one of the two goods directly influenced, is simply to reduce 6.2 (i) to its original form; for obviously we now have

$$\frac{\partial x_i}{\partial h}\bigg/ k_i = \frac{\partial x_j}{\partial h}\bigg/ k_j.$$

In short, only for the two goods 'housing and fuel' and 'motoring and travel', do we need four observations of the data, and even this can be reduced to three. For, writing v for the common

$(\partial x_i/\partial h)/k_i$ (where i is not one of the directly affected commodities) and forming an equation type 6.2 (i) from one directly affected good, j, and one indirectly affected good, i, we have

$$\frac{dx_i}{k_i} - \frac{dx_j}{k_j} - \left(v + \frac{\partial x_j}{\partial h} / k_j\right)dh = \frac{dp_j}{p_j} - \frac{dp_i}{p_i}. \qquad 6.2 \text{ (ii)}$$

Treating this as a linear equation in three variables, we may now solve for the coefficient of dh as a whole. Using then the fact that the sum of all $p_i(\partial x_i/\partial h)$ must be zero, the required parameters may be found.

The problem of introducing hire-purchase regulations as a variable is less straightforward. Essentially the real annual expenditure on durable consumer goods is the equivalent hire charge. The unit of quantity might again be £1 worth at base year prices and interest rates.† Unfortunately at the present time we have no means of measuring this. The best we can do is to accept the actual annual expenditure as the best estimate available.

Probably where consumption of durables is growing rapidly such an estimate is far too large. We may comfort ourselves with the thought, however, that in fact we want to predict the response of actual expenditure and not of the hire charge, so that any error will be in the right direction if we again interpret our prediction as actual. The assumption we make is, in short, that actual expenditure will have an invariant response parameter with the same properties as the hire charge. This probably has no theoretical foundation but the hypothesis is at least worth trying.

The hire charge is evidently dependent on the rate of interest as well as the price of the hired goods. The percentage deposit requirement and the period of hire are both devices for affecting the rate of interest; for an increase in either means that the hirer is forced to borrow from himself at a high notional lending rate rather than from a finance company at a lower rate.

It was noted, moreover, that during the period 1952–8 the percentage deposit requirement varied always in the same direc-

† But cf. Chapter 1, section 3 (pp. 41–3). The approach of this section is a statistical expedient.

tion as the rate of interest and the maximum hiring period. Probably this is a fairly general rule. The percentage deposit rate was therefore taken as an approximate indicator of all three variables, being called d. Separate indicators were initially used for 'motoring and travel' on the one hand and 'household durables' on the other, but the response in the case of 'motoring' was found to be negligible so that the appropriate indicator was eventually dropped.

The annual hiring charge p_i' for an item of price p_i with life l_i is, of course,

$$p_i' = r p_i / \{1 - (1+r)^{-l_i}\}.$$

We may therefore define a 'true' percentage price change as

$$\frac{dp_i'}{p_i'} = \frac{dp_i}{p_i} + \frac{dR}{R} \quad \left(\text{where } R = \frac{r}{1 - (1+r)^{-l_i}}\right).$$

Very crudely we then put

$$\frac{dR}{R} = \gamma_i d \quad \text{(where } d \text{ is the change in the hire-purchase deposit requirement).}$$

We have thus to compute γ_i from modified type 5.2 (i) equations. Including the hours of sunshine modification the most general form of 5.2 (i) is now

$$\frac{dx_i - (\partial x_i / \partial h)dh}{k_i} - \frac{dx_j - (\partial x_j / \partial h)dh}{k_j} = \left(\frac{dp_j}{p_j} + \gamma_j d\right) - \left(\frac{dp_i}{p_i} + \gamma_i d\right).$$

$$6.2 \text{ (iii)}$$

In treating the hire-purchase effect this way we have only to remember that the percentage price change $\gamma_i d$ is a quasi price change only. It does not, *per se*, involve more spending per unit of actual commodity purchase. This becomes important when we come to predict expenditure allocations from computed elasticities. We are free to treat any $\gamma_i d$ as a price change but in so doing we must add back the appropriate income effect. If we do not, expenditure allocations will not add to the total. (We recall that our price responses are defined as for total *spending* constant and not total *income* constant.) Strictly speaking, if the individual always borrows from himself for his durable goods, the income effect will always be present, and will be reflected by the necessary transfer of money from expenditure to saving.† In our model such an income effect will automatically be taken into account in the observed change in expenditure. It is deducted from the price response in order to avoid counting it twice.

In practice only equations involving 'household durables' were assumed to require modification on account of hire purchase effects. 'Food' was taken as the key commodity so that fourteen equations of type 6.2 (iii) could be set out. Each has 'food' as good i and one of the remaining fourteen as good j. For reasons given above only three of the fourteen ('housing and fuel', 'household durables', and 'motoring and travel') involved parameters other than k_i and k_j. The eleven pairs of goods not involving additional parameters were treated first.

Observations from 1952 to 1957 inclusive yield five type 5.2 (i) equations for each of the eleven pairs of goods. In order to see how best to deal with the problem of multicollinearity already referred to, the five equations for each pair were set out graphically. No obvious trend in the values of k were discernible so it was decided to assume these to be constant over the range. In order to find what might be called the most probable set of k's an error term was introduced into observations of the non-'food' good in each case. Observations of price changes were assumed to be correct on the grounds that these are more easily measured than quantity changes. For convenience the 'food' quantity observations were also taken to be correct. This asymmetry is, of course, completely unjustifiable except on the grounds first, that no easy alternative was obvious and second, that this was to be the first tentative experiment of its kind rather than the last.

Minimizing the sum of the squares of the error terms yields two equations of the form

$$\sum \left[(dx_i)^2 \frac{1}{k_i} - dx_i\, dx_j \frac{1}{k_j} - dx_i \left(\frac{dp_j}{p_j} - \frac{dp_i}{p_i} \right) \right] = 0$$

† Cf. Chapter 1, section 3, where the concept of notional consumption is introduced to meet this difficulty.

and

$$\sum \left[dx_j \left(\frac{dp_j}{p_j} - \frac{dp_i}{p_i} \right) \frac{1}{k_j} - dx_i \left(\frac{dp_j}{p_j} - \frac{dp_i}{p_i} \right) \frac{1}{k_i} + \left(\frac{dp_j}{p_j} - \frac{dp_i}{p_i} \right)^2 \right] = 0$$

for each pair. These also were graphed.

It was comforting to note that in most cases the solution of the two 'average' equations yielded sensible positive values for $1/k_i$ and $1/k_j$. Some symptoms of multicollinearity were still present, however, and it was necessary to use a combination of inspection of graphs and common sense to guess the 'true' value for $1/k_i$ (food) out of the eleven estimates available. In the event a figure not far from the arithmetic mean was chosen. Given $1/k_i$ and the 'average' relationship between $1/k_i$ and $1/k_j$, all $1/k_j$ were easily estimated.

The critic who objects to the use of graphs and some element of subjective personal judgement is reminded that it is never possible to guess at any stage how the choice of values for k's will affect the predictive power of elasticities computed, because of the interdependence of all goods and prices. And, even if it were, this would be a case for using the method and not a case against it.

Given a value for $1/k_i$ (food) the remaining three equations of type 6.2 (iii) are again linear in two variables (assuming 'food' is always used as one of the pair). Similar methods were used therefore to determine γ ('household durables') and all $\partial x_j / \partial h$.

Results obtained were

$$\gamma \text{ (household durables)} = +0 \cdot 00233,$$

$$\frac{\partial x}{\partial h} \text{(housing and fuel)} = -52 \cdot 9,$$

$$\frac{\partial x}{\partial h} \text{(motoring and travel)} = +64 \cdot 8.$$

Remarkably enough the two responses to hours of sunshine almost balance one another out so that the remainder when spread among all other goods is negligible. We remind ourselves also that the weather responses, as calculated, do not remain constant year by year since they depend upon prices. The figures quoted are estimates for 1957.

Table 6.2.1 sets out the matrix of price elasticities for 1957. These also are dependent on prices so that for constant k's there must be year by year changes. Income elasticities are given in the final column. The reader who is startled by the high price and income elasticities for 'food' is reminded that these results are not to be taken too seriously. Hindsight makes it clear that the high 'food' figure is largely due to the upsurge in the consumption of sugar based items and meat following derationing in 1953 and 1954. Before computations began it was felt that this effect would not be especially significant.

Table 6.2.2 represents an attempt to measure what might be called the 'fit' of changes, computed from estimated parameters, on to actual. Elasticities were in fact obtained for each of the years 1952 to 1957. The observed percentage money consumption change is shown each year, together with observed percentage price changes for each item. The actual change in consumption (measured in 1954 £ million worth) is set beside the estimate which would have been made on the basis of computed parameters.

It is more honest, of course, to compare changes in consumption rather than absolute consumption. For absolute figures seldom vary by more than 5 per cent. A guess of absolute consumption to within 5 per cent can always be made given the figure for the previous year. Indeed a result which is not within 2 per cent of actual is scarcely worth the trouble of computing. Fortunately our table shows that in fifty-one cases out of seventy-five the fit is within 2 per cent. The mean is in fact 1·9 per cent.

We comment also that some of the individual fits are remarkably close, being especially successful at points where there is a sudden switch from positive to negative changes. The reader is invited to compare estimates for 'household durables', 'motoring', and 'housing' with the figure which would have been obtained by straight projection.

Table 6.2.3 provides a slightly more objective test of goodness of fit. Estimates of actual consumption were made on the separate assumptions:

(1) that the change this year will always be the same as the change last year; and

TABLE 6.2.1. COMPUTED PRICE AND INCOME ELASTICITIES

The number in row j column i is the percentage change in consumption (as computed) of the jth good which would be caused by a 1 per cent rise in the price of the ith good, all other prices being kept constant. Income elasticity is the percentage change in consumption which would be caused by a 1 per cent increase in aggregate spending, prices constant.

	(1)	(2)	(3)	(4)	(5)	(6)	(7)	(8)	(9)	(10)	(11)	(12)	(13)	(14)	(15)	Income elasticities
1. Food	−1·127	−0·122	−0·081	0·030	−0·018	−0·015	−0·012	−0·005	−0·005	−0·006	0·117	−0·001	−0·015	−0·009	−0·061	1·345
2. Alcohol, tobacco	0·028	−0·366	−0·022	0·008	−0·005	−0·004	−0·003	−0·001	−0·001	−0·001	0·032	0	−0·004	−0·003	−0·016	0·362
3. Housing, fuel	0·045	−0·052	−0·570	0·013	−0·008	−0·006	−0·005	−0·002	−0·002	−0·003	0·050	0	−0·006	−0·004	−0·026	0·578
4. Household durables	0·121	−0·143	−0·094	−1·407	−0·021	−0·018	−0·014	−0·006	−0·008	−0·006	0·137	0	−0·017	−0·011	−0·071	1·561
5. Other household	0·048	−0·055	−0·038	0·012	−0·586	−0·007	−0·005	−0·002	−0·002	−0·002	0·055	−0·001	−0·007	−0·005	−0·029	0·627
6. Clothing	0·075	−0·087	−0·058	0·021	−0·013	−0·897	−0·009	−0·005	0	−0·005	0·084	0	−0·011	−0·007	−0·044	0·960
7. Books, newspapers, etc.	0·037	−0·037	−0·026	0·011	−0·005	−0·005	−0·413	0	0	−0·005	0·037	0	−0·005	0	−0·016	0·439
8. Other recreational	0·055	−0·069	−0·041	0·014	−0·007	−0·007	−0·007	−0·641	0	−0·005	0·062	0	−0·007	−0·007	−0·034	0·690
9. Chemists' goods	0·059	−0·074	−0·048	0·016	−0·011	−0·011	−0·005	−0·005	−0·745	0	0·069	0	−0·005	−0·005	−0·037	0·793
10. Other misc. goods	0·056	−0·067	−0·044	0·017	−0·011	−0·006	−0·006	0	−0·005	−0·667	0·061	0	−0·006	−0·006	−0·033	0·711
11. Motoring, travel	0·178	−0·208	−0·137	0·052	−0·031	−0·026	−0·022	−0·009	−0·009	−0·011	1·916	−0·001	−0·025	−0·015	−0·104	2·287
12. Communication	0·078	−0·100	−0·067	0·022	−0·011	−0·011	−0·011	0	0	0	0·089	−0·933	−0·011	−0·011	−0·056	1·000
13. Entertainment	0·018	−0·018	−0·012	0·006	0	0	0	0	0	0	0·018	0	−0·199	0	−0·006	0·216
14. Domestic services	0	0	0	0	0	0	0	0	0	0	0	0	0	0	0	0
15. Other services	0·023	−0·026	−0·017	0·006	−0·003	−0·003	−0·002	−0·001	−0·001	−0·001	0·026	0	−0·003	−0·002	−0·289	0·297

TABLE 6.2.2

Col. (1): Observed Change in Consumption (quantity); col. (2): Estimated Change in Consumption (quantity) on the basis of computed elasticities; col. (3): Percentage Error of Estimate [difference between (1) and (2), as percentage of total consumption (quantity)]; col. (4): Observed Percentage Price Change.

	1952-3				1953-4				1954-5				1955-6				1956-7				All years
	(1)	(2)	(3)	(4)	(1)	(2)	(3)	(4)	(1)	(2)	(3)	(4)	(1)	(2)	(3)	(4)	(1)	(2)	(3)	(4)	(3)
1. Food	127	88	1·1	3·9	132	132	0·0	3·8	85	75	0·3	6·3	78	78	0·0	3·9	57	114	1·4	2·4	0·6
2. Alcohol, tobacco	26	33	0·4	0·3	16	37	1·3	0·2	63	41	1·3	0·5	28	14	0·8	3·3	39	13	1·4	2·4	1·0
3. Housing, fuel	36	16	1·4	5·0	64	51	0·8	3·2	-13	-16	0·2	3·9	33	39	0·4	5·5	2	-13	0·9	5·8	0·7
4. Household durables	82	92	1·9	-2·9	89	78	1·9	-1·8	28	25	0·5	1·4	-44	-11	5·4	6·2	52	34	2·7	1·1	2·5
5. Other household	18	23	1·5	-3·8	26	12	3·7	1·4	24	17	1·7	0·0	-3	3	1·5	4·1	16	5	2·6	2·8	2·2
6. Clothing	19	71	4·7	-0·9	73	65	0·7	0·8	86	80	0·5	0·6	46	43	0·2	1·8	21	36	1·1	1·6	1·4
7. Books, etc.	6	4	1·1	0·1	2	3	0·5	3·0	-3	2	2·8	4·5	9	0·0	4·8	6·5	3	1	1·1	3·6	2·1
8. Other recreational	8	7	0·8	-1·8	8	7	0·8	-1·6	1	4	2·3	3·0	5	2	2·2	3·3	7	4	4·1	3·6	2·0
9. Chemists' goods	15	16	0·7	6·3	11	10	0·7	-0·6	7	3	2·2	5·1	-1	-2	0·6	7·1	13	4	4·8	2·0	1·8
10. Other goods	22	22	0·0	14·4	20	19	0·6	-8·9	7	5	1·2	2·9	3	1	1·2	4·8	7	4	1·7	1·3	0·9
11. Motoring, travel	86	62	3·1	2·0	77	94	1·9	0·2	119	151	3·2	3·2	-47	-47	0·0	5·3	28	19	0·9	4·1	1·8
12. Communication	3	2	1·2	2·9	0·0	1	1·2	5·2	2	1	3·6	1·2	4	-6	12·0	13·7	3	-1	4·4	7·1	4·6
13. Entertainment	-3	2	2·6	0·5	0·0	1	0·5	2·7	1	1	0·0	3·7	-5	0·0	2·7	3·1	-15	0·0	8·8	6·1	2·9
14. Domestic	-5	0·0	5·0	3·9	0·0	0·0	0·0	1·1	-4	0·0	4·2	5·5	-5	0·0	5·5	4·5	-2	0·0	2·3	4·5	3·0
15. Other services	15	9	0·8	2·3	8	10	0·3	2·5	10	8	0·2	4·0	12	1	1·4	5·4	-4	4	1·0	3·2	0·7
																				Mean	1·9
Observed change in weather indicator		-0·22				-0·46				+0·91				-0·74				+0·08			
Observed change in H.P. indicator		-5				0				+15				+2				0			

Notes: (1) Quantities are in £'s million at 1954 prices (cf. U.K. National Income blue book, 1958).
(2) Observed Change in (Money) Consumption: 1952-3, 6 per cent; 1953-4, 6·6 per cent; 1954-5, 7·1 per cent; 1955-6, 5·5 per cent; 1956-7, 4·9 per cent.

TABLE 6.2.3

Comparison of per cent error of estimate (Table 6.2.2) with similar estimates based on two alternative naïve hypotheses (1 and 2 below)

	1953–7						% deviation of 1958 projections from actual		
	% deviation of estimated change from actual								
	On basis of computed elasticities		On naïve hypothesis 1†		On naïve hypothesis 2‡		On basis of computed elasticities	On naïve hypothesis 1	On naïve hypothesis 2
	Mean§	Max.‖	Mean	Max.	Mean	Max.			
1. Food	0·6	1·4	0·5	1·2	1·3	2·7	1·8	0·3	1·8
2. Alcohol and tobacco	1·0	1·4	1·5	2·8	2·8	4·9	0·1	1·3	2·4
3. Housing, fuel	0·7	1·4	3·0	5·1	2·1	3·6	5·3	3·5	7·3
4. Household durables	2·5	5·4	9·8	16·0	4·6	6·3	2·3	0·9	0·5
5. Other household	2·2	3·7	4·0	6·3	2·0	3·8	2·4	4·3	4·8
6. Clothing	1·4	4·7	2·7	4·7	1·5	5·0	4·0	2·3	5·3
7. Books, newspapers, etc.	2·1	4·8	3·7	7·1	2·8	6·2	0·5	1·6	1·1
8. Other recreational	2·0	4·1	2·5	5·4	2·1	3·8	2·1	5·5	4·8
9. Chemists' goods	1·8	4·8	4·3	8·0	1·8	4·5	0·0	3·7	2·1
10. Other misc. goods	0·9	1·7	3·4	7·6	1·1	1·8	3·3	5·6	8·3
11. Motoring, travel	1·8	4·1	7·7	17·5	4·6	8·4	6·2	9·1	7·5
12. Communication	4·6	12·0	2·4	3·6	4·6	12·0	10·0	4·4	8·9
13. Entertainment	2·9	8·8	2·8	11·1	4·7	7·6	6·5	2·4	5·8
14. Domestic services	3·0	5·5	3·8	5·9	5·3	6·6	8·3	6·0	11·0
15. Other services	0·7	1·4	0·8	2·0	1·6	2·4	0·6	1·5	0·8
Mean	1·9	4·4	3·5	7·0	2·9	5·3	3·5	3·5	4·8

† Naïve hypothesis 1 is: 'change this year same as change last year'.

‡ Naïve hypothesis 2 is: 'all direct price elasticities −1, all cross elasticities zero, all income elasticities +1.

§ 'Mean' is the arithmetic average of the five figures of Table 6.2.2.

‖ 'Max.' is the maximum deviation in any single year.

(2) that all direct price elasticities are -1, that all cross elasticities are zero, and that all income elasticities are $+1$.

That naïve hypothesis (1) is not particularly naïve is evidenced by the existence of the multicollinearity already referred to. Moreover, this is an assumption quite commonly used by economists as a first approximation. Nevertheless, our table shows a mean percentage error of estimate of $3 \cdot 5$ against the $1 \cdot 9$ referred to above. That the method of want neutrality even at its crudest is more consistently successful is also underlined by the comparison of maximum errors set out in Table 6.2.3.

Naïve hypothesis (2) is less defensible but does take into account the possible effects of sharp changes in price movements. Again our methods give markedly better results.

As a final test computed parameters for 1957 were used to estimate 1958 consumption on the basis of published price changes and consumption. These figures became available whilst the general calculations were in progress. The result is both disappointing and encouraging. The percentage errors are again given in Table 6.2.3.

The 1958 results are disappointing for two reasons. First, the rather wider mean deviation may give the impression that the modest success for 1953–7 is due mainly to the fact that our estimates are a fit rather than a projection. Against this the reader is invited to recall that we have in fact computed only 19 parameters from 70 equations leaving 51 degrees of freedom. There is a great deal of scope for variation.

Second, our result is disappointing for the obvious reason that even though our method is shown to be as good as any other it is only just as good as naïve hypothesis (1).

On the other hand, a post-mortem reveals most encouraging signs. Above all, the main causes of deviation in 1958 *were already evident in the 1953–7 figures,* and it is now clear that a much more accurate result for 1958 would have been obtained even from the 1953–7 figures alone if a more satisfactory initial hypothesis had been chosen.

For example, the price changes in 'housing and fuel' in the early period were largely due to price changes in 'housing'. The

1958 price change, on the other hand, was almost entirely 'fuel'. Evidently 'housing' is more complementary to all other goods than 'fuel' and should have been put in a separate group. Similarly 'communication' is clearly more complementary with all other goods than all other goods are with one another. It might have been better to group 'housing' and 'communication' together.

We have already commented on the effect upon 'food' of derationing in 1953–4. It would certainly have been better to ignore the food observations for 1953–5 and use some other good as a key good. The fact that our estimate of k (food) is too high is again quite clear from the 1953–7 figures.

Again it seemed from the first that the most likely marginal propensity to consume 'domestic service' was small but negative. This is only possible within the theory if more than one group exists. The assumption of several groups would almost certainly sharply reduce the 1958 deviations although we can never be sure precisely how without trial. In short, with the one exception 'clothing', the 1958 projections do no more than underline the obvious weaknesses of our initial hypothesis. They should serve therefore to encourage us to further effort rather than the opposite.

We conclude with a remark on the reliability of the raw data examined. In some cases successive issues of the blue book have shown alterations in figures previously put out of the same order of magnitude as the deviations of Table 6.2.2. Such alterations are, of course, unavoidable. The fact is mentioned only so that it should not be overlooked.

7

TWO FURTHER EXPERIMENTS

7.1. Results of the second experiment

As the writing up of earlier chapters of this book proceeded further analyses of U.K. consumer expenditure were undertaken with the object of testing some of the conjectures of section 6.2. By this time the 1959 blue book National Income and Expenditure had become available and figures were taken from this. The fifteen commodities of section 6.2 were extended to eighteen by separating 'housing, fuel and light' into its components, 'house maintenance', 'rent and rates', and 'fuel and light'; and 'household durables' into 'furniture' and 'electrical goods'.

The extended classification was justified by the introduction of a utility tree, Fig. 12.

For the most part, of course, the compilers of the blue book have already exploited the more obvious grouping possibilities, in many cases on a basis different from that desirable from the present point of view. Without access to primary statistics there is not a great deal that the independent observer can do. There does remain, however, one important possibility. It was thought worth while to try grouping items such as 'alcohol and tobacco', 'rent and rates', and 'communication' which intuitively we should expect to have rather lower price elasticities than say 'electrical goods'. Hence group C. Group B was chosen because of the close connexion between 'domestic services' and 'household appliances' on the one hand and 'entertainment' and 'radio and television' on the other. Other groupings were made, with much less confidence, on the same basis as group C. Finally the second-order groupings (ABC) and (DEF) were made quite arbitrarily largely to see how it would work out.

Despite this there was, in the event, some evidence in support

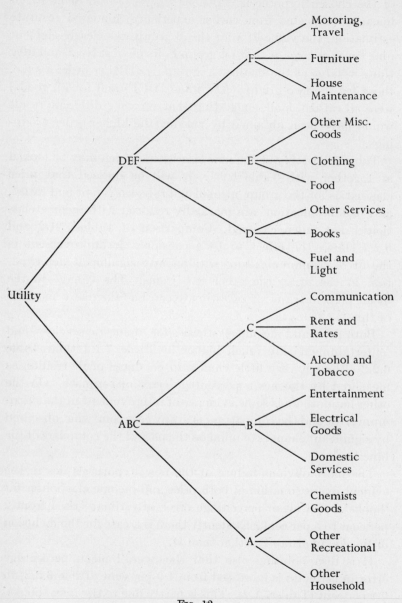

Fig. 12

of the chosen hypothesis. Although a great deal of multicollinearity (expected from earlier experience) hindered accurate
estimation, the value of λ for the B group was clearly eight or
nine times as large as that for group F, its nearest rival, and fifty
times as large as the smallest λ (group C). Higher-order λ's (i.e.
those for the two groups (ABC) and (DEF) and for all goods)
were all rather small, suggesting that no very different result
would have been obtained by varying the higher-order groupings.

Table 7.1.1 sets out the new elasticities which may be looked
at together with Table 6.2.1. It will be noticed that price
elasticities for the group 'alcohol and tobacco', 'rent and rates',
and 'communication' are markedly reduced with income elasticities not much changed. Comparison of Tables 7.1.2 and
6.2.2 shows the effect to be a considerable improvement in
the fit of 'communication' without any significant deteriora-
tion in the fit of the other two items. The change in the
mean percentage error of estimate can be taken as a measure
of this.

Both price and income elasticities for 'domestic services' and
'entertainment' are much higher in Table 7.1.2 than Table
6.2.2 although very little change in goodness of fit results, as
measured by the mean percentage error of estimate. On the
other hand, there is some evidence of improvement in the maximum error and the comparison is in any case somewhat obscured
by significant changes of mind on the part of the compilers of the
blue book.

The most obvious failure of the new hypothesis lies in the
evident overestimation of both price and income elasticities for
'books'. The mean percentage error of estimate rises from 2
per cent to 5 per cent. Evidently there is a case for the inclusion
of 'books' in group C rather than D.

It is disappointing also that the overall mean percentage
error of estimate is increased from 1·9 per cent (Table 6.2.2) to
2·9 per cent (Table 7.1.2). This is partly due to the item 'books'
already commented on, which, by itself, accounts for one-fifth
of the rise. But other causes are, first, the breakdown of the

composite commodities 'housing' and 'household durables' into smaller elements, which raises the percentage error for the same absolute figure; and second, the exclusion from the calculation of the factors weather and hire-purchase regulations.

In fact these last two causes are not unrelated for it will be seen that the particularly large errors in 'fuel and light' and 'house maintenance' which occur (if the results of the first experiment are significant), as a result of the unusually sunny summer of 1955, are greatly exaggerated by the decomposition of the item 'housing'.

Weather and H.P. changes were not included as independent variables in the second experiment partly because of the difficulties presented by the new hypothesis and partly because some evidence of their effect was already available from the results of experiment one. In this connexion it is interesting to look at Table 7.1.3 in conjunction with Table 7.1.2 so as to be able to compare the consequences of the two good summers 1955 and 1959. There is some evidence that good weather consistently decreases spending on 'fuel and light' and, oddly enough, on 'books' and 'house maintenance', and increases spending on 'alcohol and tobacco' and 'motoring'. The startling revisions for the 'motoring' figures in the 1961 blue book point, however, to the need for second thoughts. The effect of the 'Suez' crisis of 1956 is also clear.

Table 7.1.3 is in the same form as Table 7.1.2 but represents *predictions* from computed elasticities rather than tests of fit. Actual changes are taken this time from the blue book for 1961. The revisions of all figures made in the 1961 blue book imply, of course, that elasticities were computed on 'wrong' figures published in 1958. To this extent the predictions for 1959 and 1960 are made on 'wrong' elasticities. It is impossible to say without new calculations what proportion of the 3·1 per cent mean error of estimate, if any, is due to this.

3·1 per cent mean error of estimate is again disappointing although still a good deal better than we should get from predictions based on either of the naïve hypotheses of Chapter 6.

TABLE 7.1.3. PREDICTIONS

Col. (1): Observed Change in Consumption (quantity); col. (2): Estimated Change in Consumption (quantity) on the basis of computed elasticities; col. (3): Percentage Error of Estimate [difference between (1) and (2), as percentage of total consumption (quantity)]; col. (4): Observed Percentage Price Change.

	1958–9				1959–60				All years
	(1)	(2)	(3)	(4)	(1)	(2)	(3)	(4)	(3)
1. Other household . .	21	14	1·5	2·9	12	18	1·3	−0·4	1·4
2. Other recreational .	17	11	3·4	−3·5	23	8	8·4	−0·7	5·9
3. Chemists' goods . .	9	9	0	−1·0	11	8	1·5	+0·2	0·8
4. Domestic services . .	−3	−2	1·4	2·7	−5	2	9·7	+1·6	5·5
5. Electrical goods . .	69	49	4·7	−3·4	−31	+31	14·5	−1·1	9·6
6. Entertainments . .	−3	3	2·9	2·2	−2	4	2·9	+1·4	2·9
7. Alcohol, tobacco . .	75	43	1·7	−1·8	90	34	2·9	+1·2	2·3
8. Rent, rates, etc. . .	12	11	0·1	6·5	12	14	0·2	+3·5	0·1
9. Communication . .	4	3	1·1	−6·1	3	3	0	−0·9	0·6
10. Fuel and light . .	−5	54	10·9	0·6	52	59	1·3	−0·1	6·1
11. Books, etc. . . .	−10	11	12·0	3·8	11	10	0·6	+0·8	6·3
12. Other services . .	28	5	2·3	2·2	31	5	2·6	+2·3	2·4
13. Food	90	115	0·6	0·6	91	152	1·5	−0·3	1·1
14. Clothing . . .	59	59	0	−0·4	97	34	4·4	+1·6	2·2
15. Misc. goods . .	19	19	0	−3·5	15	10	2·3	+0·4	1·2
16. House maintenance .	−3	7	5·0	0·9	−2	−3	0·5	+5·2	2·8
17. Furniture, floor coverings	32	18	4·0	0·2	−18	12	8·5	+1·9	2·9
18. Motoring, travel . .	143	133	0·8	−0·3	119	115	0·3	+1·0	0·9
								Mean	3·1

Notes:
(1) Quantities are in £'s million at 1954 prices (cf. U.K. National Income blue book, 1961).
(2) Observed Change in (Money) Consumption: 1958–9, 4·6 per cent; 1959–60, 4·6 per cent.

7.2. Experiment three—the 'food' group

As a next step an attempt was made to test the hypothesis for the group 'food' defined by the more complex utility tree Fig. 10 (p. 191). In evaluating the results obtained it should be especially borne in mind that there are a great many obvious *a priori* reasons for supposing that the chosen hypothesis is not a particularly good one. Unfortunately no more satisfactory data were available. Even so predictions for 1959 and 1960 proved to be markedly better than those given by either of the 'naïve' hypotheses of Chapter 6.

Table 7.2.1 is a table of elasticities and cross elasticities as computed. It should be noticed, however, that the figures given are not partial elasticities of demand as a function of prices and *total expenditure* but as a function of prices and *expenditure on all food*. A table of ordinary elasticities could easily be prepared from 7.2.1 simply by adding appropriately an estimate of the value of the third term of equations 5.4 (xi) and 5.4 (xii), that is, the income effect due to the change in consumption of food as a whole following unit price rise in each of the nine goods of the table. Such an estimate can be obtained from the elasticity of demand for food given in Table 7.1.1 taken together with the food expenditure elasticities of 7.2.1. The change in the price of food as a whole due to a change in the price of the ith good of Table 7.2.1 is, by the argument of section 5.4, equal to the food expenditure response of the ith good.

For two reasons elasticities are set out only in the uncorrected form. First the change would affect only the second and third decimal places, mostly the third, so that the important direct elasticities can always be taken as an approximation to the more usual elasticities for the purpose of rough comparison with results obtained by different methods. Second, for the fairest test of the present hypothesis, it was considered desirable to assume that total expenditure on food as a whole could be accurately determined, so as to eliminate error from this cause. For this purpose the figures of Table 7.2.1 are already in the most convenient form.

As with experiment two, data were taken from the National Income Blue Book for 1959. Table 7.2.2 shows goodness of fit as in previous cases. The overall mean error of estimate is 3·2 per cent but this is very much exaggerated by especially large errors of estimate in the change 1952–3, due to derationing of meat and sugar. In fact the meat and sugar figures for 1952–3 were not used in computing elasticities since they could only be misleading.

Again Table 7.2.3 compares actual with predicted changes for 1958–9 and 1959–60. The mean error of estimate is 2·9 per cent. The reader is invited to consider how far a modest success might be claimed.

TABLE 7.2.1. COMPUTED PRICE AND FOOD EXPENDITURE ELASTICITIES

The number in row j column i is the percentage change in consumption (as computed) of the jth good which would be caused by a 1 per cent rise in the price of the ith good, all other prices *and total expenditure on all food* being kept constant. Food expenditure elasticity is the percentage change in consumption which would be caused by a 1 per cent increase in overall spending on food, prices constant.

	1	2	3	4	5	6	7	8	9	Food expenditure elasticity
1. Beverages	−0·244	−0·152	−0·090	−0·221	−0·240	−0·072	−0·160	−0·391	−0·046	1·615
2. Sugar, etc.	−0·063	−0·940	+0·600	−0·122	−0·132	−0·050	−0·111	−0·272	−0·032	1·121
3. Fruit	−0·129	+0·760	1·460	−0·250	−0·270	−0·103	−0·228	−0·558	−0·065	2·302
4. Bread, cereals	−0·003	+0·019	+0·031	−0·085	+0·005	−0·002	−0·006	−0·014	−0·002	0·057
5. Dairy products	−0·003	+0·019	+0·031	+0·005	−0·086	−0·002	−0·006	−0·014	−0·002	0·057
6. Oils	−0·103	−0·172	−0·103	−0·251	−0·272	−0·223	−0·187	−0·467	−0·055	1·829
7. Vegetables, potatoes	−0·043	−0·073	−0·043	−0·106	−0·115	−0·037	−0·549	+0·166	+0·024	0·778
8. Meat, bacon	−0·074	−0·124	−0·073	−0·181	−0·196	−0·063	+0·006	−0·599	−0·016	1·320
9. Fish	−0·081	−0·136	−0·080	−0·199	−0·215	−0·069	+0·007	−0·174	−0·500	1·449

TABLE 7.2.2

Col. (1): Observed Change in Consumption (quantity); col. (2): Estimated Change in Consumption (quantity) on the basis of computed elasticities; col. (3): Percentage Error of Estimate [difference between (1) and (2), as percentage of total consumption (quantity)]; col. (4): Observed Percentage Price Change.

	1952-3				1953-4				1954-5				1955-6				1956-7				1957-8				All years
	(1)	(2)	(3)	(4)	(1)	(2)	(3)	(4)	(1)	(2)	(3)	(4)	(1)	(2)	(3)	(4)	(1)	(2)	(3)	(4)	(1)	(2)	(3)	(4)	(3)
1. Beverages	9	14	2·9	7·4	2	5	1·6	23·6	23	5	9·7	16·8	5	9	1·9	-3·2	5	4	0·5	5·4	2	6	1·8	-0·5	3·1
2. Sugar, etc.	81	20	21·2	6·2	18	14	1·1	1·9	-7	24	8·0	2·4	10	15	1·3	1·7	-8	11	4·9	1·7	9	19	2·6	-1·1	6·5
3. Fruit	25	17	4·3	8·0	19	18	0·5	1·5	14	5	3·9	6·2	-2	9	4·5	3·2	8	3	2·1	3·4	-7	-4	1·2	3·3	2·8
4. Bread, cereals	-44	3	8·9	4·8	-15	1	3·3	0·0	-3	2	0·2	0·6	-6	-1	1·1	8·4	-5	-2	0·6	8·5	5	0·2	1·0	1·8	2·5
5. Dairy products	12	1	2·2	6·9	14	3	2·1	-3·8	2	0	0·6	6·3	6	1	0·8	3·0	12	9	1·9	-0·5	8	1	1·3	0·9	1·5
6. Oils	11	15	2·2	15·8	15	7	4·2	22·4	10	12	1·0	1·0	6	10	1·1	-2·7	9	9	0·0	-6·5	23	11	5·2	-11·6	2·4
7. Vegetables, potatoes	-7	18	7·2	-1·4	5	5	0·0	7·0	8	5	0·9	9·1	5	1	1·1	7·9	6	9	0·8	-1·0	11	-10	5·8	10·2	2·6
8. Meat, bacon	78	51	3·8	0·5	60	39	2·7	4·4	36	29	0·8	8·5	45	28	1·9	4·9	16	16	0·0	1·5	9	30	2·2	2·3	1·9
9. Fish	-11	7	17·5	2·6	3	5	2·2	4·5	4	6	2·1	4·0	7	2	5·1	8·8	3	0·5	2·4	4·5	-1	2	2·8	6·4	5·4
																								Mean	3·2

Notes: (1) Quantities are in £'s million at 1954 prices (cf. U.K. National Income blue book, 1959).
(2) Observed Change in Money Expenditure: 1952–3, 9·5 per cent; 1953–4, 7·9 per cent; 1954–5, 9·0 per cent; 1955–6, 6·3 per cent; 1956–7, 3·5 per cent; 1957–8, 3·3 per cent.

There is evidently no need to draw attention to the consider-able improvement of the predictions over those which would have followed from straight extrapolation. As an added test predictions were made based upon naïve hypothesis two of Chapter 6, that is, upon the assumption that all direct elasticities were −1, all cross elasticities zero, and all income elasticities +1.

TABLE 7.2.3. PREDICTIONS

Col. (1): Observed Change in Consumption (quantity); Col. (2): Estimated Change in Consumption (quantity) on the basis of computed elasticities; Col. (3): Percentage Error of Estimate [difference between (1) and (2), as percentage of total consumption (quantity)]; Col. (4): Observed Percentage Price Change.

	1958–9				1959–60				All years
	(1)	(2)	(3)	(4)	(1)	(2)	(3)	(4)	(3)
1. Beverages	10	6	0	0·8	1	9	3·4	1·0	1·7
2. Sugar, etc.	−16	−7	2·4	2·0	13	9	1·1	0	1·7
3. Fruit	28	36	3·3	−6·4	0	19	7·8	−1·2	5·6
4. Bread, cereals	−3	−1	0·4	0·9	7	0	1·5	0·3	0·9
5. Dairy products	13	0	2·3	0·6	17	0	3·0	1·1	2·7
6. Oils	−11	0	4·6	22·9	−2	13	6·2	−5·6	5·4
7. Vegetables, potatoes	16	12	1·1	−2·4	16	20	1·1	−6·0	1·1
8. Meat, bacon	15	17	0	1·1	51	24	2·8	0·9	1·4
9. Fish	6	0	5·1	5·2	−8	1	7·7	4·5	6·4
								Mean	2·9

Notes:
  (1) Quantities are in £'s million at 1954 prices (cf. U.K. National Income blue book, 1961).
  (2) Observed Changes in Money Expenditure on Food: 1958–9, 3·1 per cent; 1959–60, 2·3 per cent.

The mean error of estimate so computed proved to be 3·9 per cent as against 2·9 per cent for Table 7.2.3. To be able consistently to improve upon the best alternative hypothesis by as much as 1 per cent would be a considerable achievement. To have done so once or twice is encouraging.

7.3. Some concluding reflections

From time to time in this and the previous chapter it has been argued that tests of the theory of neutral want association have been in some degree successful. It has seemed worth while, by way of conclusion, to examine this claim more generally and to consider what might be meant in the context by the word successful.

The ultimate object of all economic investigation is to reach a position from which it is possible qualitatively, or preferably quantitatively, to predict the future. No 'explanation' of the past can be said to be satisfactory unless the principles uncovered are consistent with the events of some different past or events to come. This is no less the case with the theory of consumers' demand. But how close must a prediction be before it can be reckoned successful? Are estimates with a mean percentage error of 2·9 per cent and a range of error of 6 per cent or 7 per cent of any use?

One answer to this might be that any method of prediction, which consistently gives better results than every other, is useful, and in this event there must be some element of 'truth' in the underlying theory. Unfortunately estimates obtained by other methods of any degree of sophistication are not available for comparison. No alternative calculations of cross elasticities are known to the author and the results of elaborate studies of direct elasticities are not published in a form in which they can conveniently be used in any sensible way. In the absence of alternatives it has proved necessary to invent naïve hypotheses. What we have shown is, that both the mean and the range of the percentage error of estimate are reduced by the chosen neutral want association hypothesis to something less than they would be if predictions were made by straightforward projections, or by one arbitrarily chosen pattern of elasticities.

It might well be, of course, that market research organizations or the compilers of the statistics here analysed are aware already that they could do a great deal better on the basis of unpublished 'inside' information. Or it may be that the published figures themselves are not sufficiently accurate to justify any attempt at fine analysis. Indeed, on occasions when estimates based on elasticities have appeared more like the second thoughts of the Central Statistical Office than their first, it is hard to repress the suspicion that analysis reveals more about the principles upon which guessers guess than the principles upon which consumers buy.

For a number of reasons, however, it has always seemed worth while not to be discouraged by doubts. First, it was never possible whilst the work was in progress to seek the advice of the compilers of the blue books, and doubts may not be justified. Second, introspection and word of mouth communication of the results of other people's introspection is valid empirical evidence, so that there are good reasons for supposing that demand theory, if it fails the final test, is more likely to be incomplete than false. It seems likely that, if it is true that 'inside' information makes possible better predictions than demand theory, then the two together will yield better predictions still.

This brings us to a major point which has already been made but must be made again. The hypotheses tested are exceedingly crude. There is a desperate need to undertake an ambitious analysis of consumer expenditure with a large team of research workers who should be given access to all of the information available at the C.S.O. A utility tree of several hundreds of goods should be prepared and tested. If the mean percentage error of estimate could be reduced from 3 per cent to 1 per cent and the range of error from 7 per cent to 3 per cent by an exercise of this kind, the value to economic planners, public and private, would be incalculable.

Finally it needs to be said that, even if demand analysis as we know it should fail, and if it could be established that simpler methods yield comparable or better numerical predictions, then it might still be worth while to teach and discuss it. Many qualitative conclusions could remain valid. And even if they did not it is still true that prediction is only the *ultimate* objective of theory. Where a chain of reasoning is complex it is often the case that discredited hypotheses provide the foundation for new and even more sophisticated hypotheses which in the end succeed. The rat in the maze finds its way out by remembering its mistakes and not by deliberately forgetting them.

INDEX

PRINTED IN GREAT BRITAIN
AT THE UNIVERSITY PRESS, OXFORD
BY VIVIAN RIDLER
PRINTER TO THE UNIVERSITY